SWIFTY'S WAR

*This is a First Hand Account of the Malayan War
as seen through the eyes of Swifty.
The names of those serving with him at that time,
have been changed, so as to protect their identities.*

SWIFTY'S WAR

A First Hand Account of the Malayan War By
Keith D. Swift

First Published in Great Britain in 2003 By
Keith D. Swift.
C/O Cremer Press,
Blackburn. BB2 1JE.

ISBN 1 898722 51 X

Printed and Bound By
Edmund Mercer, Cremer Press,
45 Harrison Street,
Blackburn. BB2 1JE.

My thanks are due to my wife and children for all their help and support.

I wish to acknowledge my thanks also to Mary Williams, Geoff Philips, and Stan Donaghy for their help and encouragement.

My sincere gratitude goes to Stefan Gabrysch for designing the cover for this book.

And lastly, my thanks go to Madeleine Fish, my Editor, for all her help and advice.

Further acknowledgements are due to the authors as listed below, for quotes used as detailed herewith:-

See Cheah Boon Kheng, Red Star Over Malaya Singapore 1983); Michael Stenson, "The Ethnic and Urban Bases of Communist Revolt in Malaya" in John Wilson, ed., Peasant Rebellion and Communist Revolution in Asia (Stanford: Stanford University Press, 1974); Frank Fured, "Britain's Colonial Wars: Playing the Ethnic Card", Journal of Commonwealth and Comparative Studies Vol. XXVIII, No. 1 (March, 1990)

Robert Thompson, Forward to Richard Clutterbuck, The Long War (London 1976) p.viii.

Clutterbuck, p.9.

Rajani Palme Dutt, The Crisis of Britain and the British Empire (London, 1985) pp. 269-271, 396-397.

Anthony Short, The Communist Insurrection in Malaya (London, 1975) pp. 383-384.

For Batang Kali see Brian Lapping, End of Empire (London, 1985)

Smith, p19

Cloake, p.260.

Lawrence James, Imperial Regard (London, 1988) p155
Paul Frederick Cecil, Herbicidal Warfare (New York, 1986), p.17,

J.P.Cross, In Gurkha Company (London,1986) p.23

Sir Walter Walker, Forward to E.D. Smith, East of Katmandu (London, 1976), chs. XVII, XVIII.

INTRODUCTION

THE REBELLION

"The Communist rebellion that began in 1948 was caused by the frustration of hopes for peaceful political and social reform. During the Second World War when the Japanese had occupied Malaya, the British had allied themselves with the Malayan Communist Party (MCP) which had waged a guerrilla war against the occupation forces. Once Japan was defeated, the MCP leadership confidently expected that the British would recognize the party as a legitimate political force that would play an important part in rebuilding the country. They looked forward to social reform, a rapid advance towards democracy, and the granting of independence - expectations made all the more likely with the triumphant election of a Labor government in London. Accordingly, instead of resisting the British return in 1945, the MCP willingly collaborated with them: a Communist guerrilla unit actually took part in the victory parade in London, and Chin Peng, soon to become party general-secretary and the most wanted man in Malaya, was awarded the Order of the British Empire. Instead of mounting an armed insurrection, the MCP disbanded its guerrilla army and concentrated its efforts on building up a strong, militant trade union movement and on establishing a leftwing political movement, uniting Chinese, Malays, and Indians.

The MCP's efforts at establishing an alliance among the three major ethnic groups inhabiting Malaya was crucial. The party itself was overwhelmingly Chinese at the end of the war, but it energetically set about building support among the Malay and Indian population. In a country where only 38 percent of the population were Chinese and 49 percent Malay the MCP's success at winning over the Malays was always likely to be decisive.

The party's efforts met with some success. It allied itself with the Malay National Party, whose president was a former guerrilla fighter, and was beginning to recruit Malays directly into its ranks. The British, however, allied themselves with the Malay traditional rulers, the rajahs and sultans, who had generally collaborated with the Japanese. They bolstered their power and influence as a quite deliberate counterweight to the strength of the left. While the MCP tried to unite Chinese, Malays, and Indians against the British, the British responded with a policy of divide and rule. They combined an attack on the citizenship rights of the Chinese population that privileged the Malays with warnings that the MCP intended to establish a Chinese ascendancy. Despite this there were a growing leftwing nationalist movement among the Malays, posing a threat both to the rajahs and sultans and to the British."

*I dedicate this book
to my wife
and children.*

Chapter 1

THE LEAVING

"The British success in defeating Communist rebellion in Malaya between 1948 and 1960 has long been held up as an example for others to follow, particularly the United States. One leading British counterinsurgency specialist, Sir Robert Thomkin, who served in Malaya throughout the Emergency, argued that "the counter-measures developed and proved in Malaya...would have succeeded in the early stages in Vietnam if they had been suitably adapted and consistently and intelligently employed."

My father stopped the car outside the station entrance, but left the engine running, leaving me in no doubt that he wanted to be off quickly. On impulse I looked at him to say goodbye, but he couldn't meet my gaze. It was as if he was unable to say anything at that moment, he just stared at the car windscreen. I felt quite strange, and intensified my look, almost willing him to break the silence.

Eventually, he did. "You know what name you carry now, don't disgrace it! And remember what I've told you?"

I nodded in agreement, wondering what he'd told me?

"You'll be alright, won't you?" he said, turning his head towards me, before turning away quickly, so as to avoid the response he sought. "And don't box, it's only to amuse the Officers." He paused in order to adjust his glasses, but then continued, "I'd better get back to your mother, you know she's not well!"

He reached across and offered his hand, which I took instinctively and shook; he pulled his trilby down an inch and prepared to leave. "Write regularly, and may God bless you Keith."

I felt a little awkward and smiled to give assent. "Thank you, I'll try. Give mum my love."

Dad revved the car up, but in that instant, just before he drove away, I searched for eye contact again; an instant pang of rejection registered, but as I held my gaze, I noticed with some amazement a slight wateriness around his eyes. The old man's human after all, I thought, only to dismiss the idea as quickly as it came.

His car slowly disappeared down the hill. I watched, hoping that he'd turn and wave, but he never did. My mother's health no doubt replaced his thoughts of me.

Making my way to the station, I remembered it was Friday night, and it was late, but that didn't matter as long as I didn't miss the train, which was always a possibility with me. As I walked towards the entrance, the sounds of raucous laughter reached my ears. This somehow brought strange excitement, whilst distorting the other night noises of the town. There was a certain kind of eerie falseness, as if it couldn't last and would be followed almost immediately by some great disaster. I'd heard the frenzied laughter of the pub, and the manic laughter of the club, but this was different.

When I stopped at the barrier to show my pass, I heard a low wailing sound coming from the platform, like a bank of grief. It unnerved me, as I realised it came from a mass of people waiting on the platform for the train from Barnard Castle en route for Southampton, and the ship that waited there. People were hugging each other in desperate embraces, soldiers with girlfriends, wives, parents, grandparents, brothers, sisters, aunts, uncles and little children. In fact anyone and everyone seemed to be there.

I found a place where I could prop my kit bag up against the wall and sat on it. From there I could see the platform, and hopefully the train when it arrived. Nobody seemed to notice me at all as I sat there, outwardly calmly watching, inwardly charged to the point of emotional explosion. Then I noticed Sergeant Conelly, our new Platoon Sergeant, coming onto the station helped by two other soldiers. They dwarfed him, although they weren't particularly huge, but it amused me to hear him swearing at them in the foulest language.

"You stupid fuckin' sods, what yer draggin' me away for, ah was just getting going."

Whereupon, they both grabbed him and carried him upright onto the platform, stopping about ten yards from where I was sitting.

Almost hypnotised by his outrageous behaviour, I just stared at him wondering what might happen next. He looked old, and I wondered whether he might have been in the war? I'd heard all about the Sergeant from some of the other soldiers in the platoon, although I'd only seen him briefly, at a distance, once or twice before. He wasn't what I expected. He didn't look strong or tough, and his nose seemed to be too thin and hooked for the fighter they said he was! In fact he looked anything but a fighter. At this point our eyes met.

"What the fuck are you lookin' at?"

I looked away not wanting any trouble with a Sergeant, but I'd noticed his dishevelled uniform and rough appearance. I decided he must be very drunk. I looked again at the mass of people, while at the same time feeling the heavily charged atmosphere that seemed to have grown in the few minutes I'd been there. It gradually enveloped me, although I tried to remain aloof.

Through the crowd I saw a soldier that I knew, but try as I could, I couldn't remember his name. I concentrated everything I could on trying to remember his name, partly to stimulate my brain, but more importantly to offset any problems that might come from Sergeant Conelly. The soldier's family surrounded him in a protective circle. His father stood there, hands clasped in front of him, smiling at his son. It seemed, from where I stood, that his mother was asking him questions, and from the grimaces showing on his face, it would, I thought, be a fair bet that the questions were about his behaviour when abroad, whether he'd got everything, and the need to write regularly. I smiled, knowing that they were the questions my mother would have asked me, had she been here. I quickly stifled the smile when I realised Sergeant Conelly might think that I was smiling at him.

As I sat there on the platform floor, I saw acts of open love. So many people were crying, their tears were about departure and severance. I'd always been told that open acts of sentimentality were nearly always associated with the affects of alcohol. I saw something else that day, I realised that love has no barriers; it is simply spontaneous. However, it left me feeling uneasy at what might lie ahead. Amid the charged atmosphere, and above the noise of the crowd, the railway announcer spoke. A wave of silence came over the hundreds of people crowded onto the station, when the N.C.O.s. and others shouted for silence. The microphone was loud and distorted, and I very much doubted whether anyone could understand anything, other than the announcer himself. But, give him his due, he never allowed that to disturb him, he simply carried on with message after message. After a few seconds, the crowd, unable to understand the distorted messages, gave up trying, and the noise level reached new heights until the announcer could be barely heard at all.

I searched the crowd for someone else I knew, but saw no familiar face. Sitting there for some time, my thoughts raced to find an anchor point. Quite suddenly through the noise of the crowd I felt the earth move beneath me. It began to tremble ever so slightly at first, then became increasingly more pronounced with each passing second. I waited apprehensively until an enormous blast shook the air silencing the people around me in one stroke. My heart froze as steel upon steel developed a rhythmic sound, interspersed with great piercing screams of escaping steam. From where I stood, I saw the train appear like a great metal monster. It looked as if it couldn't stop. Squeals ripped into the night air threatening to completely pierce our eardrums as its brakes were applied. Eventually, amid clouds of bursting steam, it brought its great bulk to a standstill.

At that moment all hell let loose, as soldiers with mountains of luggage struggled to get onto the train. Emotional embraces were rudely interrupted with foul curses. Some soldiers, desperate to prolong their farewells, refused to leave the open carriage door area, making it almost impossible for anyone to pass them. Shouts and threats mingled with other noises in a garbled mass of raw emotion. In due course, all but a few soldiers had climbed onto the train.

I boarded the train and went from carriage to carriage in an effort to find a seat. I gave up when one soldier read my thoughts and sarcastically suggested that first class might suit me better. In the end, I pushed my way into an already full carriageway, intending to find a place to sit on the floor, when the train's whistle blew, and the train lurched forward sending me, and everyone standing sprawling.

"Shit! I'm sorry," I apologised, as I pulled myself up from off the floor, only to be sent flying again in the same direction.

The soldier I crashed into laughed, "Some bloody trainload hey!"

"Yes," I answered, "you'd think they'd give everyone a seat, it's a long way."

"Not in this man's bloody army; give you sod all!"

I laughed, thinking his thoughts well expressed. As the train got under way, the congestion eased, and we were able to put our kit bags on the floor and sit on them. The soldier opposite me was from Bacup, a place I'd never heard of until then. He began to tell me about the riotous time he'd had on leave. By comparison my time on leave was dead. Of course, I never told him that my parents were Evangelical Christians, with a strictness that could only find comparison in a monastery. How could I begin to tell him that my folks would see anybody, and that included the Colonel of the Regiment, going directly to hell if they were not of their fold? I knew that his reply might well be something to do with the Malayan Peninsula being hell anyway. However, my lack of response never stopped him for a moment.

He continued, "Bloody glad to be here, I am! Her bloody 'usband's looking fer me, but he'll be bloody unlucky won't he?" After which he chuckled.

"You'll have to go back sometime won't you?" I said in all innocence.

"Yeah, but he'll have forgotten by then, I bloody well 'ope!"

"Let's hope so," I agreed.

He stared at me for a moment, "Well, what about you then, get up to anything?"

I shook my head, and the subject was closed.

He paused, "Which Company you in then?"

" 'B' Company."

"Oh yeah, Lieutenant Groman's in that Company. Is he as bad as they say he is?"

I didn't answer for some time, it was a dangerous question, and one that I didn't like. Talking about officers in the corridor of a train where everybody and anybody might hear you, was not, in my opinion, a safe or sensible thing to do.

However, he persisted, "Well, go on then, what's he like?"

"If you keep your nose clean, he's okay, but if you don't, watch out!"

Lieutenant Groman had gained a reputation in the Battalion for his zealousness and meticulous attention to detail. He was a real swine sometimes, and seemed to take great delight in marching soldiers off the parade ground into the cells for the smallest of misdemeanours. A button undone, a beret slightly adjusted at the wrong angle, or the wrong sort of knot in a tie could land you in real trouble. I remembered a time when I became the centre of his attention for a short while. We were on the parade ground being taught how to drill. I felt that things were going very well, when the Sergeant Major decided to teach us how to salute. He went to great lengths explaining how to raise the right arm properly, how to hold the thumb close into the hand so that no daylight could be seen between the two. He got us to practise saluting stood to attention, then on the march, heads turning toward some imaginary figure, all hands shooting upwards together to salute, while continuing to march. I felt extremely confident about the whole thing.

However, before he dismissed us, he decided to test us one last time, "Company," he shouted, "Salute!"

We all shouted at the tops of our voices. "One," and stretched our arms out. "Two," and we all brought the outstretched arm across onto the forehead in one movement, the palm of the hand facing outwards, while our eyes rested on that imaginary figure directly in front of us. I never flinched, moved or dared to think about anything but the last order. I waited and waited before I began to wonder why it had never been given.

Then I heard the Sergeant scream at the top of his voice, "What 'ave we here then?" He walked across the parade ground.

I could hear his boots scrunching on the hard surface of the ground. Not daring to even attempt a guess at what had gone wrong, or to whom he was referring, I waited thinking that some silly sod had got it all wrong. I listened for the inevitable stream of abuse that would come from the Sergeant's lips, but it never came. All I heard was the continued scrunching of the Sergeant's boots getting closer and closer. Apprehension, together with some puzzlement enveloped me, until he stopped directly in front of me, crashing one boot past the other in a perfect halt. With no answer forthcoming or necessary, he shouted again, only this time he was about an inch away from my face. I could see his face twitching as he summoned reserves of venom. Fearfully engulfed, I waited for him to start; I didn't have to wait too long.

"Why are you insulting the Queen soldier?"

I didn't know how to answer him.

He continued, "Everyone 'ere is saluting the Queen with his right hand soldier, but you've decided to salute her with your left hand. Now if that's not a fuckin' deliberate insult, I don't know what is!" He waited for a moment.

I blurted out, "I didn't mean to Sergeant M…"

He interrupted me before I had time to finish, "You didn't bloody well mean to! I fucking well 'ope you didn't mean to! And keep your shitty little eyes to the front soldier, don't move," he shouted, as he peered right into my face, so that I could see the veins standing out in his eyes, looking as if they might burst. His spittle was by this time, on his lips, on his teeth and on my face. I stood rigidly to attention.

"Company," he bawled at the top of his voice, "except for this soldier 'ere." He stopped and snapped at me. "What's your bloody name soldier?"

"Swift, Sir."

"I am Sergeant Major to you soldier. I'm not a bloody Officer yet. What am I soldier?"

"Sergeant Major, Sir," I answered.

He laughed, but his laugh was not genuine, it was a laugh of triumph, not of humour, "Funny as well as friggin' stupid then are we?" He paused for breath, "Well, I asked you a question soldier?"

By this time I was so utterly confused by his aggression and his sheer speed of questions, I began to stammer, "Yes Sir, Sergeant Major, Sir."

He then moved even closer to me until I could feel the warmth of his breath, "You taking the piss out of me soldier?"

By this time I was a stammering mess.

He turned to the Company of men watching, "Company, except this 'gobshite' Private Swift, who will standfast, will gather round 'ere and witness this terrible exhibition of a soldier insulting our gracious Queen. When I give the order that is!" He took one pace backwards, "Company!" he screamed, "Dismiss! Now gather round," he said, when the sound of the last command had drifted away.

The whole Company eagerly gathered round, some half embarrassed, others quite gleeful. I stood there still in the act of saluting with my left hand. The Sergeant waited until everyone had had a good laugh, "Now take a good look will you," adding with mock desperation,

"What can we do with this little shit?" He stopped speaking and gestured to me with his hand.

I thought, "That's it! It's the guardroom for me."

The very next minute, he changed, and in a quiet voice he asked me a question. "Well, Private Swift, will it 'appen again?"

"No Sergeant Major," I shouted at the top of my voice.

He slowly repeated what I'd said. Then boomed out like thunder, "It bloody well better be no Private bloody Swift, or your balls will rot in hell." He returned to the Company. "Get fell in, at the double!"

He then turned to me, "Private Swift! As you were."

We assembled in ranks again and marched off the parade ground before he dismissed us. However, as I was walking back to the barracks, a second sense told me that I was being watched. I experienced that interminable problem of wanting to look, but somehow being warned not do so. For some strange reason, try as I may, I couldn't contain it and looked as I came to my quarters. What I saw unnerved me. The Sergeant Major was pointing directly at me, and he had Lieutenant Groman at his side.

"Shit!" I thought, "I'm in for it now."

Sure enough, on Inspection Parade the next morning, when Lieutenant Groman was doing his rounds, he stopped when he came to me and proceeded to examine everything that I had on in minute detail. When he'd finished, he stood back a pace and looked me in the eye, "I believe we'll have to watch you Private Swift, you have a nasty habit of insulting people, I'm told." He paused for breath, then looked away as if it didn't really matter, before whipping back with all the fury that he could muster within him. "Is this true?"

The sheer hostility in his voice threw me into a blind panic. I stammered, "I never insulted anybody intentionally Sir!"

He repeated what I'd said, slowly rolling each syllable where it was possible. After he'd finished he laughed softly, "Slightly educated are we? We'll see." He moved on to inspect the next soldier.

A moment later, while seemingly inspecting his cap badge, he suddenly looked at me. I saw him out of the corner of my eye, and an involuntary shiver ran down my spine. He was a dangerous man, who seemed to use power to intimidate and humiliate the men under him. No one trusted him. He often asked questions that were inappropriate, and designed to gain information about other Officers and N.C.O.s, which soldiers were generally eager to give. However, should such information be volunteered at some other time, he could become almost demented in his abhorrence at such intrusion into the private lives of Officers. He was sinister, and I felt that I had good reason to fear him.

"What's your name?"

I came back to the present with a jolt as I heard an awful sucking noise coming from somewhere under the carriage. The sound drowned every other word and made it impossible to speak. We gave up trying and just smiled and stared at each other. He lit a cigarette and offered me one which I accepted. The noise the train was making ceased just as it had begun.

"What did you say your name was?"

"Keith," I replied. "What's yours?"

"Alan, but they call me Al."

"Yeah, well they call me Swifty," I responded.

Al was a strange looking creature, almost elf-like, slightly under average height, and as skinny as a mountain goat. But most distinctive of all were his ears, which stuck out like a couple of wing mirrors. Every time I saw him I had a childish impulse to flick them. I found myself looking at his ears in horror, thankful they weren't mine. Slowly, I sensed he knew my thoughts, whereupon I tried desperately to mask them by casually looking at his nose, which was slightly long and looked as though it had been broken at some stage. It was then that I noticed a faint scar running right across from the top of his ear to his mouth.

"I'll have to watch him," I thought.

We became friends. He told me that he was now in 'D' Company, having been transferred from 'A' Company. I knew that it was unusual for Private soldiers to transfer from one company to another, although Officers and N.C.O.s did so regularly. However, I didn't pursue it further, thinking it might be embarrassing for him. What I did know was that 'A' Company had a reputation as a hard company, and that impressed me. I also knew that their Commanding Officer had a distinguished war record, and he expected a lot from his men. However I kept my thoughts to myself. We settled down and slept somewhat fitfully as the train sped towards the south coast.

During the night it became increasingly difficult and irritating trying to sleep, as soldiers continually came through the passageway, pushing and shoving their way through the closely packed bodies and luggage, inevitably standing on someone's extended legs.

"C'mon, Swifty, I've had enough of this," I heard Al say, as yet another argument erupted.

"Where to?" I asked.

He ignored my question, jumped to his feet; grabbing his kitbag and luggage he began to muscle his way down the carriage shouting, "Let's have a look down the train and see."

Much to my surprise, the train had cleared to an extent. It would seem that they'd all found seats. We pressed on down the train, going from one carriage to the next, hoping that we'd find some empty seats. I opened the door of one carriage, and saw to my delight, that only two soldiers occupied it.

"Piss off!" came from under a newspaper in the corner.

I sat down and stared at the paper covering his face. He must have sensed it, as the newspaper came down and his eyes peered over the top.

"I thought I told you to piss off!"

"I heard you," I said, continuing to look at him.

He looked away and turned to read the paper as if nothing had happened.

"Shove up! You can't have all the seat to yourself." I watched as Al gently moved the legs of the sleeping soldier, which were sprawled out over the seat.

He must have been soundly asleep, but the next minute he suddenly sat bolt upright. "Are we there yet?" he asked.

"Are we hell! replied Al, and everyone laughed.

The soldier reading the newspaper put it down. "We're miles from Southampton." He then looked slowly around.

As I watched him, not knowing what he might do next, something clicked in my memory and I felt that I'd seen him somewhere before. Then it came to me - Billy Sway. I'd never seen him since leaving Junior School. I smiled only to draw a quick response.

"Something bloody funny then?

"Yeah, you're Billy Sway, right?"

A somewhat perplexed expression came onto his face as his mind raced among memories. "Swifty! Ribby Ave. Junior School, yeah? I remember! Well bugger me Swifty, didn't know you were in the Army, never mind at Barnard Castle. Heard you'd gone to a boarding school, that's the last I heard. Ribby Ave. too rough for you then?"

I smiled, "What happened to you then Billy?"

"Everything," he said. Then, as if he'd had enough of the conversation, he turned to Al. "Who's yer mate?"

"Oh, this is Al out of 'D' Company.

Billy just nodded at him. Al nodded back. I watched, knowing that they were sizing each other up. They didn't speak for some considerable time.

Then Al broke the silence, "Hi Billy, how yer doin'?"

"This bloody train's goin' in the wrong direction fer me," he said, visibly relaxing.

Nobody spoke for some time. I knew Billy must have had a skinful of ale. I could smell it on his breath as he spoke. Later, as he slept, the smell of putrefied beer drifted across the carriage, helped along with huge farts as he dozed off. I gave no indication that it bothered me. It wouldn't have mattered anyway. We all fell asleep.

I don't think I slept much, partly due to the carriage light which seemed to shine straight into my eyes. Billy had a go at removing it when we came into the carriage earlier, but couldn't quite reach, so after much swearing and cursing, he left it. We settled down into fitful sleep again, when suddenly the train came to a juddering halt. Metal clashed, wheels hummed as they seized up and slid along the track, while the carriage buffers continually groaned and grated as they were pushed back to their full extent. An air of expectancy breached the walls of sleep. Thoughts raced through my mind making me feel insecure and nervous at what might happen next. I'd never liked trains, they seemed great cumbersome things to me. It seemed to take such an enormous effort to get the things going, and even more to get them to stop.

Al read my thoughts, "You worried Swifty? Maybe it'll be Korea instead of Malaya; could even be Suez if things go bad for us there."

"Yeah, we don't know do we?" My reaction hid my fears. I couldn't possibly tell him that I'd been thinking about the dangers of trains.

"Anyone for three card brag then? Aces high, come on!" Billy brought a worn pack out of his B.D. pocket and began to shuffle them. "One pound limit, right?"

Everyone agreed. We played cards for what seemed hours. I don't really know how long we'd played for, but what I did know was that I was sick of playing; not to mention the fact that I'd lost ten shillings. I decided that I wasn't very good at cards. It always seemed to me that the biggest rogue won, which made sense because Billy had a pile of money in front of him and a sickening grin on his face.

"I'm out," I declared.

"Yer what?" said Billy, his response a challenge I readily understood.

"I'm out," I repeated, as our eyes met briefly.

His grin turned to a grimace as he ran his hands through the money in front of him, "You givin' me this then?"

"Yeah, that's okay by me, but you're not getting any more."

They played on, but that didn't stop him from giving me filthy looks now and then, followed by a muffled expletive just loud enough for me to hear the first letter. I watched him, hoping he'd lose, but he never did. Eventually, I moved to the corner of the carriage away from the windows. Resting my head on part of my luggage; my thoughts went back to the day when I was chosen to play rugger for the Battalion. We played at Catterick. Things hadn't gone right from the start, not as I wanted them to go anyway. I'd intended to make a name for myself by playing hooker, although I'd usually played in the backs. We played the South Lancashire Regiment. Early in the game I went down for a loose ball. Stooping down to grab it I was met by the boot of one of the opposition intent upon clearing it. The boot connected with me right under the jaw. I went down, but got up almost immediately. The rest of the game was a blur. I remember coming to intermittently, asking other players what position I was supposed to be playing, vaguely recalling their verbal and non-verbal irritation mixed with anger and despair, we were losing quite heavily I was told later.

"That silly sod doesn't know where he's supposed to be playing."

The comment came from my Platoon Commander Lieutenant Roy Kutchen, who apologised to me five days later in Catterick Military Hospital. I finished the game and somehow made my way back to the NAAFI. I'd changed, but hadn't showered. Upon entering the NAAFI, I went to the counter. Through an intense blur, I remember the lady looking at me and asking if I was alright? Sitting down at a table, I was joined by two soldiers.

One of them said, "You've got blood running down yer chin pal. You alright?"

I remember saying that it was nothing, and seeing them look at each other.

He persisted, "Don't look like nothing to me!"

He went, leaving his friend gazing at me. Quite unable, in my state of mind, to understand why he kept on staring at me, I looked around and thought others were also watching me, until I felt that I had become the focus of everyone's attention. I sensed a conspiracy and left. The next thing that I recall was a bright light shining in my eyes. I was lying flat on my back on a raised bed with two people wearing white coats, looking over me.

One of them noticed me coming to, "Don't worry soldier, we're here to help you."

At first I wasn't at all afraid. Even so a numb feeling began to creep over me slowly, making me feel that I was losing control. I began to experience real fear, not only for my life, but also for the soundness of my mind. My eyes must have told the story.

"What's your name?"

I remember the question piercing the numbness. I didn't know. I didn't think about the question. I simply didn't know who I was. It never occurred to me that it was vital to know my name. "I don't know Sir," I said quietly and apologetically.

"Don't worry son, don't worry. What Battalion are you in?"

I thought for a moment, but I didn't know what he meant. "I don't know Sir," I replied again.

He smiled and spoke to his colleague who was stood next to him. The questions continued.

"Where do you come from?"

I intuitively knew that I should know, but I didn't. A kind of inertia feeling came over me making me completely dependent upon the two men present. I must have looked a sorry sight. "I don't know Sir," I said in a whisper, realising that the continual repetition of that phrase was fast burying me.

Some time past and I dared not close my eyes. I lay back. No thoughts, nothing but numbness. Suddenly, and without fear of contradiction, I recognised the man in the white coat to be a Doctor, an Army Doctor. I sat up.

The Doctor smiled at me and asked me to lie down again, "What is your number, soldier?"

"23293210," I replied without hesitation.

"Told you!" said one Officer to the other.

I could tell that they were Officers by their accent and the authority in their voices.

One of them addressed me, "Right son, we're going to send you to another hospital where they'll make you better." He paused, leaned over me and stared straight into my eyes, "Right?"

"Yes Sir," I replied, "thank you." I lay back and waited for the ambulance, but it never came. I entered a large pool of swirling water. Confident I would rise to the surface, I waited patiently going round and round. The water felt warm and made me feel comfortable, too comfortable, only to be followed by a sudden urge to surface. This urge became desperate. I nearly broke the surface many times, only to sink back into the comfort of the warm water. The sense of urgency persisted, becoming ever stronger, until summoning every effort I eventually broke the surface. Enveloped by the exhilaration of finally succeeding, I relaxed, then sank back into the pool and the abyss of nothingness. Almost immediately, I felt a strange sensation as if someone was stroking my arm and saying something to me.

"You coming to Private Swift?"

I opened my eyes and saw the Ward Sister. I looked into her roundish face as it creased into a smile. Words wouldn't come. I must have looked quite ill.

She patted me gently on the top of my head, "Lie back now and don't you worry your head, you'll be alright now."

I was baffled by the thought that with nothing hurting, how could I possibly be ill?

The Ward Sister spoke to the nurse by my bed, "I think he'll be alright now nurse, but keep your eye on him, he's had a nasty…"

I couldn't quite catch the last word before I drifted off again, but not before it had registered that she was Irish. Some time must have passed before I came too again. I awoke with a startle. Sitting up immediately I looked around, and saw that the ward was full of soldiers talking and laughing at the tops of their voices, or so it seemed. I watched in utter amazement. I'd no idea how I came to be here, I had no recollection of arriving or being put into bed, but what was worse, I had no idea what was wrong with me. A nurse turned in my direction and noticed that I was awake. I felt like an intruder and looked away.

He came straight over to me, smiling as he came, which made me feel better. "Okay then? Back with us. You've been coming and going for the past three days."

I couldn't reply straight away because I had difficulty trying to move my jaw. Eventually, I mumbled through my teeth, "I'm alright, but where am I?"

The nurse laughed, "Catterick Military Hospital son and you've a broken jaw."

My hand instinctively found my jaw and the huge bandage around it. Why hadn't I found that before, I thought.

"Here, I'll get you a mirror, and you can have a look at yourself." He went and came back with a large mirror.

I looked at myself. A bandage had been placed under my jaw and then knotted on top of my head. I laughed at the sorry sight. "Will you leave me like this?" I muttered through my teeth.

The whole ward laughed at my question. I laughed too. The nurse put his arm under me and lifted, putting a pillow under my upper back as he did so. I suddenly felt very tired as if I was slipping back into unconsciousness. I also felt quite panicky and nauseous, but nothing could stop its march as it crept up to, and over me, enveloping me in its mist. It was a slow dive, as if water was swirling all around sweeping me in its spin. I sank gently as if being caressed, but all the time I had that dreadful feeling of being lost, which sent disturbing vibes throughout my mind. From hidden depths came a desperate urge to break out, to rise above the water that was holding me prisoner. I tried time and again to surface, almost getting there, but always sinking back down again. The urge came and went periodically, as if to remind me that I was in mortal danger. Tired beyond exhaustion, but comfortably lulled by ecstatic sensuous movements that seemed to satisfy nearly all my emotions. I settled, only to be stabbed by that innermost need to survive. The desire to surface became ever greater and greater, until with one great effort, I pushed my head out from under the water, emerged and entered the world of the conscious, only this time I seemed to be much more aware of the unconscious. I was also aware that I could slip back into the void. I looked around, it was night, the curtains were drawn and the dim night-light cast shadows along the green walls. Muffled voices came faintly from across the ward.

Looking in the direction of the voices I was struck by the greenness of the walls. I questioned the colour, wondering whether it was me that placed the eeriness upon it, or whether it was simply standard Army paint. I tried looking at the night-light, and became almost obsessed with it, thinking that it was too dim, when the thought crashed into my brain that I couldn't see properly. Panic sent involuntary shivers down my back and through my legs. I wanted to shout and scream that I couldn't see, but the whispers coming from further down the ward stopped me.

Just as I was about to get out of bed and make a run for it, the night-nurse, having finished his conversation, was making his way back to the office; he stopped when he saw me looking at him.

"You back with us then Swifty?"

"Yes, I suppose I am," I muttered.

"Amnesia, that's your problem, but it'll go, just relax."

The word relax unsettled me, as this was something which I felt I couldn't do. I must be on my guard all the time otherwise I'd be entering that world of darkness again.

"Bring you a drink in a minute." The night nurse moved off.

I watched, hoping that the day would come quickly.

The train jerked forward, jolting me into the present. I looked around; the lads had finished playing cards and were in various states of sleep. The air in the carriage was beginning to get putrid, so I got up and went into the corridor which was empty. The first signs of dawn escaped the foreboding sky with needle-like slivers of piercing light. I stood watching in the corridor, trying to keep my balance as the train hurtled towards its destination. No great thoughts came to me, only that I was going to war and I wasn't sure what that meant. Somehow I needed to look at the land, even though we were hurtling past it. It was as if I was satisfying some inner primeval need. I was frightened without really knowing why. What I did know, was that some on the train would never return, and that was a hard thing to cope with.

A soldier pushed past me, "We're nearly there," he said, "about half an hour." He carried on, never as much as giving me a second glance.

I returned to the carriage; the air was sticky, thick with body smells. I sat down in the corner. The others were still asleep. Closing my eyes, I too fell into fitful sleep until the train jerked to a standstill. Everyone jumped to their feet as if an alarm had gone off. We all waited, knowing that we had arrived, and that the command to get off the train was imminent. Nobody spoke; tenseness grew as expectancy raged. Suddenly, and seemingly without a command being given, the train began to empty onto the platform. It was cold as the chilly February wind swept through the station. Nothing in the immediate surroundings suggested that we were in the port of Southampton. I thought maybe they'd got it wrong and sent us to another port, until an N.C.O. started assembling us in neat rows on the platform, where we began a long wait. The coldness of the morning brought about silence among the men. After waiting for some considerable time, low curses could be heard as the icy wind chilled us to the bone.

Sergeant Conelly walked up and down clapping his hands as he went, "Don't worry lads, we'll be on board this bloody ship in no time."

As I listened to him, I couldn't help but notice the red blotchy patches on his face, with protruding veins that criss-crossed his nose, making it look purple and discoloured.

He saw me looking at him, "What the hell you lookin' at Private Swift, you've seen me before haven't you?"

I looked away, pretending that I hadn't heard him. Others had informed me that he was a dangerous man to cross. I also knew that he was an alcoholic and quite unpredictable.

"Well Private Swift, I asked you a question, aren't you going to answer me?"

"That's enough Sergeant!" The cultured voice of Lieutenant Jamieson came to my rescue. Sergeant Conelly moved away as the Lieutenant came over to see me.

"You trying to take the whole Army on Swift?" he asked.

"I only looked at him Sir," I answered.

"Yes, but it's the way you look Private Swift, you can be interpreted as being quite provocative at times."

"Yes Sir," I conceded, not entirely sure as to what he meant.

"Right, well watch your step in the future, I won't always be around."

I nodded, and he moved on. After he'd gone, I looked around to see who might have heard, only to meet the stare of Sergeant Conelly. A shiver ran down my back as I heard him mutter expletives directly at me.

Corporal Docherty, who was standing next to me, whispered in my ear, "Swifty for God's sake cool it, or he'll have you."

"What have I done? I've only looked at him."

"Well don't! You bloody fool. I'm telling you, he'll have you!" After which he shook his head slowly to illustrate the point.

The column I was in began to move toward the entrance to the harbour. The air suddenly became charged with excitement as it gradually came into view. We emerged onto the quayside with our kit bags slung over one shoulder and our rifles in the other hand.

Chapter 2

THE SHIP, THE STORM AND THE VOYAGE TO SOUTH AFRICA

"Thompson was to head the British Advisory Mission to Vietnam from September 1961 to March 1965 and later became a special advisor to President Richard Nixon. Another specialist, Major General Richard Clutterbuck, similarly argued that Malaya in 1948 was comparable to South Vietnam in 1957-1958 but whereas the British responded with decisive counter-measures, in South Vietnam the government was "strangely complacent" and allowed the Communists to establish "clandestine control over much of the population before any serious shooting began."
Clutterbuck, p.9.

The biggest ship I'd ever seen in my life greeted us lying against the quayside. I read its name, *'The Empire Orwell'*. It seemed a strange name to me, and I wondered where it came from? Everyone began talking at once as the excitement grew. We were told that the ship weighed 20,000 tons, but it looked a great deal heavier. Looking up at the huge mountain of steel, I wondered how it could possibly float?

We waited on the quayside for what seemed an eternity. Whistles blew, followed by shouts as Officers rushed around, occasionally congregating in small groups for heated discussions.

Eventually, we moved up the gangplank and onto the ship. I couldn't help but notice that everything was made of steel; steel doors, steel floors, steel railings and steel walls. The noise of our boots on the steel floor was ear-piercing as the Company made its way down innumerable staircases until we arrived at our deck. We were housed in three-tiered bunks, and a mad scramble ensued as soldiers claimed a bunk. I'd decided not to get involved in the scramble, so I took whatever was left, which unsurprisingly turned out to be near the toilets. After settling down, we were told that the ship would sail on the tide. With that I lay on my bunk and slept until vibrations, and the sound of deep powerful engines awoke me. It seemed that the whole ship shook with the power released.

Shouts of, "We're off," started a mass exodus to get on deck. It somehow felt important, yet quite strange to be intent upon seeing the last of England. It was as if I wanted a last picture. I questioned why I might want to do this, it wasn't an emotional response; it was deeper than that. It came from something within me that drove rather than questioned. I found myself standing there, before I had time to think. I wondered whether I was fulfilling a tradition that had been set before me.

Upon clambering up endless staircases, I emerged onto the deck some fifteen or twenty feet above the quayside. From this vantage point I hoped to see everything. My hopes however were forlorn, for the crush was so great, I couldn't see a thing. The upper deck seemed a good idea, but it proved to be even worse.

Frantically I scrambled back to the lower deck, and waited at the back unable to see a thing until some grew tired, after an hour or so of total inactivity, and left. Taking up a position against the ship's rail next to a Sergeant out of 'A' Company, whom I vaguely recognised, I waited. The moment arrived when the last rope was hurled off the quayside and drawn up into the ship. The ship's whistle blew ear-deafening blasts again and again as the massive steel hulk slowly eased itself away from the quay. I watched totally mesmerised by the spectacle. It made me feel small, insignificant and totally dispensable. Strangely fearful, I continued to watch. The ship's screws suddenly came to full life, sending the steel frame into a violent shudder. The water boiled around the ship as the power of the engines increased.

"This could be forever," I'd heard that phrase somewhere before, but it still held a powerful meaning for me as I felt and understood, to some extent, the reality of leaving. My mind started playing tricks; was it reality, or was it a just a dream? Another dimension of fear crept over me as I thought of the amnesia I'd suffered in hospital, with someone ending up saying, "Don't worry soldier, you've been out for a while, but you'll be okay, just relax!"

I felt quite isolated not being able to disclose my thoughts to anyone, for they'd undoubtedly think me mad. My father had always advised me to keep well away from anyone displaying strange ways, saying that it could be infectious. I could never tell when he was kidding and when he was serious, but I knew that he voiced the opinion of many. Again and again strange thoughts kept coming into my head, always interlinking with fears associated with Catterick Military Hospital, where bouts of consciousness and unconsciousness had driven me to the point of questioning my sanity and my identity. Sweat started to surface on my forehead as the uncontrolled world of dreams presented itself. Could I decipher between the two worlds, or were they fusing into one? Great beads of sweat began running down my face. I felt like shouting, "I'm all right, you know!" But that would tell everyone that I wasn't. How could it give the opposite meaning, I thought, for it would convey the idea that I was quite mad. Was I going mad? The very thought sent shivers through me. I shouldn't be thinking such things.

"You alright?"

I turned sideways to see the Sergeant's concerned look.

"Yes Serge, I'm okay, thanks."

"Difficult time, difficult for me," he looked away toward the quayside.

"Wow!" I thought, that was a near one. I recalled the Doctor telling me at Catterick that I'd had an enormous bang on the head, and that I should be very careful as it could lead to all sorts of complications. I wondered whether these thoughts were part of those complications he had in mind? I looked at the Sergeant again, and wondered whether he had any strange thoughts; and then the thought struck me that he might have some very painful answers. Realising that I must stop talking to myself, it occurred to me that no one could possibly know my thoughts. A voice inside seemed to answer that I should know anyway. I felt sick as waves of nausea made me think I might be in the first stages of madness. "Do other people think like this?" I asked myself, but knew I would never dare ask anyone. I gripped the rail tighter, it was an instinctive reaction to secure some kind of reality. I looked at my hands on the rail, they were white with strain and effort. As I continued to look, they seemed to become totally detached from my body. "Those *are* mine?" I thought. "Don't be silly of course they are," a reply came from inside my head. This detached view persisted in a frightening way. I questioned whether I was the person they said I was, or was I an impostor? The Sergeant looked directly at me again and our eyes met. He stared at me intently without saying a word. I could tell that he knew something, but wondered how much he really knew.

"Hey Serge, do you ever have strange thoughts?" I realised how stupid the question was immediately it left my lips.

He continued to look at me, and in that look I saw something that startled me.

I tried to regain my composure. "Yeah, well I mean..."

He interrupted, "Don't worry son, beneath all the bullshit we all feel strange in times like these."

As he turned away, I thought I saw a tear fall from his cheeks. This show of emotion from a Sergeant really shook me, but in a way it made me feel more secure. You never expect to see a Sergeant weep. I tried hard to suppress my inner thoughts, but quickly realised it was beyond me. As long as I never owned up to them, and as long as I never showed any outward signs of their existence, I'd be all right, otherwise I'd be a marked man.

I recalled a young man who lived near to my father's butcher's shop, who had psychological problems. He was, according to popular understanding, a clever boy at school and was destined for great things. However, he always behaved oddly. As he walked he would periodically stop and look at the bottom of his shoe, screwing his torso round while standing on one leg.

My father would call his men together to witness the event. Nobody laughed, that would be uncharitable. Then my father would lecture his men on the dangers of education. "That's what too much education does for you," he'd say, "sends you crackers," Then he'd look at me, "Think we're alright with you though, not much danger of that!" And a big grin would come onto his face.

As I recalled the event, I began to realise that I was no different than that boy, and my father would no doubt have said the same thing about me if he knew that I was talking to myself. Then the thought suddenly occurred to me that the tears that I thought I saw on the Sergeant's face were a sure indication of something going on his mind. What was he saying to himself, I wondered? I remembered the emotion my father tried hard to suppress when he dropped me off at the railway station in Preston, before I caught the train to Southampton. I realised that he was no different than the Sergeant or me for that matter; he just pretended to be. I reasoned that most people were just like me, having hidden conversations in their head. It had nothing to do with a bang on the head at all. However, the golden rule was that you never showed it, or admitted to it; otherwise you'd end up being ridiculed like the boy who passed my father's butcher's shop. I felt happier, and the strange thoughts about my amnesia drifted away, but not before the idea occurred to me that if all people felt as my father did, and they all suffered from it, then we must all be nuts!

We stood there and watched the ship begin to ease itself away from the dock. My thoughts were centred on the immensity of the occasion. Almost a thousand soldiers lined the decks of the ship. However, it was the destination and intention that really played on my mind. A phrase I'd remembered from my English Literature class at school came back to me, *'Soldiers and a beckoning foreign land,'* the phrase came to me again and again. The meaning escaped me, but somewhere within the phrase came back to me all the ingredients of danger and excitement. Was I to die there? Thoughts flitted across the surface of my mind evoking memories of my school days. I'd read Graves and Sassoon, and although they'd shocked and impressed me with the horrors of war, I'd always read them in quite a detached sort of way; never once thinking it could ever happen to me. The horrors hadn't arrived, but all the signs were there. I looked all around me, and noticed with a new understanding the significance that khaki held by way of uniformity. In a way we'd lost our individual identity and had become part of a whole.

Standing there holding onto the ship's rail, looking at the land of my birth, life became much more than just the 'here and now'. In some strange way it enabled me to be part of a historical whole, and to understand that I was part of that whole whether I wanted to be or not. This revelation, for that is exactly what it was, brought no panic and little emotion, but I did wonder how many of my ancestors had felt the same way throughout history?

"This really is forever, I may never come back!" As the thought surfaced again I felt a sickness in the pit of my stomach. "No, it can't be true. How do I get rid of such a thought? Think of an antidote! It's bad luck to think of such things in the first place. Why can't I control the things I think about? Perhaps I will die." These thoughts sent shivers down my spine. "How can you?" Came from somewhere in my brain. "I shouldn't be arguing with myself like this, it's ridiculous."

All the time this was going on, the ship was slowly turning until its bows were facing seawards. Uneasy and on edge, I risked a look at the Sergeant. His gaze was firmly fixed on the quayside; great tears were rolling down his face. Shocked, I stared at him. It confused me to see such raw emotion coming from a Sergeant. As I watched, almost hypnotised, my thoughts went back to an emotional experience that had become indelibly stained upon my mind. I knew that it would be a very painful one to relive, but watching the Sergeant, I gave in.

It happened on the first day I arrived at boarding school. I was ten years old. I'd agreed to go after much persuasion from my parents. However, I had no idea what going away to school really meant, nor did I understand that once there, that was it, you couldn't change your mind. My mother and father painted an idyllic picture of the school, set in beautiful grounds surrounded by woods just waiting to be explored, with fields that stretched for miles. Of course this was all true, but what I'd failed to understand was that I couldn't come home until the term had finished. I willingly agreed to go, having little or no understanding what the idea of boarding entailed. I remember feeling very confident kissing my mother goodbye, catching the train to Crewe and then another one to Whitchurch accompanied by my father. It all seemed really exciting. It never occurred to me that boarding meant severance. I'd been away before when I was seven, although it was only to the local hospital with scarlet fever. I never allowed myself to think of that though, it was too painful.

Upon arriving at the school by taxi from the station, my father paid the taxi-driver, tipping him generously.

"You sending him to the school then?"

"Oh yes," replied my father. "It's his first time."

I saw in his face that he was pleased to be able to say this. I knew that he was proud to be able to afford to send me. I looked at him and his face beamed.

"I think he'll be alright now," he said addressing the taxi-driver. He then turned to me wanting some confirmation. "Won't you Keith?"

"Oh yes," I replied, not quite understanding what he really meant, because one school was very like another to me.

After saying goodbye to the taxi-driver, we made our way along a gravel path lined by huge trees, the likes of which, I'd never seen before. They made me feel very small as I looked up to them. Their branches gave the impression of huge great arms with a massive green spread at the end of each branch.

My father saw me looking. "Cedars of Lebanon," he said with great certainty. He always spoke like that when he wanted to emphasise a point to me.

"Where's Lebanon?" I asked, only to receive a stare that suggested I was being too clever. He obviously doesn't know, I thought.

"Lebanon is in the Middle East."

His response startled me, for I'd deduced from his reaction that he didn't know. Funny people parents! Ask some questions and they say you're bright. Ask others and they say you're being cheeky, or trying to take the mickey, as my father would put it.

We went to the headmaster's study where I was formally introduced to him. The Reverend Harold Norton Duncan was by far the biggest man that I'd ever set eyes upon. He looked like two men pushed together. He put his hand out, and offered to shake hands with me. I was immediately taken aback, for it wasn't customary for adults to shake hands with children in the circle that I was familiar with; they would simply nod their head at you in recognition of your existence and leave it at that. Instinctively my hand went out to meet his proffered hand, disappearing in his huge grasp.

"Hello Keith," his voice boomed out. "Are you looking forward to your stay with us?"

I smiled. It seemed the safest thing to do in the circumstances, "Hmmm," was all I could manage.

He turned his attention to my father for a minute before he addressed me again, "Keith, would you like to look around the school?"

I agreed, and a senior Prefect was summoned, and off we went on a tour of the school. He took me around the junior dormitories, the gymnasium and the classrooms.

After a while I became quite bored, "Where are the boys of my age?" I asked.

"Oh they're down at the kitchen gardens, would you like to go?"

"Yeah, I would," I replied, eager to see what they were like.

"Do you come from Lancashire?" he asked, with a half amused look on his face.

"Aye, I do! I answered believing that there was nothing unusual about the question.

He followed it up with, "I thought as much, smoke and chimneys and all that, what!" After which he laughed uproariously.

I didn't understand his amusement and stood there quite perplexed, although I obviously sensed he found me funny. We walked to the gardens in almost total silence, except for the sound of our shoes on the gravel path. The route took us through some of the biggest trees I'd ever seen.

"Wellingtonia's my boy," the Prefect informed me, with a confidence that both frightened and astounded me.

Eventually we arrived at the gardens, which were situated at the back of the school. They proved quite amazing, for they were walled and had pink or red paths running between each plot of ground. It seemed that the whole school was down there working feverishly like ants, some digging, some weeding, whilst others were engaged in what seemed to be deep discussion. I found it an exhilarating sight and desperately wanted to be part of it. I made friends quickly and helped as best as I could.

A boy about my own age stopped what he was doing and came over to me, "I'm Leo," he introduced himself, "Would you like to see my garden? I've some lovely spring onions."

Now spring onions were new to me, and all vegetables represented something that was supposed to be good for growing children, and therefore to be avoided at all costs. "Yeah," I said, "what are they like?"

He gave me a confused smile, "You'll see."

So off we went to his patch of garden. Before I knew it, he had me weeding while pointing out all the various insects that might spoil his crop. He had traps for snails, slugs and rabbits; perfume from certain wild flowers to ward off other unwanted visitors. He lectured me on birds and animals, some of which I'd never heard of. I nodded dutifully in agreement every time he paused for breath. Before he'd finished I'd realised that he was a genius. My father had often spoken about certain people who had received God-given gifts. I suppose I'd always secretly hoped to be one of those few, but in my heart I knew that I never would. However, I'd done the next best thing, I'd become friends with one who had.

The sound of a bell suddenly interrupted his steady flow of words. He stopped, and looked urgently towards the main building, "That's the supper bell, let's go."

"What supper bell?" I asked, somewhat apprehensively.

"For supper, before we go to bed."

"Bed!" I exclaimed, "but where's my dad?" Tears welled up in my eyes at the thought of going to bed without saying goodnight to my mum.

Leo screwed his face up into a frown, "But you're here now until the end of term."

"The end of term," I screamed, "but when's that?"

"In about eleven or twelve weeks, I believe."

With a cry, I ran off to find my father, but he'd gone. "Oh why didn't he say goodbye?" I said out loud.

"Because he most probably didn't want to disturb you," said Leo, who'd caught me up. "Most likely didn't want a scene."

I looked around to see the Prefect who'd shown me round the school. "You'll get used to it, it's hard at first, but with time you'll be alright." He paused, smiled before putting one hand under his chin with the other supporting it underneath.

"He's imitating a teacher," I thought.

He spoke again, "I too was homesick when I first came here some years ago now."

I looked at him, knowing that it was important to show that I was listening, but inwardly I wasn't really listening at all, I had other ideas. "I'll ring my mum, my mum will get me out of here I'm sure, she'll never say no." I pretended that I wanted to go to the toilet and walked away. Once out of sight, I ran as fast as I could down the drive and onto the main road to find a phone box. I'd never used a public phone before, but I'd seen other people use them. Frantically, I searched for the right money, which I found and laid out on the tray in front of me. Lifting the receiver, I dialled the operator. Nobody answered for a while. Eventually, I heard a voice on the other end. Without listening to what they had to say, I shouted down the phone, "Is that the operator?"

"It is," came the standard reply.

After some delay and many questions, I managed to get through, "Mum! Is that you?"

My mother answered in her unmistakably gentle way, but before I could tell her anything, I broke down in tears. From inside the hand piece of the phone came a gentle but firm voice, "Where are you Keith?"

I couldn't answer the question, it just wouldn't come out, the emotion was too great. "Will you have me back home mum?" I pleaded.

"Keith, where are you?" she asked again.

"I'm on the road just outside the school mum."

"Does anyone know you're there?"

"No," I replied, "you won't tell them will you?" Again I collapsed into uncontrollable tears. "Don't you want me? Why did you send me here?"

At this my mother began to cry too, but she was adamant, "It's for your own good Keith, your dad thinks that it'll make a man of you!"

"Make a man of me!" I screamed down the phone. "I only want to be with you."

"Yes, I know that sweetheart, but you'll get used to it, and it is the best for you, just you wait and see."

The pips went before I had time to say anything more. I cried bitterly into the empty hand-piece of the phone for some time. It was the last time that I cried from my heart. I felt abandoned, yet I knew that sending me to school was costing my parents a small fortune. It was all very confusing.

A sharp pain in my kidneys ended my dreaming and brought me back to what was going on around me on the ship. "Don't do that!" I cried turning round as I shouted out.

"What's bloody well going on Swifty?"

"Tony Robins. I might have known it was you." "Go on, tell me what's going on?"

"Nothing's going on all right. Nothing that you don't already know about that is."

"Well what are you looking so worried about?"

"Do you mean what am I looking at? I'm just watching the last of England."

He gave me a funny look as if to make allowances for me, but as he did so, I thought I heard someone singing. Naturally I never mentioned it to Tony who would just take the 'mickey', but again I heard it as every one else did around me. Silence came over us as we strained to listen. It grew louder and louder as more people began to sing. It was a song I'd heard on the radio.

Then I heard the words or some of them, *'I never felt more like running away',* from the song *'I never felt more like singing the blues'.* The words hit deep into me as I felt their significance, for I knew that many on board ship would be feeling the same way. Waves of nausea swept over me as I realised that wanting to run away constitutes a major part of life. Me at school some years ago, and here and now, leaving the dockside on board ship, for others. I also realised that it would continually happen throughout life, as people found themselves in positions and situations they had no control over. I also understood that it was the realisation of knowing that caused so much pain. No doubt it would happen again in the future as people found themselves in positions they couldn't come to terms with. There was no escape, and no running away now. I looked toward the Sergeant for strength and saw tears. Great beads of tears ran down his huge face as he sang for all he was worth. By this time all the ship's company joined in the singing with a passion that transcended anything that I'd ever experienced. The words of the song seemed to hang on the wind as the ship started to turn in the dock.

The Sergeant suddenly stopped singing, drew himself up to his full height and started to wave for all his worth at someone on the quayside. My eyes followed his and I saw the object of his emotion - a lady and three small children were frantically waving back to him. I cried. I cried for him as well, careful not to let anyone see of course; but I realised he really was singing the blues.

The ship turned quickly now, and seemed to give a new-found volume to the singing, which reached new heights for me as I really let myself go in this experience of deep emotion. My body tingled with excitement; rivers of feeling flew down my skin, sending shocks to all parts of my body. My whole body rocked with a carousel of different feelings, each one registered individually, yet were in some strange way connected. Excitement followed deep depression, followed by some sort of heroism, followed by intense fear, in a continual *ad hoc* way. I was out of control, unable to contain myself any longer. In that moment I would have killed someone if told to do so. I would most certainly have given my life if necessary. The experience frightened me upon reflection. I somehow retained a picture of myself completely out of control. It stayed with me, ever present, almost as a warning for future reference. I had given myself over to the overwhelming forces that melt down individual thoughts and actions, in order to take on the identity of the crowd, or the unit in this case; for I was one with them as they were with me. The ship turned its bows to the open sea and it was all over. The wind increased as the ship cleared the headland. Soldiers around me departed quickly, but I stayed, I had too many thoughts, too much pain, but I was very much aware that it had to be hidden, just as a secret.

I couldn't quite believe the enormous size of the *Empire Orwell*. When I'd viewed it from the dockside and now on board, it seemed like a great lump of steel, and that's what it proved to be. Its form was quite repulsive, yet in some strange way almost majestic. This was due not only to its size, but to the lines of the ship which were not too pleasing. It looked cumbersome and awkward; in fact it looked as I imagined a troop ship should look like, ugly but strong. It proved to be a warren of passageways that seemed endless. I remember walking down the passageways, wondering which poor sod had to paint all that steel. Everything was newly painted, but it didn't take a genius to see that it was a rush job; it had that kind of look about it. It was painted, but only just, with signs of the old paint showing through in places. The restricted areas for ordinary ranks were clearly marked, and this made it easier to get used to our quarters; although I still managed to get lost on numerous occasions. Our bunks were in the bowels of the ship. I'd managed to get a bunk in the middle, but the space between the top and the bottom bunks was so minimal it made me feel quite claustrophobic. This and no privacy reminded me of school, where everyone knew everything about everyone down to the smallest trivial thing. However, some found it extremely difficult and tempers flared. I never counted how many men were on our deck, but there must have been three hundred or more. The air was stuffy and the smell was foul at times.

After some time had elapsed and we had settled down, we were suddenly brought to order by C.S.M. Bullock, "Stand by your bunks," he shouted above the general noise level.

Some heard him; others didn't or didn't want to.

"Stand by your bloody bunks you load of bloody gobshites!" was his immediate response to being ignored.

Gradually the whole deck came to attention and silence. "Right you men. Listen and listen carefully. This is not a bloody Sunday school outing, and I'm not your bloody teacher. So come to bloody attention at once when I speak to you! Got it?"

"Sir!" came the dutiful reply.

He then turned to the Officer behind him and spoke briefly for a moment before addressing us again, "The Major would like to speak to you."

"Major, Sir!" He bellowed at the top of his voice.

"Thank you Sergeant Major," came the reply as the Major stepped forward to speak to us. "Right men, we're off to war, and you know what that means? We're to be alert and fit at all times. Yes fit!" He paused, looked around the assembled group before him and waited, watching all the time for those who might not be giving him the attention he wanted. His eyes darted around the group, almost daring anyone to show the slightest disinterest or boredom, before he continued, "Your Officers have devised a routine for you. In this routine there will be P.E. Drill, Rifle practise at the rear of the ship where we will be firing live ammunition; and…" He turned to one of the Officers standing near to him and said something that I couldn't quite hear.

The Officer responded rapidly.

"Oh yes!" he continued with a smile, "there'll be some games as well as a Boxing Tournament. I believe that is right Colour?"

The Colour Sergeant confirmed it.

The Major continued, "By the way let me confirm what I said before. Rifle practise will be with *live* ammunition, so you'll have to look lively now. I do hope that you men will do the Company proud during our time at sea. Join in all the activities with enthusiasm and participate as best you can in order to get the maximum benefit possible. We want to see zeal and a willingness to give it a go. So that later in combat you will be able to give a good account of yourselves. Got it?"

We all shouted, "Yes Sir," at the top of our voices.

He turned to Sergeant Major Bullock, who was about to take over and dismiss us, when he stopped in his tracks. He'd obviously forgotten something. "One moment Sergeant Major, I'd almost forgotten. There'll be a roll-call every morning." He smiled at us, "See if anyone's fallen overboard in the night. Also, there'll be the usual Company inspection on deck every morning before breakfast. Twice a week there'll be an inspection by our Commanding officer Colonel Harrison. Finally, it is my duty to warn you of the dangers of drink and the general excesses of alcohol, but I'm sure you all know them, and I'd be probably wasting my time lecturing you." He laughed, thus allowing us to do so too, because it was common knowledge that he liked his booze. With that he left followed by all his entourage.

After we'd been dismissed, I turned to my friend Arnie who was 'B' Company clerk. Arnie was a strange looking guy, built like a toy bulldog, squat with square shoulders and a paunch. His head seemed too big for his body, and what was more, he was losing his hair. But, oh! what he lacked there, he more than made up for with his tongue. I never dared mention any of my thoughts about him, even in fun; the repercussions would be too painful.

"Well, Arnie, what do you make of that?"

He looked at me with a half smile on his face. "Yeah, what do you make of that? I don't bloody well know. But what I do know is that they'll be working our bollocks off. What a thousand men on board? Bloody hell, they'll keep us busy, you can count on that!"

The Sergeant Major reappeared again and stood in the centre of the floor, then bawled at the top of his voice for our attention, which we gave him in quick time. "Right! Listen! It's getting rough and the forecast is for a stormy crossing. So, if you feel sick, get to the ablutions, and don't spew up in your bunk or you'll have to lie in it, not to mention that it will stink for the rest of the voyage." He stopped for a moment as he saw some puzzled looks.

"You!" he pointed to a private soldier stood at the back. "You got a problem soldier?"

"The crossing Sir, which crossing is that?"

"Don't get bloody clever with me soldier. The Bay of Biscay, that's what I'm talking about. What's your bloody na…"

Before he could get the last word out, a huge wave hit the ship sending him and us off balance. We stumbled around while trying to stand up straight, but every time we managed to do so, we were sent flying again. Eventually the Sergeant Major found himself sat on the floor. Soldiers went rushing to his aid, but a suppressed gurgle of laughter could be clearly heard above all the obscenities coming from his lips. He jumped to his feet as soon as he realised that some found it funny and tried to speak, but the ship was rolling really badly by this time, and it was nearly impossible for anyone to stay upright. It was quite a spectacle watching him swaying this way and that in a desperate effort to keep his feet. He eventually left shouting obscenities at us, assuring everyone he hadn't finished with us and he'd be back. Everyone laughed heartily when he'd gone, but the ship's incessant movements began to take over our attention, it was getting serious. Everyone took to their bunks. I lay there and tried to sleep. Eventually, unable to relax enough to sleep, I sat up and looked around to find the lights had been dimmed and I could hardly see a thing. Sitting there in the semi-darkness, I became aware that a number of people were making gurgling sounds in and around the ablutions.

"They're being sick." The thought crossed and recrossed my mind, as I lay back on my pillow trying desperately to come to terms with the extremely violent movements of the ship. I must have fallen asleep, because the next thing that I remember was an upward movement of such proportions that I thought I was going up in the air. This was followed by an almighty shudder as we reached what must have been the top of some huge wave. The boat then began the descent which proved to be equally awesome, as we plunged down, ever down, until I felt we'd never be able to get back up. When the ship hit the nadir of its plunge, it shuddered to such an extent I thought the steel might come apart. Later, I learned that this incredible plunge had occurred because the ship had turned its bows into the storm, and been hit by an enormous wave that had demolished some of its super structure. All hell broke loose on our deck. Some got up in panic and tried to walk, ending up on the floor in a heap, only just managing to claw their way back into their bunks. The ship then began to pitch. The bows of the boat rose until I felt that I was stood upright while still lying on my bunk. It then crashed down until I felt like I was stood on my head. It was really frightening. Each time I waited with baited breath, thinking the ship may never come up again. It was like being on the 'Big Dipper' in Blackpool, only we weren't paying nor wanting the thrill. More and more soldiers were becoming seasick, and the groans became cries for help. Soldiers rushed to the ablutions that were just by my bunk. Others were being sick where they lay, much to the disgust and annoyance of the soldiers above and below them.

The storm couldn't last, but it did. After a while, the smell of sick filled the air. At that point I began to feel squeamish. Arnie Wilkin, who was in a bunk near me gave in, and went to the ablutions, spewing up as he went. I was about to follow him, when I remembered some advice my cousin Colin had given me. He'd said, from his wartime experience on ships in the Atlantic, that a good cure for seasickness was to go and stand in the spray on deck. With this in mind, I clambered up the innumerable steel stairways to the top deck; all the other decks had been closed. When I eventually arrived, I found that the door to the deck wouldn't open; such was the force of the wind. After much swearing, I was about to give up when there must have been a lull in the wind and I managed to force my way on deck. As I took my first step, a gust of wind took all my breath away, the second one slammed me against the railings so hard I thought I'd been hit by someone. I clutched the railings and looked down, it must have been a hundred foot to the water below. Grasping hold of the rail in fear of being blown into the sea, I looked toward the bows of the ship. The roar of the wind and the sound of the sea were deafening, obliterating any and every other sound. I watched the bows of the ship go down, until I felt like I was going to be pitched into it; when I saw the greatest wave imaginable loom up. It hit the ship and completely enveloped the most forward parts, only to be stopped by the superstructure. The spray from that great wave not only reached me, but it wet me through. One minute I was feeling sick, but dry, the very next, I was sick and wet through to the skin! I just stood there completely immobilised, not quite knowing what might happen next.

The sea was enormous, great waves developing in front of the ship, then crashing onto the bows sending spray hundreds of feet into the air. The ship was being tossed around like a cork; I'd never seen nature as raw as this. The immense power of the sea was frightening yet eerie, and in some way beautiful. Standing there almost too frightened to move, I continued to watch the bows rise and fall, becoming almost hypnotised with the rhythmic movement. Incredible sounds came from the ship as the wind shrieked through the rigging hurting my eardrums. Suddenly feeling very cold, I decided to get back inside just as the bows of the ship ascended with the impact of another gigantic wave. The door refused to open. I pulled as hard as I could, but it refused to budge. I tried again, easing the handle down gently, thinking that I might get it open that way, when through the small glass in the door, I saw a face looking at me from the other side. I yanked the handle as hard as I could, losing my balance in the process, the door opened and I fell inside at the feet of the soldier, much to his amusement.

It turned out to be Corporal Stan Docherty out of 'D' Company. "What's it like out there Swifty?" he shouted in my ear.

"Go and see. It's wild. Blow you off your feet."

The noise of the storm was so great I don't think he really heard what I'd said, although he nodded. He struggled to open the door just as I had done. After watching him struggle for a bit, I decided to help, between us we just managed to prise it open. The wind, if anything, was even greater than before. He went out swearing at the top of his voice but barely audible. Looking through the window, I couldn't help laughing, even though seasickness kept me continually retching. Stan's face was screwed up. His eyes were almost closed. I could see his mouth forming obscenities that he aimed at the wind and weather. He eventually came back inside wet through to the skin, but full of the excitement of the storm.

"Did you see them waves Swifty?" he asked. "You wouldn't last long if you fell in!" He looked intently at me for a moment, "I hope this bloody thing stays afloat or we've shit it."

I nodded; my seasickness was so bad I could hardly speak. We stumbled down the staircase as the ship was thrown about in the gale, vaguely noticing that the air was getting hotter as we descended. However, what became more worrying was the smell. I stopped twice to retch; all that came up was foul green bile. It was strange stuff, and I remember being quite worried about having such foul looking stuff in my body. When we arrived near to our deck Stan stopped and sat down on the stairs groaning in some distress, I would have genuinely liked to help him, but my own sickness was so great, I couldn't, and pressed on to my bunk where I collapsed in a heap. By this time the air was like porridge. Shuttlecock, who was in the bunk above me, leaned out over the passageway and spewed out onto the deck below. Soldiers swore at him, as I did, but nobody was in a fit state to do any more. Tommo was sick where he lay. The groans and moans were such that anyone would have thought they were in a First World War Hospital instead of being on a troop ship.

Sometime later during the night, I desperately wanted to go to the toilet. So I stumbled out of my bunk and lurched towards the ablutions. As I opened the door, the water spilled out over the two-foot step and over my legs into the passageway. All the outlets for the toilets and the urinals were blocked up with sick. This meant that the water from them was sloshing around in there with all the filth one could imagine. The smell was so abominable I nearly passed out. I slammed the door quickly and received a torrent of abuse from the soldiers nearby.

"Use the toilets on the next deck up Swifty."

Looking down onto a bunk nearby, I saw the ashen face of Corporal Mick Grantley. Without replying I staggered off to find them.

The storm in the Bay lasted for three days, during which time two soldiers turned up for breakfast, dinner and tea. One of them was Pop Quint, who'd been in the Merchant Navy since leaving school. Pop was one of those unfortunate people who seemed to always be in the wrong place at the wrong time. He'd been on the Seaman's Strike in 1955, when the Government in power decided that anyone on strike who was of relevant age became automatically eligible to do National Service; whereupon, he received his call up papers and reluctantly joined the Loyal Regiment.

On the day after the storm had finished, still feeling very sickly, Sergeant Conelly turned up on our deck and informed everyone that duties would have to be done and he had me down to work in the kitchens, washing dishes. I really felt too ill to work, but there was no alternative.

At roll-call the next morning he read out the orders for the day, "Private Swift, you're with Private Calburn in the kitchens."

"Are we cooking Sergeant?" Calburn asked with a twinkle in his eye.

Sergeant Conelly walked over to him, "Are we being our shitty little self Private Calburn? Or are you just fuckin' stupid!"

"I was only…"

Sergeant Conelly didn't allow him to finish what he was saying, "Shut your flaming mouth Calburn before I stick something in it!" He turned to the assembled men, "Now you know where to go after Inspection, and remember, I'll be coming round to see that you're doing a good job, so be warned!"

He turned to where Lieutenant Kutchen had been standing, our Platoon Officer, but he'd gone. "Right, dismiss."

We all turned to the right, snapped our left foot down, and went to our allotted tasks. Jeff and I made our way to the kitchens, where we were greeted by a crew member who introduced himself as 'Bugsy'. He was quite the most formidable looking man I'd seen. He must have been six feet six inches tall and about twenty odd stone. What was more frightening, he had a personality to match. Apparently, he held some rank among the crew that I never really understood, except that crew members scurried round when he gave them orders. What quickly became apparent was that when he told us to do something, he did so with all the authority of an Officer. His voice boomed out advice and rebuke, in a string of well-practised phrases, quips and well-chosen words, that provoked immediate action throughout the ancillary department of the cookhouse. I quite liked him for his quick wit and repartee. The result of which saw him coming over to us frequently to talk as we washed up.

"I reckon he fancies you Swifty!" Calburn said as we saw him making his way towards us.

What do you mean?" I asked not really understanding what he was on about.

"He's an arse bandit, a wufter you know!"

"Seems like a nice bloke to me, whatever he is."

"You one of them Swifty?"

Now Calburn was a pretty small man and he wasn't a fighter. The idea of thumping him crossed my mind, but I knew from past experience that it would only lead to further trouble and I'd have to explain myself to my Officers yet again. "Shut up Calburn, yer mouth's too big!"

"Shut up yerself Swifty, yer think yer an Officer."

At that precise moment I was violently sick. I leant over the slop bucket, which was as big as an oil drum, and retched for some time. I could hear Calburn swearing and cursing at me, but there was nothing I could do, I was so sick.

When I eventually pulled my face out of the drum, he stuck a wet floor cloth into it.

"Do that again Calburn and I'll stick your head up your arse-hole, was all I could manage."

"Well I'm doing all the work around here, you lazy sod."

This was true, and I knew it and felt guilty, but there was nothing I could do I was so ill. However, I resolved to remember the incident and get him back at some later date.

The storm passed, and with it the whole atmosphere on the ship changed. The skies cleared from grey to blue as did the water, the whole Regiment settled down to enjoy the voyage. We were told that the ship would be putting in at Las Palmas in the Canary Islands. As we approached them at daybreak, the mountains looked just like needles pointing toward heaven. It was quite the most idyllic sight I'd ever seen. As we drew ever nearer it resembled 'fairyland' coming from wintry Britain.

About two hours before we were due to dock, the ship's bells sounded for Inspection Parade. We all lined up in our various companies, while our Officers scurried around carrying out various duties, looking as excited as we felt. Sergeant Major Bullock drilled us while we waited for our Commanding Officer to attend. He eventually arrived with his usual entourage and we were stood at ease.

Major Coker came forward, "Now listen, and listen carefully. You are to be allowed shore leave, and for those who have little or no experience of this, I warn you that behaviour unbefitting of British soldiers will not be tolerated." He paused, "Do you understand me?"

Silence pervaded, nobody thinking that he needed an answer.

"Well do you?"

Still there was no answer.

"Sergeant Major I really believe we should cancel shore leave!"

To which we all responded with, "Yes Sir."

"Yes," Major Coker said, "I wondered what it would take to make you wake up. Now at least I'll know that you'll be of a good mind to behave yourselves, but I also know that some of you will drink too much and forget your intention. What I will stress to those is that..." He paused and looked at the Sergeant Major with a half smile, "Why should I bother it's all been said before without any bit of use. However, I will say that the Army takes a dim view of British soldiers molesting foreign women; for a start you never know what you'll get!" He suddenly realised what he'd said. "Well I mean, it can lead to a number of unpleasant experiences, sometimes International incidents and very serious trouble. I warn you again, anyone causing disturbances will be dealt with very severely. Do you understand me?"

"Yes Sir," we shouted at the top of our voices.

He turned to the Sergeant Major again, "Dismiss them Sergeant Major and remind them about the Inspection before being allowed shore leave."

The Officers led by Major Coker left. We were standing at ease waiting to be dismissed.

The Sergeant Major shouted: "Parade!"

We all drew ourselves up to the alert in readiness for the next command.

"Parade! Shun!"

The parade came to attention. The Sergeant Major saluted the retiring Officers who returned his salute. Sergeant Major Bullock really enjoyed his rank and revelled in his position of power. He was a natural bully and had crafted the art to a fine degree.

He returned to the parade again, "Anybody who brings disgrace on 'B' Company brings disgrace upon me." He looked at us for a moment before continuing, "I bloody well 'ope you bloody lot understand me? That includes Private Morgan, are you listening?"

"Yes Sergeant Major," came the standard reply.

"Good, there'll be an Inspection and nobody's going ashore if they're not properly dressed, got it? Now as you were."

We all stood at ease and waited for the command to come to attention yet again.

"Ssshun!" came the command, and we all came smartly to attention.

"Dismiss!" He always stretched the word to an incredible length, hanging onto the first three letters for ages, allowing it to reach a crescendo before spitting out the last four.

We went away intent upon getting ashore. However, in order to do so, we all knew that we'd have to be 'bulled up to the eyebrows'. This term meant that the creases in our trousers would have to be razor sharp, our brasses on belts and caps would have to be shining like 'the noonday sun' as the Sergeant Major would put it. Lastly, and perhaps more importantly, our boots would have to be gleaming with the application of 'spit and polish'. This application always secretly amused me. You spat on the boot, made small rings with the liquid by rubbing furiously in a circle before continually adding more polish and spit. The exercise was repeated time and time again until your arm felt like it might drop off. The result witnessed a mystical shine, and what the Sergeant Major would call, 'A reasonable shine lad keep trying.'

His own boots were quite something to behold, you could almost see your face in them.

The ship docked and we all lined up ready to disembark. I was at the back of the queue waiting patiently. However it allowed me to have a bird's eye view of the island. The island seemed strange with so many differing colours. It represented something I'd never seen before, a completely different landscape. I was quite stunned by the mountains that were so clearly visible in the clear blue sky. They rose like great church spires providing a beautiful backdrop to the town on the side of the hill.

I went through the gauntlet of Inspection carried out by the Sergeant Major and the N.C.O.s under the watchful eye of Lieutenant Kutchen. They scrutinised me from top to bottom.

The Sergeant Major couldn't help himself in the end. "You've only just made it Private Swift, so you can take that bloody grin off your face."

I wasn't aware that I'd been grinning, it must have been because I was so nervous, but I couldn't help responding instinctively, "I'm only happy Sergeant Major."

The Sergeant Major screwed his face up in annoyance, "Piss off Private bloody Swift you fucking well annoy me."

I joined my friends on the quayside. They were talking about Johnny Neilson out of 'A' Company. Johnny had a reputation throughout the Battalion as a carefree laid back sort of guy, who just couldn't care less about Army discipline, nor the punishments that went with it for that matter. I'd often seen him marching around camp in Barnard Castle, under guard, having been sentenced to time in the Regimental jail. His crimes were always the same - being scruffy on parade, answering N.C.O.s back, never Officers, he just never seemed to rate Non Commissioned Officers, they never had any status with him. However, he was very undisciplined. When sentenced to do 'jankers', which meant fatigues, and having to report to the guardroom at six in the morning and ten at night in full battledress, he'd refuse to do it, and would actually ask the Officer presiding to put him in jail, which he invariably did. Whenever he passed me under guard, he'd always have a big smile on his face, one hand holding his trousers up while marching as fast as he could. I knew that most of the Officers liked him for his courage and pluck, but I also knew the N.C.O.s hated him.

"Hey Swifty, you missed it!" said Arnie with a huge grin on his face.

"Missed what?" I asked.

"Johnny Neilson, you should have seen Bullock's face, he nearly had a heart attack, no kidding. His face went as red as a tomato."

"Go on tell me what happened?"

Arnie Wilkin fell about laughing, even after trying to compose himself enough to tell the tale. When he started to speak he'd suddenly begin again, gurgling uncontrollably.

"What's so funny then?" I asked getting slightly annoyed.

At that exact moment Sergeant Conelly intervened and the mood changed. "Go on tell *me* what's so bloody funny then. You can tell me."

"Nothing really Mick," said Arnie not thinking.

"Mick!" he shouted. "I'm a bloody Sergeant to you, and don't you bloody well forget it."

We all clammed up. Sergeant Conelly was largely an unknown quantity. Nobody ever knew what he might do next. He was, according to popular understanding, an Ex St. Helens Rugby League Player, and an expert on small arms weapons. He was also an alcoholic. At the time I just thought he was a big drinker, who was always broke and borrowed off anyone and everyone. I never lent him anything, which made him instantly loathe me.

He looked at us all, "Where yer goin' to?"

"We're going to see the sights Sergeant," I said, partly to annoy him, and I got the required reply.

"You dog's fucking bastard Swift!" He turned to the rest of the group. "What you lot doin' with him, he'll get you into trouble! Come with me?"

"And pay for your drinks Sergeant," I mouthed almost inaudibly, but he must have heard something.

"What was that *Private* Swift?" he responded, emphasising the Private bit.

"I said we'd buy you a drink Sergeant."

"No you bloody well didn't; what did you say?"

I repeated what I'd already said, whereupon, he pointed a finger at me.

"Watch him you lot, watch him! He's a wrong un! Especially you Thomkin." The Sergeant walked away and wandered up the road, presumably to find the nearest bar.

"Why me?" said Tommo, when he was safely out of hearing range.

Arnie turned to us, "Well where are we going?"

"Let's wander up to town and have a look at the local talent," suggested Bill Tatlow.

"What language do they speak?" interrupted Tommo.

"Spanish you silly sod," Arnie answered with an air of supreme knowledge.

"Can't they speak English?" Tommo asked quite innocently.

We all laughed at Tommo, who must have felt it, because he wouldn't let it drop. "Not properly civilised, can't be, if they don't speak bloody English."

"Coming from bloody Rishton you'd know all about that, I'm sure." said Arnie with a grin.

I thought, "I'm keeping out of this argument," it was just too quick for me.

Arnie's wit was revered and feared. It hurt, I could see it on Tommo's face but there was no way you could hit back. I'd tried, and although I knew some big words, I could never get a chance to use them, he always came away with the laughs, and it was always at my expense. I wouldn't have minded so much, but he was nothing physically.

We went up to town on foot, resisting the offers of the many taxi drivers who were touting for business on the quayside; we needed our money for other things. However, the taxis did captivate our attention for some time. They were old pre-war vehicles, immaculately kept, gleaming in the bright sunshine. The drivers were shouting for business in broken English.

When no business came their way quickly enough, they'd resort to attracting our attention by other means. "You wanna go town Johnny?" followed by, "You wanna woman Johnny?"

It never really occurred to me that they were serious and I could have got a woman. I just thought that they were desperate for business and would use any means to get some. Anyway, the island seemed too idyllic for that sort of thing. We declined their offer and walked in the direction of the town. When we got to the main street, or what looked like the main street, I was shocked by what I saw. The place looked worse than the slums of Preston or some other Lancashire town. The roads were dirty, with open sewers running by the side of the road that stank to high heaven. The houses were in very poor condition, with what looked like plaster peeling off the outside walls. As we walked along the street, the occupants began to come out of them to see us. In this way we were able to see inside their houses. What I saw was evidence of poverty that exceeded anything I'd seen before in Britain. They seemed to have little in the way of furniture, no carpets on the floor, and wallpaper seemingly in tatters, coming off the walls. I was utterly disgusted with the place, never for one minute thinking that being near to the docks, it would be naturally rough and ready, and that the better parts would be somewhere else. The people, who came out of their houses, were rough, poorly dressed, and undoubtedly poverty stricken.

"Bloody hell! It's just like Ribbleton Lane in Preston!" I exclaimed.

"No it's not, it's a bloody sight worse." replied Bill, who gave me a withering look, which confused me until I realised he came from there.

"Come on let's find a bar," said Tommo who was striding out in front.

Arnie looked at him, "Yeah, preferably one without Sergeant Conelly in."

"Piss off Arnie, he'll be in 'em all," I replied.

We headed towards a bar when a young boy came running out of a house towards us. "You want 'jig-a jig' Johnny? Me nice sister." He must have been barely ten years old at the most.

Bill told him to piss off, but he continued to follow us before he finally got the message, whereupon he transferred his attention to another group of soldiers.

We managed to find a bar eventually and settled down with some drinks after debating the price for what seemed hours. Within no time the bar was full. The noise got louder and louder as more and more soldiers came in. We finished our drinks and were about to leave when someone began shouting in the entrance. I couldn't see who it was, but the voice was unmistakably that of Sergeant Conelly.

"He's arrived," announced someone.

I looked at my three friends and saw that Arnie had begun to panic.

"Is there a back entrance? There must be some other way out of here. I don't want to be in here with that bastard, he'll have all our money off us."

"He won't get mine!"

Arnie made a face at me, "You know Swifty; you're such a clever sod. Fight anybody eh? Well you're going to have to learn that there are people that you can fight, and there are people you can't fight in this outfit, and you don't seem to know which is which."

My reputation for fighting followed me around wherever I went. It started in basic training when I was pitched into the middle of an intake of recruits from Liverpool and East Lancashire. I'd fought in order to survive, although I must admit I didn't mind fighting, and was probably to blame for some of the fights I got into.

Arnie continued, "When are you going to learn?"

"Yeah, that may be the case, if you say so. But he's getting no money off me."

Arnie smiled, "Well let's get out of here then."

Bill looked around and tried a door, but a Spanish guy rushed towards us shouting and gesticulating that he shouldn't be doing that. By this time we were all standing together, desperately trying to think of a way out in order to avoid meeting the Sergeant, when to our horror, he elbowed his way through the crowd. His eyes were glazed, he'd obviously had a lot to drink in the short time he'd been ashore.

He saw us, "C'mon lads. Yer not bloody well leavin' without buying yer old Sergeant a drink now, are you?"

Arnie looked at me as did Bill and Tommo, and Arnie's look spoke volumes.

"They may be, but I'm not!" I said.

The Sergeant stared at me, then lurched towards me with his fist, as if to hit me. I stood my ground not really knowing what would happen next. At the last minute he pulled back, due to his mate Corporal Becker pleading with him not to get into a fight; but it didn't stop him from pushing his head close to mine until I could smell his foul breath. "You Dog's bastard! You're a wrong un Swift an I'll fuckin' have yer yet."

I looked at him without speaking before I pushed past him followed by my three friends. He tried to follow, not wanting to let it drop, but Corporal Becker pulled him back. We left him shouting obscenities and threats.

Once outside, the heat of the day hit us and made us want to get out of the sun as quickly as we could. I expected to get a hard time from Arnie who'd almost predicted what would happen, but he never said a word, although he kept giving me furtive glances.

Eventually, he could hold it no longer, "He'll 'ave yer Swifty, make no mistake, you bet he will, even though he were pissed, but drunken men always remember!"

"Yes," I answered. "That's what they say, but it's not always the case 'cause I never remember anything when I get drunk."

Bill and Tommo laughed, but Arnie remained deadly serious, "But that's why they call him the two pint wonder isn't it lads."

They all laughed; I joined in because I knew it was true. We made our way back slowly towards the ship. The island was beautiful, but so poor. It was the contrast of such beauty and poverty that hit me. By comparison Lancashire, and particularly Preston, was grey, dull and ugly. It's the weather I thought, but I knew in my heart it was much more than that.

Arnie guessed my thoughts, "Too bloody hot to work here, that's why there's no money around and everyone's so poor. Too bloody hot for me!"

The sun beat down on us, by the time we were near the docks I was wet through with perspiration.

"It's only the British Army that could send you out in this heat in battledress, bloody hell! I'm roasting!"

Bill remarked as he began to remove some of his uniform.

"Hey! If 'Big Mick' sees you, he'll have you Bill!" Arnie said with all the certainty of a company clerk.

'Big Mick' was the notorious Regimental Police Sergeant, who administered the law as Moses might have done. He stood six feet four inches, must have weighed something well over eighteen stone, being enormously fat.

It was so hot, that by the time we arrived back at the docks, we'd taken off our ties and B.D. jackets and had them slung over our arms; and still felt most uncomfortable. However, we also knew that the Regimental Police would be waiting for us at the gangway, scrutinising everyone coming back on board, and they'd be in a foul mood looking for trouble, having been stuck on duty while everyone else was out drinking. With this in mind, we all spruced up our appearances behind one of the warehouses, before attempting to board the ship again.

"Hey, I think we're first back," I said looking directly at the Provo-Sergeant.

"One of the first," he said with a grin. "Some of those bastards didn't last ten minutes before they got into trouble. I'd have liked to have gone ashore," he almost whispered with a resigned smile, "but that's the bloody Army I suppose."

I felt for him, he seemed quite human compared to the rest of them.

Arnie would have none of it. "A hyena always acts like a hyena in the end," he said, with a look of profundity.

I didn't know exactly what he meant, but I had no intention of asking him, so I let it go.

We went to our bunks exhausted and lay down. I dropped off to sleep to be awakened later by the lads who were going up on deck to see the latecomers returning. Apparently, rumour had it that there'd been some trouble and it would be a sight to behold. We scurried on deck. It was going dark, some were saying that the ship should have put to sea, but couldn't because a considerable number of men had not returned. The Regimental Police were out rounding them up. We saw some returning under escort.

"They've shit it," said Arnie with a look of one who knows.

Then, from round the corner of the warehouse came the sight we'd all been waiting for, Sergeant Conelly being dragged along by three burly Regimental Policemen. He was fighting, swearing and cursing the Policemen at every step, and was being really roughed up badly. We all laughed at the sight. Drunk, dishevelled with all his clothes torn and dirty, he resembled something out of a comic strip, or even a horror film.

"He won't be a Sergeant in the morning," said Arnie quietly in my ear.

"He'll be bloody lucky to be alive in the morning. See that bloody great lump over that Policeman's eye? I bet our Sergeant did that." I observed as Colour Sergeant Stock tapped me on the shoulder:

"Be careful what you say Private Swift, you're just a bit too clever at times."

"Colour Sergeant, I was only saying what I think you already know," I replied.

"Yes that's the problem, most people don't. They're more careful. I'm only trying to give you some good advice. If what you're saying gets back to Sergeant Conelly, heaven only knows what he'll do. Bollock you up hill and down dale for starters I would think. And what's even worse, he doesn't seem to like you anyway. So, if I were you I'd shut it, and shut it tight, right?" With that he moved away.

Arnie, ever the sage, offered his advice when the Colour Sergeant had moved out of hearing distance. "You should watch your mouth Swifty; you have too much to say. You never think about what you're saying or who you're saying it to."

"I just can't believe it. Talk about jumping on the bandwagon. Sod off will you? You sodding little garden gnome."

Arnie smiled at me sardonically before turning to Bill and Tommo, "Did you hear that, resorting to his usual filth, can't conduct a reasonable conversation, must always resort to filth or violence." Then he turned to me, "Go on threaten me now; c'mon isn't that the next step?"

I felt completely demoralised and rejected, and walked away. Soldiers are not supposed to cry, but I felt like I would, I was so upset, not with Arnie, because I knew in my heart that there was some truth in what he said, but with myself. Everything in my upbringing went against the language that I was using. I didn't like it, but everyone used it except the Padre. It wasn't like this at home, I rarely swore, and never in my father's house. A sense of guilt bit deep into me, yet within me was the need to conform, and in doing just that, I'd arrived at my present predicament. Then it dawned on me that I hadn't sworn, so what was he on about? However, I realised that it was too late to bring the matter up; the chance had gone. I did however make a resolution not to swear, it didn't last long, but the inner voice never stopped pricking me in moments I never expected. I decided that soldiers were one thing in the Regiment and another thing at home on leave. How else can you come to terms with all the training that goes into teaching soldiers how to kill without hesitation and mercy? Particularly when the so-called enemy haven't done you any harm, and you don't even know them. It was as if we had two split lives, one for war and one for home and normality, being kind and reasonable. In this way, I came to terms with everything that was being demanded of me in the Regiment.

I remembered bayonet practise at Fulwood Barracks. We had a young soldier in our Company who was quite effeminate. He was a strong young man in many other ways though, holding to his strict religious beliefs that put many to shame. However, he was gentle and non-aggressive, and came in for a lot of stick off the N.C.O.s who found him easy meat. During bayonet practice he'd run at the dummy gurgling with half suppressed laughter, much to the annoyance of the N.C.O. in charge, who was intent upon getting his charges to scream at the top of their voices in the most blood curdling manner.

The response of the Officer in charge was usually nothing short of amazing, "You're not in bloody church now soldier. You're out to kill the bloody thing, not to bloody well convert it. Stick the fucking bayonet into the bag, just as you would have stuck it into a German in the last war." He would shout until I thought he was going to have a convulsion.

Whereupon Private Tooby would inform him that he was too young to have been in the last war. This would lead to the Officer almost losing control of himself. I thought at one stage he was actually going to hit him, but he never did. He would then make him do it again and again, shouting the most obscene things at him; but it made no difference, he just couldn't satisfy the Officer who simply gave up in the end.

The ship sailed with fifteen men in the ship's jail and no deserters. The men in jail were to be charged with numerous offences from being drunk and disorderly, to the very serious offence of striking a superior Officer. I comforted myself with the thought that I wasn't one of them, speculating endlessly with my friends as to the fate of the men charged. With those thoughts I climbed into my bunk and fell asleep.

Reveille was early the following morning, or so it seemed. After which we were summoned to the deck for Inspection, where our Officer Commanding read the riot act out about the disgraceful behaviour of some of the soldiers on shore leave; leaving us with the knowledge that those soldiers who were in any way involved in the disturbances at Las Palmas, would not be getting any more shore leave in the near future. After we'd been dismissed, we made our way up to the dining room for breakfast.

Arnie made out that he'd saved me from getting into deep trouble. "You ought to be bloody grateful to me Swifty," he said. "I 'ope you know that but for my influence over you, you'd be in the 'nick' right now. Think about it!"

"Piss off Arnie," I answered. "I know enough not to associate with that crowd."

"Yeah, that is true, but what are you like when you've got a bit of ale down you then? You'd be fighting and farting all the way up to 'Big Mick's' knee caps, wouldn't he lads?"

All the lads looked at me and laughed. Arnie made such a fool out of me I couldn't answer him.

The canteen had a large window, through which we could see the sea as the waves brushed past the ship. The sea was quite beautiful, rich in all the different shades of blue and green. Green predominated, but the shade changed every time you looked at it. Sometimes, and for no apparent reason, it changed to blue. I'd never seen anything like it before, and found myself continually staring at it. I also noticed other soldiers did the same which made me feel better.

The days passed with drill, endless parades, followed by incredibly boring lectures on jungle warfare. I developed a great strategy for coping with this by pretending to listen to every word without hearing one; I just concentrated on my own thoughts. However, this let me down when any questions were asked, but I was astute enough to keep my head down when that happened. When we weren't in lectures, we'd be stripping Brens, Stens and F.N. guns down. The crunch came when we were put into teams, and competitions were held in order to speed up the process. Nobody wanted to let his team down, so great concentration became necessary. I learned fast and became quite expert in stripping and reassembling the various guns. When we used live ammunition, we would fire at balloons that had been released over the stern of the ship. This proved very popular, although they were extremely hard to hit. I proved to be hopeless at this, partly due to the fact that I was more concerned about dropping my rifle in the sea as I rested my elbows on the ship's rail.

We sailed into the tropics, it was so hot, the heat below the main deck was especially stifling. The lads stayed on deck until late before descending below to their bunks. Some actually found it so uncomfortable below decks they slept on the deck itself and were allowed to do so. The days when we had free time were spent just lounging around on deck in the sun. However this proved disastrous for some who fell asleep, or simply stayed around too long in the sun.

"Have you seen Dave Munthy's back Swifty?"

"Why should I?"

"Look at Dave Munthy's bloody back."

I stared at Bill wondering what he was on about.

"See the bloody blister on his back, it's this size." He gesticulated with his hands to show me how big it was. "That's what comes from too much sunbathing. It must cover ninety percent of his back."

"Really," I said.

"Yeah! really!" he replied with a sneer.

I knew then that he was serious. I'd never seen anything like that and wanted to know more, so I rushed off to find Munthy. After speaking to some of his friends I found out that he was in the ship's medical room being looked after by the Medical Officer. After a few enquiries I found it, and hovered around nosey enough to risk the wrath of the Medical Officer should he see me. Plucking up courage, I put my face round the door and asked if I could speak to someone?

"Yeah, what do you want?" came from the orderly.

I didn't meet his eyes; my eyes were looking beyond him to where Munthy was sat at the far end of the room. The Medical Officer's body shielded his bare back, so I couldn't see a thing.

"C'mon, be quick, what's the matter with you, or are you just noseying about Munthy?"

"No! No! Corporal, my leg's giving me a lot of pain."

"Yes, well so is my arse, get out of here before I put you on a charge for wasting my time."

I closed the door and waited outside. Eventually, the orderly appeared followed by Munthy and the Medical Officer.

The Corporal approached me, "You still here?"

"Me Corporal?" I answered.

"Yes you. I thought I told you to piss off!"

"I just want to see Munthy for a minute."

Munthy came forward when he heard his name mentioned, "Me? What's it you want Swifty?"

"What's your back like Munthy?"

Before the Corporal had time to intervene, Munthy had turned round. He was bare backed and unable to get any clothes over the largest blister I'd ever seen. It stretched from the top of his back to about three quarters of the way down. All the water was hanging in the skin at the bottom. It might well have been a balloon filled with water.

"Does it hurt Munthy?"

"Na not a lot," he replied shortly before the Corporal came over to me.

"I thought I told you to get out of here!"

I went quickly after hearing the Medical Officer suggesting to the Corporal that he should charge 'that man' for persistently ignoring him. It left me feeling uneasy, because my name had been mentioned. I'd have to hope that they couldn't remember, or in fact they'd never heard; but I knew that Munthy would never grass.

It appeared that many soldiers had suffered from too much sun. Many men in our Company went sick with either blisters or suspected sunstroke. This situation led to the Colonel of the Regiment addressing the whole Battalion. We were all squashed together on deck when the Colonel and his entourage appeared. He was a small man, but he had that military bearing that produces great aloofness, which in turn demands instant respect.

The Regimental Sergeant Major bellowed out, "Parade," at the top of his voice followed by, "Attention!" which was lost in the thunderous roar of boots slamming down together.

There we stood rigidly to attention in the blazing sun until the Colonel told us to stand at ease, "It has come to my notice that some of you men have been sunbathing. Yes, well it does seem the thing to do. However, the sun being what it is, can be both healthy and unhealthy at one and the same time, if you understand what I mean. Let me explain, we are damned near the equator here. Now that means that the sun is directly overhead, and that means it's hotter and you get burnt. Now, as some of you most probably know, some soldiers have not shown the respect they should have for the sun, probably because they have some strange idea that they can stand it better than others." He paused, then carried on when he thought it had gone in, "I know that some kind of silly competition to get brown goes on amongst you, can't see the point myself, but I know it goes on. Let me tell you," his voice began to rise as his intensity grew, "I consider it a stupid thing to do, to go and get burnt even if it is by the sun. There can be no possible excuse. Therefore, I consider it to be a self inflicted injury, and you all know what that means I'm sure?"

Arnie looked across at me with a slight grin on his face, I knew that he was thinking that I didn't have a clue what the consequences might mean, so I gave him a sign that he had no possible way of misinterpreting. He understood with a grimace.

By this time the Colonel had folded his arms and was looking around the assembled gathering. While we waited in silence for him to speak. "Having a self inflicted injury means that your pay will be stopped while you are sick. Also, time will be added onto your service, so let's not have anymore of this stupidity. Keep your shirt on your back and sit in the shade if at all possible." He turned to the Sergeant Major, "Dismiss the parade Sergeant Major!"

"Sir," came the instant reply.

With that the Colonel left, followed dutifully by his entourage.

The Regimental Sergeant Major then addressed us, "Right men. You heard the Colonel. Anybody going sick with sunburn from now on is not going to be too popular. Got it?" He then bellowed at the top of his voice at us, "You've all seen Munthy's back, I'm sure. The Medical Officer says that it needs skin grafts. Do you bloody well understand that?"

"Yes Sir," came the standard reply.

"Good. Now as you were!" At which point he dismissed us.

We made our way back to our bunks discussing the fate of those already suffering from sunburn and those who might suffer from it in the future.

The sun continued to beat down upon the Southern Ocean as we gradually sailed nearer to Cape Town. It was a relaxing time, seeing the flying fish and watching the dolphins chasing the ship. It seemed so peaceful and settled, it was hard to believe that we were going to war. Everyone on our deck seemed so happy. I never saw any fights, nor did I get into any arguments. However, as we approached Cape Town a strange feeling of expectancy seemed to come over us, and gradually change our psychology. Perhaps we'd been at sea too long and the cramped conditions had taken their toll; or maybe it was the phenomenon of rounding the Cape that lay unconsciously under the surface? Whatever it was, the mood changed.

I thought about the prospect of seeing Table Mountain and discussed it with my friends, who all agreed that it must one of the greatest sights in all Africa, with clouds covering its flat top making it look like a tablecloth. As we neared this most southern African port, excitement began to build up among the general body of troops. However, the immediate need was to have a hair-cut. Word had gone round that any soldier with untidy or long hair would not be allowed shore leave at Cape Town. Arnie, my mate, had already had a haircut. He always seemed to have an incredible ability to anticipate everything, as if he somehow knew what was going to happen next. By comparison I never seemed to be able to develop this ability, and correspondingly, found myself scrambling with the masses at the back. Hearing that someone was cutting hair on the second deck, I hurried there. The queue was so long, it went round the corridor and down the stairs. If my estimate was anything like true, there must have been fifty or sixty men waiting. I waited for an hour, but patience was never my virtue, so I left.

"Hey, that's a fine haircut, Swifty lad," said Arnie pointing his finger at me with a laugh.

"Piss off smart arse," was all I could manage by way of reply.

After more sarcasm and laughs at my expense, he eventually told me about someone in Headquarter Company who would occasionally cut hair. "Tell him that I sent you, and he might do it for a small fee. His name's Bill Bosby."

"Right," I said, "We're due in Cape Town tomorrow, so it's getting bloody serious."

Brian Shuttlecock, who'd been listening while lying flat on his back, offered his opinion, "I'd tell you to bugger off Swifty, if it were me."

"Well it's not you Norman. And anyway you haven't a brain Mr. Shuttlecock, and if you had, you wouldn't be able to find it. You couldn't find a brothel with a tart as a guide."

Shuttlecock jumped out of his bunk, "My name's not Norman, and I'm bloody well sick of you Swifty. I'll flatten yer, if yer don't keep yer mouth shut."

"Well come on then, do it." I waited.

He backed off and climbed slowly back into his bunk. "Another time Swift. Another time."

"Piss off Shuttlecock, you're like the barber's cat - all piss and wind!" It was a saying I'd learned from one of my father's workmen; it brought a few laughs and made me feel good. However, it didn't solve the immediate problem of getting a haircut, so I went in search of Bosby.

Arriving at what I considered to be the right place, I asked if anybody knew where Bill Bosby might be? Nobody answered.

"Are you deaf? I shouted most irritated by the silence.

A guy sat up in the bottom bunk. "Yeah, I'm Bosby. What do you want?"

"Arnie Wilkin said you'd cut my hair if I asked you."

He brought his legs slowly over the bunk, placing them on the floor, before slowly bringing his eyes up to meet mine. "Two and six. That's what I charge, money up front and I'll do it now."

I hadn't any money, but I knew we'd be getting paid before getting off the boat, also I expected a five pound note from my mother in the post at Cape Town. "Right, Bill, listen. I'll give you two and six when we get paid and…"

"Listen, I don't know who you are but I don't cut hair for nobody without money up front. Get it?"

"Yeah," I answered, "but let me finish..."

"No money now - no haircut. Okay?" he answered before I could finish.

I was desperate, he was proving to be very stubborn and wouldn't let me explain. "Bill! I'll give you three and six. Ask Arnie Wilks, really, he'll tell you I'll pay."

A voice called out, "Tell him to piss off or I'll piss him off for real."

I wondered who it was that was speaking. Although I couldn't see the speaker, I knew the voice was coming from the bunk above Bill. Being quite annoyed at his intrusion, I gave vent to my feelings. "Mind yer own business, it's nothing to do with you."

I'd barely got the last word out before he'd jumped down, grabbed my hair, pulling it downwards while bringing his knee up into my face. He kneed me again and again as he dragged me like a dog across the floor. I didn't know what was happening to me at first; nobody had ever attacked me with such ferocity before. I remember a strange feeling, a feeling that told me that everything was a farce. This sensation soon disappeared as the brutality of the attack dragged me into an appalling sense of stark reality; a strange and ominous thought occurred to me that I might die. For the first time in my life I felt abused. Certainly, I'd been hit many times before, but I'd always had some freedom to fight back. This attack was quite different; through his constant grip on my hair, I was helpless to hit back. Eventually, he let me go, only to elbow me in the face as he did so. As much as I tried, I couldn't summon up enough venom to respond. It was as if I just waited submissively to be hit, to be abused again and again. I hadn't to wait for more than a second before he grabbed the lapels of my jacket and pulled me roughly towards him, putting his head down at the last minute. The intention was to bang the top of his skull into my face.

However, to my utter surprise he somehow missed and lost hold of me. "That'll teach yer, yer bastard!"

He'd hardly finished the last word before I'd hit him. The surprise and puzzled look on his face told me that this was the last thing that he expected. I still don't know how I managed to summon up enough energy to hit him. All I knew was that I really thought he might kill me and if I hit him and kept on hitting him, he wouldn't be able to hit me back. On this impulse, I launched everything into a desperate counter attack. It took me beyond any point I'd ever been before. Instinctively I knew I couldn't win, but a sense of the sheer need to survive demanded from me an intense determination to fight. I remember little of what occurred in the ruckus which was to follow.

Two emotions managed to pervade my consciousness, fear and the vaguest sense of hope that my own ability to fight could not be rubbished so easily, or so cruelly. Punches rained in, it seemed that they were mine, in a dream-like haze where instinct seemed to take the place of any strategy I might have learned in the ring.

"Right you two stop fighting. And that's an order!" The voice of Ex Sergeant Corporal Conelly brought us to a sudden halt.

I looked at my adversary and saw a huge swelling near his eye and blood round his mouth. I felt greatly satisfied that I'd managed to fight back, especially when I realised how big he was, well in excess of six feet against my five feet seven inch frame. The sense of satisfaction was short-lived however as I felt and tasted blood running down my face and into my mouth. It was then that I felt the pain. During the fight I must have been so desensitised as not to feel a thing. The feel of my own blood was nauseating, with its bitter taste and stickiness, that I began to tremble and shake. I felt my face and ran my fingers across rising bumps. My nose felt twice as big as it should. Bits of skin were left straggling on the inside of my mouth caused by blows to my cheek which had cut on my teeth. They proved to be extremely painful; and in an effort to relieve the pain, I eventually yanked at one, only to experience excruciating pain and an immediate resolve not to bother further.

Bernie Rend came across to me, "Hey Swifty, you surprised that bastard Spendler."

"Did I?" I answered, somewhat pleased by the observation, but more than thankful I was still in one piece.

"Yeah, but he's the Colour Sergeant's best mate, so watch your back."

"Did you see what he did to me?" I pointed to the swellings around my eyes and cheeks.

"Yeah, but have you seen him? You've loosened his teeth, one of 'em's hanging out."

I didn't say anything; I couldn't remember hitting him that hard. Of course I never disclosed that to Bernie. What he was saying sounded too good to be spoilt. I made my way back to my deck and my bunk.

Arnie was there, sitting on the end of the bed. He laughed when he saw the state I was in. "What did I tell yer?" He looked around for an audience, "Can't take me bloody eyes off him for a moment before he's trying to fight the whole bloody ship."

"But Spendler set on me…"

He didn't let me get any further before he interrupted me. I knew the lads were all ready to have a laugh, but suddenly Arnie got very serious. "Spendler! Spendler's about six foot bloody three. You trying to commit suicide Swifty? You've got mixed up, it's an apple a day not a fight."

All the lads laughed.

By this time I could hardly see out of one eye and the other wasn't so good. My mouth was bleeding profusely on the inside and I felt sick; so without answering, I made my way to the ablutions to clean up. Washing my mouth out with cold water was painful, then I noticed Arnie had followed me in.

"Don't get sore at me Swifty, I was only taking the piss."

I realised that because I'd walked off to the ablutions, he'd got the idea that I was upset. I laughed, "I'm not upset Arnie, I'm just sore."

He waited around until I'd finished and we made our way back to our bunks.

On the way back, through swollen lips, I felt a sudden impulse to justify myself, "Arnie, I didn't even know Spendler, and I'm sure he didn't know me. I thought I was being okay with Bill not getting mad or anything like that, when he just went mad. He had no need to get involved at all, 'cause I wasn't saying anything nasty."

Arnie stroked his chin and looked away. "It happened before you had time to think, yeah?"

"Yeah, that's right," I said.

"Well work on your thinking then, I never get into scrapes like that do I?" With that he walked away.

The next morning on roll-call, as C. S. M. Bullock was making his inspection, he stopped at me. "Private Swift. Now tell me lad are you intent on committing bloody suicide? You know it's a bloody offence don't you?"

I thought I recognised a hint of Arnie's influence in the retort. "No Sir," I responded.

"Then perhaps you'd like to tell me what the hell you're doing fighting Spendler?"

I looked him straight in the eye, "Because he attacked me Sir."

He proceeded to examine my face, "You're a bloody mess. And I mean a bloody mess. After this inspection get yourself to the M.I. Room. You never learn do you Swift?"

"No Sergeant Major."

"After you've been to the M.I. Room, you can report to the Boxing team, then we can all have a bloody good laugh watching you beat the hell out of each other, can't we?"

I didn't answer, which brought an immediate scream from him, "Answer me damn you?"

Through swollen lips I spat out, "Yes Sergeant Major."

"Yes Sergeant Major," he repeated slowly. "If I were you boy," he slowed his speech down to the point where he was pronouncing every syllable, "I'd save some fight for the Commies. They like a good fight I'm told."

Thankfully he moved on, only stopping when he came to Spendler. I couldn't see him, but I could hear every word. "Well, well Spendler, you look a mess." After which he laughed uproariously, yet it wasn't a laugh of amusement, it was a cynical laugh and it revealed anger.

Spendler didn't say a thing; he stood there as I did upright and helpless.

The Sergeant Major continued, "Have you heard of Goliath, Spendler?"

Spendler must have answered, but I couldn't hear him.

"Well you're fuckin' Goliath Spendler, and you've just got yourself flamin' hammered by a little shit. Haven't you boy? Room for improvement I'd say, don't you think?" He paused for breath. "Well, Spendler we have a Boxing Team and you've just joined it."

Out of the corner of my eye, I saw Bullock point in my direction, "You'll have to watch him Spendler. He's not like all the rest. He'll hit you back you see. Surprised you that, didn't it?" He laughed cynically.

After we'd been dismissed, I saw Spendler coming towards me. At first I panicked inwardly, although I knew that I had no need to; he wasn't likely to start something. Even so, I was on edge.

"Hi Swifty, what goes on?"

"Nothing much," I answered, wondering where it might lead. However, he did seem friendly, so I felt slightly more confident. "What do you think about the Boxing Team then?" I asked.

"Wait until my teeth have settled down, won't I?" He looked at my face. "You'll be no good either, you can't see properly, can you?"

I touched the swellings around my eyes. "It was a bit daft wasn't it?"

"Yeah," he said. "Don't know what happened really. I was a bit pissed off!"

"Yeah, I somehow got the message."

He grinned at me and looked me straight in the face before speaking, "We can be mates, you know."

"Yeah," I said, "let's forget it?"

He slapped me on the back so hard it nearly knocked all the wind out of me, but I didn't let on. I just smiled as if it was something that happened to me quite regularly. As I walked away I began to think that I was too small for my own good, and immediately laughed out loud at the stupidity of such a statement, so much so, that other soldiers began to regard me with some curiosity. However, they hadn't been nearly flattened by a simple slap on the back, and what was more they hadn't fought the guy who'd just done it.

Some good did come out of it. Bill Bosby came round to my bunk and offered to cut my hair provided I paid the agreed sum upon being paid before leaving the ship. I felt the bumps on my cheek bones and around my eyes again, and ran my tongue around the inside of my mouth and wondered whether the price was worth it.

Later that day we saw our first glimpse of Africa. I watched for hours as we drew ever closer to land, until I saw what I thought were twinkling lights in the far distance. I stayed watching as we approached the land through the darkening skies, until the extent of my tiredness led me to my bunk knowing that I'd be in port the next morning.

As soon as I awakened the next day, I rushed up on deck to get my first look at Africa and Cape Town. A strange sense of expectancy had given way to a sense of the sublime, "I was here!" In my mind I'd built up an incredible desire to see this most southern city, which held for me a fascination bordering on the mystical. I couldn't explain this attraction to my friends, partly because I didn't have the vocabulary to describe it, and partly because I was afraid they wouldn't understand me, and find it amusing.

My interest stemmed from the geography and history classes I'd had at school. The Elizabethan period had always attracted me, particularly those brave men who'd sailed in the southern oceans. I think that must have been the first time I'd made some connection with something I'd learned at school. It wasn't all meaningless drivel after all!

I looked at the city nestling at the foot of the mountain, and tingled with excitement as if it were Christmas. The smell of the place was different to the odours that I was used to, but it wasn't repugnant, just different; it was Africa. Letting my eyes roam at will, I saw Table Mountain clear and huge, like some giant overseeing the city below. I decided there and then to write home and tell my folks that I'd seen the greatest sight in all Africa, and there **was** a tablecloth on the mountain. Deep in thought and wonder, I was rudely brought back to earth upon hearing Arnie's voice.

"C'mon Swifty where the bloody hell you bin, I've bin lookin' all over for you; Pay Parade in half an hour." With that he walked off.

I rushed after him, "Hey Arnie, where are we going when we get ashore?"

"Let's get ashore first, shall we?" He stopped, looked at me, running his eyes up and down my whole frame. "Listen, I'm going to tell you something you're not going to like."

"Go on," I urged.

"I wouldn't let you go ashore dressed like that."

"What's wrong with me," I said quite hurt.

"You look scruffy." He waited for my response which never came." Right," he carried on, "I know a guy who'll lend you some boots. Just look at them," he said pointing to the boots I had on, "they're a disgrace."

I was taken by surprise, I really didn't expect to be criticised by him. "Right," I agreed, "let's go and get them then?"

We made our way to where he bunked.

On the way Arnie continued to talk to me, "Remember the fight you had with Spendler?"

"Yes," I said, wondering why he'd brought it up.

"Well Mick Conelly broke it up didn't he?" He spoke, looking at me intently, "That true?"

"Yeah, he did, that's right, but what are you getting at?"

"Well he must have been watching you all the time."

"That's true, he must have been, I never thought about that."

"Well you wouldn't. No disrespect, but you wouldn't, would you?"

"Well I'm warning you, he's out to get you, so be careful. He wanted Spendler to give you a good hiding."

"Well he didn't get to see it happen did he?"

"No but there'll be other times. You know he got busted at Las Palmas for being drunk and disorderly? He's a Corporal now and as sick as a parrot."

"Yeah, I know he got busted, but I thought he was lucky not to get reduced to the ranks."

"I think that's precisely why he hates you so much. You have this wonderful idea of speaking the truth that makes you say what yer think to anybody and everybody. Only what makes yer think, heaven only knows. You go around telling people things that can only lead to trouble, and when it comes, you wonder why. I give up with you Swifty, yer just thick. Mick Conelly is a regular Army man, anybody else would have got six months. They get away with murder, we all know that. But we don't go around telling everybody. Get it? Best method when in deep trouble, sign on for twenty-two." Arnie had all the answers.

I made a mental note to see Arnie if I ever got into really serious trouble.

Arnie got me fitted up and I ran the gauntlet of inspection with Lieutenant Kutchen giving me some good advice about keeping out of trouble and not fighting. The fighting bit was really starting to get to me. It was all a bit sickening, it was beginning to sound like I always looked for trouble which was not true, as I saw it.

I mentioned this to Arnie as we stood on the quayside waiting for Tommo and Bill to join us. Arnie was watching the gangway looking for them coming off the ship.

"Did you hear what Lieutenant Kutchen said to me? I think he must think that I look for trouble."

"Well you do, don't you? And if you don't, you'd better explain in words that I can understand, why you're always fighting? And what's more, you give me the impression that you actually like it."

"Because I don't let people walk all over me. That's why I get into fights," I said emphatically.

"Okay, neither do I, but I don't get into fights do I? You really don't get it do you. Are you thick or what? There are other ways; it would seem that you haven't tried any of them out as yet!"

"Shit!" I thought, I wished I'd never asked him. Then I began to think about how many fights I'd been involved in since joining the Army. I realised that at Fulwood Barracks during basic training, I'd moved beds and barrack rooms nearly every week for fighting. It seemed that they were always picking on me. My intake consisted of about seventy-five percent Liverpuddlians with most of the rest coming from East Lancashire. Not being one of either of them, I must have presented an easy target. They thieved off me quite openly, on occasions inviting me to do something about it. I recall a time when I'd got everything ready for an inspection. I'd laid my kit out on the bed feeling very proud that it was immaculately presented, before going to the canteen for a break. When I returned, I found to my horror that someone had taken some of it and replaced it with some of theirs which was scruffy. With little or no time before the inspection, I had no alternative but to go round everybody's kit in a desperate attempt to find it. I found it on the bed of a 'Scouse' called Hardshaw. I asked politely why he had taken it, and he, very predictably, told me to bugger off, whereupon, I picked it up. His attack was expected unlike some of the others. The fight came to nothing, Corporal Rutherfield intervening after he'd decided that we were serious. I gave as good as I got.

Then there was an awful time when I was watching a fight between a Liverpuddlian and a guy from Burnley. They were going hard at it when Ditchworth, the Liverpuddlian, went down on the floor. Pickle, the guy from Burnley, picked up a chair, raised it above his head, and was about to bring it down on Ditchworth who was helpless. At that precise moment I stepped in with a cracking punch, knocking Pickle over a chair and into the fire. He went into the fire momentarily, but he didn't get burnt, it just singed his hair.

However, it resulted in me being charged and going on orders in front of the Officer Commanding. He listened to my tale and much to my relief dismissed the case against me. The incident made me very unpopular with the lads, who thought that I should not have interfered, especially when Pickle had a chair in his hands and was unable to defend himself. I argued that Ditchworth might have been seriously hurt if I hadn't have done so, but they'd have none of it. To some extent it was true, and I certainly made an enemy of Pickle, who for weeks afterwards followed me round wanting another fight, but I always refused, allowing him to save face to some extent, not to mention the fact that he was a tough guy, and would most probably have given me a hard and painful time.

"Hey, Swifty c'mon," I came too as Bill shouted for me to join them.

"He's dreaming again," I heard Arnie say.

"He's either dreaming or fighting," said Bill with a laugh.

Now that was a bit much without Bill jumping on the band wagon, I couldn't let that go. "Hey Bill, less of that, don't you think that one big mouth's enough without you joining in?"

He looked upset by my quick retort, "C'mon Swifty, let's get going, I didn't mean anything by it really."

It seemed that the whole city had turned out and were offering lifts into town. We declined many offers of lifts deciding to walk instead. We walked from the dock toward the centre of the city. It was hot, but a gentle wind made the heat bearable. It took us longer than we expected to get to the city centre. As we began walking, I experienced a strange feeling that somehow I'd been there before at some time. This sensation persisted, even though I tried hard to dispense with it as being ridiculous. It became creepy, for nothing I saw held any of the freshness and sparkle that I expected, and so desperately wanted; it was as if I'd seen it all before. At first it unnerved me, not to mention that the lads had noticed that I knew my way around.

"You bin here before Swifty? You normally have difficulty finding the bloody toilet," remarked Arnie with half a smile.

We carried on walking until Tommo started making cryptic comments too. "No he hasn't been here before, it's that bloody school he went to. Leading the way and all that."

I turned round to Tommo. I hadn't much choice about Arnie taking the 'mickey', but I could most certainly stop Tommo. "That's enough from you Tommo! Stop taking the piss. You can't afford to coming from Rishton Ragged School."

"Hey, he's getting really smart now isn't he? Must be my influence."

We all laughed. Arnie always had to have the last word.

The Regiment's arrival had caused a big stir in the city, and upon seeing us walking up from the dock area many white people came to talk to us. Some even stopped their cars and begged us to accept a lift to wherever we wanted to go. It was all a little too much, it was hospitality beyond anything anybody had experienced before, and as such made us wary and unsure. We declined their offers, but exchanged the usual pleasantries and carried on towards the city centre. We'd been told about 'Apartheid' during the voyage, and been advised about the conditions that existed in South Africa. I didn't listen very much to the talks, mainly because it was quite obvious that the Officer giving the lecture had no first hand experience. However, it did bring to our attention the seriousness of the situation, and the need to respect it, simply because we knew the ship could sail without us. The whole idea made us a little on edge and nervous when being approached. I didn't really have an opinion about the rights or wrongs of 'Apartheid' at the time, other than it seemed nonsensical, for I had made great friends with many black children in the school I'd gone to in Shropshire. However, such was the warning we got from our Officers that we went ashore with the intention of not causing any waves.

I was walking ahead, intent upon finding a decent bar, when an elderly lady stopped me.

"Hello," she said in a very frail voice."

I stopped and returned her greeting.

"You've come from England? Did you know that I came from England in 1905 when I was twenty-eight and I've never been back."

"That's a long time ago," I said, casting a worried glance at my friends who were disappearing up the road.

"Yes," she said. "I came out here in order to marry you know, they did things like that in those days. I'd never even met my husband to be. All I knew was that he was a farmer with no wife and forty-two years old." She looked at me for a moment. "How old are you?"

"Oh," I said quite surprised, "I'm only nineteen."

She smiled, "I came from Bolton you know. Do you know Bolton?"

"Yes I do a bit," I answered. "My cousin's a vicar there at St. Paul's and something, I can't remember."

She thought for a moment, her eyes never for one second leaving mine. "Oh yes, I think I know that church." She asked me many questions about Bolton that I desperately wanted to answer, even though I had little knowledge of the place. What I didn't know I made up. I think she knew that I was bluffing on occasions, but acknowledged that I'd been there, and that seemed to be enough to satisfy her.

My friends eventually stopped and began to saunter back when they saw me deep in conversation with her, eager to know what was being said. I introduced them and they exchanged greetings very formally, which tickled me when I saw Arnie's worried look. Eventually, and after a prolonged farewell, we took our leave, but before we departed she pulled out her purse and gave me some money. I tried to refuse, but she'd have none of it, and pressed the money into my hand. I thanked her profusely and watched her walk away.

When she'd gone, and I was sure she was out of hearing distance, I thought I'd wind the lads up a bit. "You know, I should have two drinks to your one," I said holding up the notes that she'd given me.

"You bloody well would, wouldn't you," said Bill.

"Well don't you think I should, after all I did all the talking there?"

"He's not a tight bastard, not with his mates anyhow," said Tommo.

I could tell that Tommo was thirsty. Arnie, on the other hand was quiet, but he kept looking at me to see if I was serious.

However, it didn't last long, "Are we getting a drink then, or are we expected to kiss your arse first, hey?"

"Don't rush me, I'm deciding, and I must say it's nice being in the driving seat for a change."

Arnie was beside himself and I liked it. However, my joy was short-lived.

"Well, I've seen it all," he said, "C'mon you lot, sod him. Let's put our money together, we've got enough for a few drinks. Let's just ignore that tight swine."

"No," I replied, "I was only kidding," but they ignored me and walked off in search of a bar. They were playing my game now. I followed them but they'd have nothing to do with me. After trying one or two bars they eventually found one that took their fancy. I followed them in, but they told me to sod off again.

"Don't be so bloody childish, I was only having a laugh," I said quietly.

"Well it wasn't funny pal. That old lady wanted us all to have a drink, not just you."

"Yes I know she did."

"Well," said Arnie, "give us the money then."

I pulled the money out of my pocket and gave it to him.

He took it, "Right now, let's see." He counted the money out and gave each of us a share.

I watched, wondering why I hadn't had the presence of mind to do that. I thought, "It should be me that shares the money out not him," but it wasn't, it was Arnie, it was always Arnie.

After drinking in the bar for most of the afternoon, we emerged almost broke, but relatively sober.

"Let's go up Table Mountain," suggested Bill.

"Good idea, but you know how much it costs, don't you?"

We all looked at Arnie thinking that he knew. He always said things with such confidence you expected him to know.

He read our thoughts, "Don't look at me like that, I don't bloody well know, but what I do know is that it'll be too much for the likes of us. I'll tell you what though, we could walk up towards it, get a good view of it and the city up there."

With that, Arnie set off briskly, and we all followed. When we got to a fork in the road or some crossroads I'd tell him which way to go.

"Hey Swifty, you bin up here before?" enquired Bill.

"No," I answered, "I haven't. Nor have I a clue how I know, but I seem to."

After walking for some time, the going began to get much harder. We hadn't a clue where we were in relation to the city centre, although I made as much as I could about my new found sense of direction. We stopped and looked at the city below us; it was simply amazing, with the tall white buildings looking as if they'd been specially painted, standing out against the deep blue of the ocean, then we looked at Table Mountain and its astonishing beauty. The exceptional visibility allowed us to see the hue of the multi-coloured flora on the slopes, as well as people climbing. We stared at the sight for ages before deciding to move on.

"Right lads, that's enough, I'm knackered, I don't know about you? Let's rest here, then get back to the ship."

"Arnie, why are we always first back?" I asked.

"Because we're not pissed, and we don't like trouble, and that's why you won't be in trouble. Got it? You wait and see the brave lads returning at the last minute, you just wait. They'll be fighting and farting and carrying on, and what have they seen of Cape Town? Nothing, they won't even remember it."

"Okay, I've got your point," I replied; but secretly, I thought, "neither had we, but I daren't say so."

We made our way back to the ship. Occasionally we passed some of the lads, who were well away, singing and shouting and generally revelling in the freedom bestowed upon us by the people of Cape Town, and cheap brandy of course. The city seemed to have gone mad. We pressed on to the ship, continually refusing drinks that were being offered to us freely by some of the people we passed. Eventually, we arrived at the ship and walked up the gangway past the Regimental Police who were really peeved at being on duty; you could see it written all over their faces and they were out to make as much trouble as they could. As I passed them I saw the Policeman at the bottom of the gangway look at the Policeman at the top.

"Look out Larry. The choirboys are back." He then looked directly at us to see our reaction. I met his look.

"What you lookin' at me for soldier, you fancy me or somethin'?"

I continued walking, but smiled at him while raising my eyebrows an inch, whereupon, he shouted for me to stop, but I'd heard that one before and just kept going until I got on deck when I darted down the stairs, knowing he'd be reluctant to leave his post and follow.

After lying on my bunk for some time, I announced my intention to go up on deck in order to have a last look at Cape Town, and to see the fun as the stragglers returned under escort. It must have been near to midnight, and all we could see of Cape Town was a mass of lights in the distance. We'd been told that curfew was ten-thirty; but I could see at least thirty or even forty soldiers weaving their drunken way back to the ship.

"Can't charge all that bloody lot," said Arnie in my ear. "Nearly the whole bloody ship'll be on 'jankers' tomorrow."

"Except us," observed Bill, with a smile, never taking his eyes off the returning troops for a minute.

"Hey. There's 'Sniggy Heald' at the back. See him?" asked Bill.

He leaned over the ship's rail in order to get a good view, at which point Tommo grabbed his legs and pretended to throw him over the side. It must have been fifty feet to the quayside. Bill let out a howl thinking he'd gone, but Tommo hauled him back and he thumped back down on the deck frightened out of his wits.

"So who said I'd never saved your life? Look at that you were a gonna."

"You'll be a bloody gonna, you stupid sod! Stop farting about, it's dangerous."

After that, I noticed that Bill kept looking at Tommo, but Tommo was no fool, and kept well away from the rail. We all laughed and watched the returning drunken soldiers.

"Hey, there's Sergeant Becksey." I pointed to a dishevelled Sergeant being escorted back to the ship by 'Big Mick' the Provo Sergeant, in handcuffs. As the escort got nearer, and we saw the state of Sergeant Becksey, any smiles we had on our faces disappeared. His face was a mess, his nose was bleeding profusely, his mouth was swollen and his uniform was in absolute tatters. By this time a huge crowd had gathered on deck and were watching in almost complete silence.

"Look at 'Big Mick's face," someone shouted.

"Hey Mick! Did he get a gooden in?" shouted someone else.

Sergeant O'Shan had a lump the size of an apple over his right eye. We all laughed, until he looked up at the crowd as he came up the gangway.

"I know some of you shitty bastards. And I'll be seeing you tomorrow."

The crowd began to thin out as his words sank in, causing concern in some, and blind panic in others. Sergeant Michael O'Shan had that kind of affect on most soldiers. We stood some distance from where the remark had come from, so we felt relatively safe. We watched them literally haul Sergeant Becksey onto the ship, fighting, swearing, spitting and biting like a demented animal.

"That's what they call fighting drunk, some say it's Boddington's, others say it's Tetley's, but I say bollocks, it's just a gallon too much of anything."

Arnie couldn't take his eyes off him.

"I hope I never get like that," I said.

"Sergeant Becksey has spilt more ale down his tie than you've ever drunk, or ever will drink, so don't give me that crap," said Arnie, a little more than irritated.

Now this confused me for one minute, Arnie was seemingly disgusted with Sergeant Becksey for being totally incapacitated through drinking too much, the very next minute he was displaying great admiration for him, and his incredible capacity for consuming ale. I'd learned something though, to say nothing.

Next morning the ship sailed. Everyone was on deck and all the dignitaries in Cape Town had come to see us off. As I watched I heard the voice of a lady singing as the ship eased itself away from the quayside and its moorings. Straining to see through the crush of people, I saw the figure of a lady standing on a podium. She looked old and frail, and her voice faltered in the wind, but she carried on. The song demanded some high notes, which she reached, but others were way beyond her, and she squeaked out strange sounds in a shrill screech. For the life of me, I couldn't understand why she was doing it, though nobody laughed, so it wasn't funny.

"Hey Serge, who's the singer then?"

Sergeant Bodlin, who was standing next to me smiled, "Don't you ever listen to anybody Private Swift?"

Before he could explain, Corporal Standring, who was stood next to him interrupted, "She used to sing to the troops as they left port during the last war on their way to fight the Japs."

"Right, thanks Corporal," I said, "but why is she singing to us?"

Corporal Standring was a Liverpuddlian and a regular Army man. He looked at me for a moment. His look was one of deep concern, followed immediately by one of deep disdain, "She's not singing to you Private Swift, she's singing to me, because I'm going to fight the Commies."

"Well that's what I'm going to do, isn't it?" I answered somewhat perplexed.

"No," he retorted, " you're only a tin soldier; you'll only be *trying* to fight the Commies. Heaven help us all! And that's only if you manage to stop fighting the whole fucking Battalion first."

"He'd obviously heard about Spendler," I thought.

We all listened to her singing as the ship gently drew away from its berth and entered the main channel, until all we could see was her silhouette in the distance.

Arnie sidled up to me, as I was about to leave, "Anybody would want to fight the Japs after that racket wouldn't they?"

"I suppose they would," I replied.

We settled down knowing we'd be in Durban in two days or so, and there would be shore leave. I stayed on deck for some considerable time watching the African coastline recede as we made for the open sea, and the Cape of Good Hope. I felt quite strange, as if I wanted something to happen in order to mark the occasion. Nothing did of course, except the violent shuddering of the ship as she hit an extra large wave. I wrote to my father and mother later that night to tell them all about Cape Town and the journey so far. I stressed how strange I'd felt about the city, and how I seemed to know my way around it, as if I'd been there before.

Some time passed before word got around that a court-martial was to be held. Twelve soldiers were to be tried for various reasons ranging from hitting Non Commissioned Officers, to being drunk and disorderly. They were being held in the ship's prison. I thought about them as they sweated in the bowels of the ship. We arrived in Durban two days later. It seemed altogether different than Cape Town. It somehow looked more European than Cape Town; I didn't like it at all, and the people weren't as friendly.

My group of friends split up, Arnie and Bill went off together to see the centre of the city, while Tommo elected to stay on board ship. I chose to go to the beach on my own. After finding a stretch of beach which wasn't too crowded, I did what countless others must have done before me; I watched the magic of the Indian

Ocean until a young South African guy came up and enquired what I was doing? He grimaced in disbelief when I told him I was just watching the ocean He asked me about England. It seemed strange trying to describe Lancashire to him, and I'm quite sure he wasn't the least bit wiser when I'd finished. I went on to try to describe a typical industrial town, which sent him into fits of laughter, indicating to me that he didn't believe one word of it. He eventually said that he was glad to live in South Africa.

After I'd finished, he went on to tell me about the problems in Durban, not that I was in the least bit interested; but my lack of interest didn't deter him for a moment. He mostly complained about the Indian community, who he said, ran all the businesses in the city, and had a complete stranglehold on all the trade. I argued that this couldn't be true as this ran counter to my understanding of 'Apartheid'. His face changed colour when I mentioned the name. He told me, that in his opinion, they were inferior in every aspect of life. I asked him to explain how he came to hold this opinion?

He ignored my question and entered into a tirade against them, "Listen my friend we have learned, through bitter experience, to treat our blacks the way we do; if a black as much as speaks to a white woman in the street it would be like trying to commit suicide. It just wouldn't, and doesn't happen. You understand me? Blacks are not the same as us, they're different."

"Okay," I nodded, " But what about Indians and half-caste people then?"

He looked at me in exasperation, "They're neither one nor the other."

"You mean Indians or half-castes?"

By this time his face had gone a shade of pink. "You bloody awkward man; I'm about sick of this subject. You don't want to understand."

"Oh I understand alright, but you can't accept that I don't agree with you." I could see his anger rising, so I backed off and changed the subject.

Before he left, he asked me if I'd like to live in South Africa? I said that I wouldn't, because I had many black friends, and I could never accept the laws of his country. His response was abrupt, and he advised me that it wouldn't be very wise to even mention my views to anyone else, as they may not be as tolerant as he was.

Back on board ship, I learned that one of our black lads was being held in jail for simply speaking to a white girl in the street. Major Harrison refused to leave without him, so he was escorted from the jail to the ship just before it sailed. I saw Arnie and the lads sometime later, and they all agreed that the place wasn't nearly as good as Cape Town and we were all glad to be leaving.

A rumour that the Battalion Boxing Championships were going to take place on board ship in the next few days circulated around the decks causing some excitement, not to mention a lot of speculation. I found the news intriguing and was duly signed up to compete, being a member of the Battalion Boxing Team. However, I did wonder where they would put up the ring? As it turned out, it wasn't the ring that should have worried me, it was the weighing scale. When it was my turn to step on the scales, the needle rolled around with the movement of the ship. I didn't pay any real attention to it, because I thought it would be the same for everyone. Little did I realise that scant attention was paid to weight when it was thought a good fight might come of it. All the contenders trained together. I met Spendler there, and we both laughed about how we came to be there. I told him about the advice my father had given me about not providing amusement for the Officers.

"Yeah," he added, "we'll both probably find ourselves in the ring with professional boxers Swifty."

He was right, for both of us eventually fought professionals. Some time later, the list of bouts to take place was pinned up on the Company notice board. I was to fight someone out of 'A' Company. The bouts were to take place the following day; I couldn't help smiling at the length of time they gave as notice. Arnie speculated that it was in order that those soldiers with second thoughts wouldn't have time to go sick. He was probably right.

It was blistering hot in the Indian Ocean, and it seemed that the ship's screws caused the only movement on there. I weighed in with the soldier that I was to fight. As I stepped onto the scales, I immediately noticed that the motion of the ship affected my balance. The needle, on the weighing machine, swung backwards and forwards with the swell of the ocean and the corresponding movement of the ship. I watched as the Sergeant Major tried to decide what weight we were, by roughly trying to calculate the middle of the needle's swing.

"Great!" I thought, "I could end up fighting anybody here."

As it happened, I fought a rank novice and the fight only lasted one round before the referee stepped in to stop him taking any more punishment. The next fight was quite different; the guy I fought was a physical training instructor, who was, according to Arnie, a better footballer than a boxer, playing for some major football club before joining the Army. As I entered the ring I certainly hoped so, because it was about six months since I'd broken my jaw playing rugby; and those strange unrelated thoughts kept coming back, which worried me. I had always to balance this with being in the Battalion Boxing Championships, which meant that I was excused normal duties, giving me lots of time to myself.

It was during this time that my thoughts strayed back to some of the bizarre characters I'd encountered in Catterick Military Hospital. I met Corporal Bob Harley and his friend Lee, who had sustained broken jaws in drunken brawls. They always stressed that it wasn't as a result of fighting each other, but the truth, I suspect, was that they couldn't really remember. I remember them telling me about the time they'd been allowed to go out of the Hospital for a walk in the grounds. They actually went through the grounds and down to the local pub where they got absolutely plastered, returning blind drunk at some unearthly hour of the morning. The next morning Sister O'Sylvan confronted them with bared teeth, frightening the life out of them as she explained that should they have been sick, they could both have died due to their jaws being wired up, not allowing the vomit to escape fast enough in order to allow them to breathe. Word had it that both of them realised the truth of her words and were sheepish for days. However, seeing the error of their ways didn't stop the Sister from placing them on 'shining parade'. This entailed the polishing of all windows and brasses in the ward and corridors. They were continually chivvied along by the incessant banter of the Sister, who never let them rest for a minute.

Then there was the soldier who'd been wounded in Cyprus. He'd been accidentally shot in the face, and was lucky to be alive. The bullet had entered his face by the side of his nose, hit a bone, and veered off coming out behind his ear. Apparently he'd been cleaning his weapon, as were the rest of his platoon, when a soldier, sat opposite to him, cleared his rifle not thinking that he still had a bullet up the breech. He shot him and lengthened his service by six months.

Another time, during a visit to the Red Cross Club, I met a soldier who quite disturbed me, not because he threatened me physically or intellectually, but because there was something very sinister about him. I couldn't really explain what it was, or how I felt about him, but there was something not quite right. I met him on my first visit to the place when he came to sit next to me. He introduced himself in a whisper. I never gave him much thought at that time, and just nodded in recognition of his greeting, which I thought was an appropriate response. He leaned across and began to chat. Before long he'd told me all about himself. I listened slightly perplexed, not quite understanding why someone would want to disclose intimate details about themselves so soon after meeting. However, such analysis only comes with reflection. At the time, I just had an uneasy feeling that all was not quite what it should have been. Eventually, on our third meeting, he launched into what I believe was his main objective, namely, to get out of the Army. He said that he was purposely acting stupid and hoped to get out of the Army on medical grounds. I was quite horrified, although I tried not to show it. He went into great detail as to the lengths he'd gone; it included wetting the bed, not eating, not speaking, although I very much doubted the latter, being generally disorganised and other acts which were purposely designed to get him out of the Army. I eventually told him about the time that I'd gone to see the M. O. and he'd told me that I could get out of the Army if I so desired. He was totally intrigued as I told him about the skin disorder I'd had in basic training caused by the khaki shirts that made my skin continually weep. The skin on my neck was a weeping mess after three weeks. To overcome the problem, my mother sewed cloth onto the inside of the shirt in order to make it smooth, and this did the trick. He listened aghast at the story, completely unable to understand why I'd gone to all that trouble to stay in the Army. He told me that I was mad and should see a Doctor. I never told him that I desperately wanted to be normal, even if that meant being in the Army.

On my return from the Red Cross Club, Bob Harley came over to me. "Hey, saw you talking to Spider Ketley!"

"Who's he?" I asked.

"That 'nutter' who's working his ticket on mental grounds. Be careful of him lad it's catching you know."

I laughed, "Well he didn't get far with me."

"Maybe not, but the truth of the matter is that although he's acting nuts, he is nuts. He thinks he's sane and putting on a good show, get me?"

I nodded, quite shocked by what he'd said. "Do you think he'll get out of the Army then?"

"Oh, aye, he'll get out of the Army all right, into a 'nut-house' the Army'll see to that."

Pop Quint, a fellow boxer, nudged me and brought me back into the present. "Swifty, C.S.M.I. wants all boxers in the lounge in five minutes. He held up five fingers to illustrate his point.

"Okay, I'll be there." But I didn't hurry because I felt quite important now; boxers were very much aloof and generally held in high regard. Later that night, I fought the physical training Instructor out of 'A' Company.

I remember stepping through the ropes and the second shouting above the noise of the crowd. "Watch his left hand, it's fast okay?"

I nodded indicating that I was aware of what he'd said.

The bell went, and as the second had predicted a rapier like straight left hit me flush in the middle of my face making my nose bleed. I went after him, but he was fast, and moved out of reach quickly before moving in again to throw left jab after left jab straight into my face. The crowd loved it and roared their approval. He won the first round by a mile; I knew I'd have to do something very special to turn the fight around.

The second round started just as the first finished, he'd jab and move, leaving me to hit air. However, towards the end of the round I noticed that he was blowing a bit, and instinctively looked towards my corner. Pop Quint and Chuck Farmer my seconds, were almost out of their minds trying to tell me to take the fight to him. I hurled myself after him, and much to my surprise he didn't move away, but traded blows. I scored with some really heavy shots, he winced and decided to go back to his original plan of hitting and moving. As we came to the end of the second round, I noticed him really gasping for air, so I immediately threw a massive uppercut from miles away. Instead of leaning back out of reach, he put his head down thinking he was well away from it. When he came up seconds later, he was covered in blood, which began to drip onto the canvas. The sight of blood made me go for the kill, but the referee stepped in and stopped the contest. Jimmy had six stitches in the cut above his eyebrow. The crowd were unhappy about me winning because I was so far behind on points; but I didn't care because I was through to the final.

About a week later I found out that I was to fight a guy called Johnny Shaker out of 'A' Company. I learned that he had gained a reputation for being difficult to manage in his Company, I was completely amazed when one of his Officers came to me and wished me good luck before the fight. This wasn't the normal action of an Officer and it made me feel uneasy. The night came, and the crowd gathered on the deck of the ship where the ring had been set up. My turn came; I entered the ring to the roar of the lads out of my Company. We both came to the centre of the ring to touch gloves and the first thing that struck me was his size. He must have been three or four inches taller than me. I thought this guy couldn't possibly be a Light Welterweight; then I remembered the weigh-in, together with the advice that my father had given me about boxing in the Army. I realised that it was too late to back out, so I got on with it. When the bell went, I tried to get close to him and stay there. We had a hard fight, it certainly wasn't stylistic stuff, but he won on points. After the fight, I went to the toilets nearby to wash some of the blood out of my mouth and to bathe my nose, which was bleeding. After swilling water over my face, I looked into the mirror and much to my dismay; I saw my eyes actually closing up, until I had great difficulty seeing properly. A visit to the Medical Inspection Room revealed a broken nose.

"Excused duties until you are told otherwise Private Swift," said the Medical Officer.

I was excused duties for a week, which meant I could lie in my bunk after roll-call in the morning. Later, that same night after the fight, there was great revelry as some soldiers celebrated victory, while others commiserated losing. Whatever, alcohol flowed freely and resulted in many soldiers wandering about quite drunk. I felt really bad, my head ached and my vision was impaired by the swellings around my eyes, so I went to lie down on my bunk. I wondered if that would be it, as far as the Boxing went, since I'd lost to Shaker; I reasoned that he would now represent the Battalion, but he never did, and I never found out why.

The ship sailed on towards Columbo. The Indian Ocean was like glass, with hardly a movement. All we could see was a clear blue sky without a cloud in sight, and feel the gentle breeze caused by the forward movement of the ship; but the heat was becoming oppressive and seemed to sap all our energy.

One night the alarm bells went off and we had a roll-call on deck; it must have been three o'clock. I wondered what could have gone wrong? We stood there for ages as the Officers counted and recounted the men under their charge. Bill said that they were just being bloody awkward, but someone else said that it was more serious than we thought. We were dismissed without any reason being given. We later heard on the 'grapevine' that someone had fallen overboard and the ship had circled all night. No matter how hard I tried, I never found out any more about it; the Army kept very tight secrets of which I was to learn more about in Malaya.

Another incident that caused some concern was when we had a film show on deck, in the open air. Suddenly and shortly after the film started, great plumes of smoke began to come out of the hold, under where some soldiers were sitting. The cry went up 'fire!' and pandemonium broke out as everybody scurried to get away in panic. Seats were overturned in the desperation that ensued, the ship's siren blew loud ear-deafening blasts again and again, adding to the already charged atmosphere. We were ordered to get to our lifeboat stations, which we promptly did, waiting there for ages before being stood down.

"It constitutes the biggest 'cock up' I've seen for years," said Arnie, having been asked what he thought.

It quickly became obvious that no one seemed to know what to do, nor it would seem, who was in charge? The Officers thought that the crew would take command; the crew thought that because it was a troop ship, the Officers would naturally take control. I saw soldiers ready to jump into the sea. I saw others rushing around with fear-filled eyes at the thought of the ship sinking. Some even ran below, against all orders, in order to retrieve valuables. The whole thing was over in a couple of hours, but it had a lasting affect upon me. Never again did I believe that all things were under control when those in command told you so.

Later, we were told that there had been a small fire in the ship's hold. However, much later, in Columbo harbour, I learned from one of the crew that it was still burning when we entered the harbour. Whatever, on the night of the film show, we were told within ten minutes that the fire had been put out and the show began again; and if, as the crew member suggested, the fire was still burning, we must have been sat on top of it.

Arnie, always the wit, said the Officers had done it purposely so that their wives could get better seats. Sure enough, when we returned, there they were, sat at the front waiting for the show to start.

"Told you," he said. "Look at them in our bloody seats. I tell you. That's how to get better seats. Have a bloody fire."

Chapter 3

THE EAST

"Communist hopes for peaceful reform were quickly dispelled. Far from the introducing social and political reform, the Labor government had allied itself with the most reactionary elements in the Malay community. The British made it quite clear that democratization was not on the agenda and that independence was not going to be granted in the foreseeable future. Moreover, their plans for Malaya did not include tolerating the increasing influence of a Communist-led leftwing movement or the growing strength of militant trade unions. Far from reforming British imperialism, the labor government actually proceeded to intensify the exploitation of Malaya and other dollar-earning colonies. The reason for this was quite simple; the bankrupt British desperately needed the dollars that Malayan tin and rubber could earn and nothing was to be allowed to get in the way."

As we approached Colombo, we all felt excited at the thought of seeing land again; what we didn't expect was the odour that goes with the east, which was gradually getting stronger as we got ever nearer. After some grousing, the initial shock wore off in the excitement of seeing it.

The whole Battalion was ordered on parade and the Colonel addressed us. He told us that the ship was only stopping in order to pick up fuel, so he limited us to six hours shore leave He then proceeded to lecture us on our general behaviour, but he needn't have bothered as far as I was concerned, because for some reason I couldn't explain, I didn't want to go ashore. What I couldn't shake off was the incredible stench of Colombo harbour, even though the overpowering nausea diminished to some extent, it was always there catching the back of my throat.

I asked a crew member what it was, he just grinned, "Oh, that's Colombo, don't worry, you'll get used to it."

It was a sweet oily smell that seemed to permeate everything around us. The ship, once at anchor, was quickly surrounded by small open rowing boats. The boats sold everything and anything to the ships in the harbour. They operated their business by shouting to us, whilst holding up the various goods they had for sale. If you gave any indication that could be vaguely taken as approval, they'd throw up a small rope with a weight tied to the end. We'd then pull on the rope, and the goods would come up tied in a basket. Trust was a major part of the operation; as we were obliged to place the money for the goods in a bag tied inside the basket, which would then be lowered back down to the rowing boat.

Many problems followed such a delicate operation. Money didn't arrive down at the boat, resulting in anguished cries and dire threats, all completely lost by the soldiers on the ship who thought it great sport. Some of the rowing boats nearly turned over as the lads started to pull the rope as hard as they could; it resulted in a 'tug of war'. The occupants of the rowing boats refused to let go of the rope and hung on for dear life. Some of the men in the boats tried to climb up the rope. The soldiers let them, until they got near the top, then let go of it, hurling them into the sea below. The whole thing really got out of hand, when some of the lads wrenched a metal bench from the deck and hurled it down at one of the boats, narrowly missing it by inches; the screams of fear from the boat people made for even greater laughter.

Luckily an Officer saw what was going on and intervened, the men responsible were arrested on the spot, and spent the rest of their time in Columbo harbour in the ship's jail. They were also made to pay for the damage to the deck where the seat had been wrenched from, and for its replacement.

I asked Arnie if the boat people would get any damages?

He sighed after hearing the question. "You baffle me Swifty, are you really thick? Will the Army pay out? Of course it will. But how can it pay out to those poor bastards, they can't sign for it, get me?"

"Oh I see, if you can't sign for it, you don't get anything. Is that right?"

"Well have you got anything out of the Army without signing for it?" he replied.

"Now you mention it, no. We even have to sign for our pay, don't we?" I said, quite satisfied with his explanation.

Next day we sailed for Singapore and the Far East. The former Sergeant, now Private Becksey, joined our Company after his spell in the ship's jail. I tried to speak to him about his court-martial after the Cape Town incident; but he just shrugged his shoulders and called me a nosey little bastard. I didn't take offence because being a former Sergeant, he still had friends who could make life really unpleasant for anyone who might upset him. I later learned that the big drop in pay would be a big blow to his family back home. I also heard that the Army appreciated the fact that others would suffer for his stupidity, and intended to promote him up the ranks as quickly as possible. He was a small man with a large ginger moustache. He'd fought in the Second World War; and though he was only tiny, he had a reputation for being a rough character. He intrigued me, and I tried again and again to get friendly, but he'd have none of it. He kept himself to himself, with all the aloofness of a Sergeant without stripes. Later, in Malaya, I was to learn that his personal habits left much to be desired, and in many ways he was just like Ex Sergeant Conelly, only not as dangerous.

The next few days were uneventful as the ship steamed towards Singapore. It was extremely hot and uncomfortable, even though we were all now dressed in tropical kit. As our destination got ever nearer, so the tension mounted as everyone considered what might lie ahead. We had talks on every aspect of jungle warfare. We studied the social, economic and industrial problems that faced Malaya in the past, present and future. It seemed to me that rubber and tin constituted the main problems for us. By this, I mean that it was mentioned so much, and so seriously, that I decided that it was the main reason we were there, so that it wouldn't fall into Communist hands.

We docked in Singapore harbour and almost the entire ship's company viewed the city from the ship's rail. I thought it looked quite similar to Colombo, only larger, but Arnie obviously disagreed as he gave me a derisory look that indicated that I was making a fool of myself. He endorsed this when he announced that the city looked breathtaking.

A strange calmness came over us as we made our way down the endless iron steps when disembarking. I became anxious by the unfamiliar noise of the city, and its pungent smell, as it wafted to the ship on the gentle breeze. A distinct feeling of inevitability, combined with a heightened sense of apprehension, made for explosive outbursts among the lads, resulting in punches and angry words. After waiting in almost silence for what seemed hours, a huge convoy of trucks drove towards the ship. We all guessed that it was our transport and cheered. I couldn't understand why I cheered with the rest of the men, but I did notice the Officers didn't, they watched, then smiled at each other.

"They're treating us just like school children," I thought. They were smiling at us like parents might do with their children.

Upon disembarking, we lined up in ranks along the quayside before clambering onto the trucks. Somebody said that we were going to the Jungle Warfare Centre at Kota Tinggi near Johore Baru in South Malaya, where they trained soldiers to fight in the jungle.

After waiting in the trucks for what seemed hours, we eventually sped off through the city towards mainland Malaya. The city looked so large and over populated it made me feel anxious and vulnerable. I just sat on the transport in complete awe. It seemed thousands of people were all going to the same place at the same time; I was tempted to ask whether there was a big event going on somewhere? I'd never seen so many people together. It was really quite alarming. What I did find out quickly was that most people actually lived on the streets, they hadn't a home, so they wandered around until the early hours of the morning when the city closed down for the night; then they put up their makeshift beds under the verandas outside the shops. They had to be gone by the time the shops opened up early the next day. The scene was entirely new to us, and was instrumental in bringing about a demeaning attitude towards Asiatic people generally. It didn't really matter whether they were rich or poor, educated or uneducated; if they were Asiatic then they were considered inferior. This attitude was reinforced by the N.C.O.s who took every opportunity to humiliate them whenever they could. Although I went along with the general position, I couldn't help thinking it ironic that most of the soldiers in the Battalion came off some of the roughest housing estates in Britain.

After crossing the causeway into mainland Malaya, the scenery changed dramatically. The road ran through the jungle, which grew right up to the roadside. Villages were dotted around along the road edge. They gave me the impression that they were impermanent and quite unlike anything we'd been used to seeing in Britain. After some time on the road, we could smell a village before it appeared. It was a sickly sweet pong that filled the air making us gasp and swear as it filled our lungs.

"The dirty bastards! What is it?" Bill asked without looking at anyone in particular.

"It's the problem of having no proper sewage system, that's what the problem is!" We all looked at Lieutenant Kutchen and gasped in disbelief."

"You're joking Sir," said one of the lads.

"No," he said, they store it up and put it on the fields as manure, why not?"

"But Sir, you could be eating your own shit," cried Tommo in total disbelief.

"No you couldn't," he said, but nobody was listening, they'd all decided that the natives were dirty and inferior.

We watched the natives working in the paddy-fields with a new understanding, and a lot of revulsion. It was all very different, and before we knew it we were in Kota Tinggi.

The camp was situated on the edge of the jungle not far from the town of Johore-Baru. The geographical location of the camp was designed to give some idea of the life ahead of us. We lived under canvas and everything was raised off the floor in order to allow the rains, in the monsoon period, to flow freely through the living quarters. The camp was located on two hillocks with a slow moving stream flowing in a culvert between them. The main body of the Battalion was located on one hill, while the NAAFI and stores were on the other one, together with the Officer's quarters. Meals were cooked over open fires and eaten outside. It was certainly different, and gave us all an air of expectancy as we entered into a new phase of experience.

The heat and humidity were so great that we were given two weeks to acclimatise. I couldn't really believe that the weather could have such an affect upon me until

I tried to walk to the NAAFI on the first night. I was so exhausted that I turned back wondering if there was something physically wrong with me? However, looking at the others who were also suffering, I realised we simply needed time to adapt to the conditions.

For the first week, we lay on our beds, slept, played cards, joked and drank 'Tiger' beer in the NAAFI at night. Gradually we acclimatised, and with it the programme of events increased. The team who trained us began to introduce us to the jungle, and we began to make small incursions into it. Learning the jungle code wasn't easy; no speaking, no unnecessary movement, everything done by stealth. We learned to communicate in sign language, and how to move with some meticulousness care, while always thinking ahead. It proved difficult, and some found it more taxing than others. They taught us how to deal with mosquitoes and other insects. But the thing that was impressed upon us most of all, was the need to maintain absolute silence because the jungle was as still as death during the day, and any sound would give our position away. After our very first patrol in the jungle it became patently obvious to all that silence was synonymous with survival. During the day, six a.m. to six p.m. nothing moved, nothing could be heard, all was total stillness, and so we too moved around as quietly and as silently as possible, so as not to be heard. However night was quite another thing; darkness in the Malayan jungle meant that you couldn't see your hand in front of your face, and we crawled about under our groundsheet shelters, or slept, while contemplating the coming dawn.

They took us into the jungle for one night, then for two nights in order to allow us to get used to the problems to be found there. Every soldier carried a groundsheet, which had many uses. Normally two soldiers teamed up together so that their two groundsheets could be used to make a shelter. They did this by suspending one groundsheet on two poles to serve as the roof, while the other covered the floor. We quickly learned to place the poles at the right angle, so that the shelter would provide adequate protection from the monsoon rains. At first we practised all the skills in camp at Kota Tinggi, and later for real, in the jungle. Within a short time we became quite expert, and remarkably quick at setting up camp. The roof was most important of all, and we all knew that it must be strong enough to withstand the enormous force of the monsoon rainstorms.

Leeches caused great discomfort at the beginning of our jungle training, mainly because these tiny worm-like creatures latched onto your body and sucked your blood. It was their stealthy intrusion, and the way they were able to penetrate through any garment, that alarmed most soldiers. They were somehow able to find their way through the most tightly textured clothing, to cling onto the most delicate organs. Later, they became an acceptable part of jungle life, due to the fact that they didn't hurt, and were an inevitable occurrence in the jungle. We just let them have their fill of blood, then when they became bloated they fell off. The thought was always there, that it was your blood you could clearly see filling them up like a balloon, but after a while nobody seemed to care. Should a leech find a sensitive place, and quite often they did, a touch of a lighted cigarette was enough to get rid of the creature.

Kota Tinggi was a great learning experience for all. We were taught what weapons were appropriate for the jungle and what were not. For example, grenades were never used due to the foliage, which could catapult the grenade back in the direction it came from. We were taught how to hack our way through secondary jungle. This was jungle that had been stripped of trees, and had been left for some time, with the result that a mass of foliage had grown in great profusion, in a desperate attempt to get to the light of the sun. It grew in such abundance, and at such a pace, that in places it was totally impenetrable. When we came up against it, the Patrol Commander would make the necessary calculations on his fixed compass bearing, then make a detour round the area. We slowly learned the patrolling procedure. One Company would go out to a certain point and make a base camp, choosing the spot carefully in order to make sure the camp was near water and couldn't be attacked easily. One platoon would always stay in camp in order to guard it, and reinforce the other platoons on patrol, should they make contact with the Communist terrorists. Each platoon comprised of about thirty men. A camp would be established at a prearranged grid reference, and the remaining platoons would split up into sections and go out on patrol. This procedure ensured that great areas of ground were covered by the various patrols. Each section would have a leading scout who would be a crack shot. He would generally carry a Remington automatic shotgun. The scout paved the way for the patrol, being continually

132

directed by the Officer in charge who would be right behind him. The next soldier would be the number two leading scout. He would carry an FN rifle and would take over when the leading scout was exhausted. Behind him would come the Bren gunner and his number two; while bringing up the rear would be the remaining soldiers in the platoon. An Iban tracker would also accompany the patrol if possible. The Ibans came from Borneo and were renowned for their expertise in the jungle. In our Company we had two who were called Gendang and Igo. Every Company I knew prayed that they would be given Iban trackers when going out on patrol. However, we had to wait until we went to North Malaya to meet them, for no trackers could be spared for training camps.

In the NAAFI one night, I heard that a patrol was going out on a night ambush. After some enquiries, I also heard that the ambush was the result of information received from a reliable informer. The camp was agog with excitement. The patrol was chosen from 'C' Company, and I remember the thrill and delight on the faces of the men as they prepared for action. They had the look of the chosen ones.

Arnie, Bill, Tommo and myself had split up on arrival at Kota Tinggi. Arnie had temporarily joined Headquarter Company and was now in camp on the other side of the stream. Bill had been offered the post of O. C's Batman and had accepted it, which left Tommo and myself together. In the tent we shared we had soldiers we hardly knew, but we made friends quickly, and very soon it was like old times. I brought back to the tent the news of the intended ambush, and it caused a lot of discussion as each individual gave their views of its worth.

"Better stopping the last bloody bus from Johore Baru on a Saturday night, more Commies on that than in the bloody jungle," said Arnold Rushan from the end bed.

We all agreed, knowing that the terrorists needed the help of the local population to survive. That same night, in the NAFFI, speculation was rife as we contemplated who would be going out on the next ambush? The beer flowed freely, and I had my first pint of Tiger beer. It made me feel really heady, and after two pints I started to slur my words. Everyone laughed, so I left.

The next day, during the afternoon, I heard that someone had been killed on the ambush. Desperate to know what had happened, I asked everyone I came across, but nobody knew anything. Then I remembered a guy I vaguely knew in 'C' Company, so with no more ado I approached 'C' Company lines. As I drew near to them I sensed the depression they were experiencing.

"Have you seen Roy Slokes?" I asked putting my head into one of the tents.

"What do you want him for?" came from one of the beds, shortly before a Corporal walked over to me.

"Go on, what do you want?" he asked with a hint of irritation in his voice.

"Oh, I just wanted to ask him something, that's all, nothing important really."

"Well if it's nothing important really, it doesn't matter then, does it? Forget it! It's a bad time right now, okay!"

"Okay, I'll see him later," I said.

"Do that," he stated, but his eyes gave indication that he knew what I wanted to know.

That night nobody from 'C' Company came to the NAFFI. They kept to themselves. It was as if it was their grief and nobody else's.

I'd never ever contemplated being killed, it had always been unthinkable, but shortly after the incident, it made me recall some words my father once said to a friend of his over dinner.

"Young men make good soldiers because they think they'll live forever."

I couldn't really appreciate the full significance of it at the time, but it was slowly coming into focus.

In the NAFFI some days later, I saw Roy Slokes sitting by himself with a beer. Very casually, trying to hide my real intent, I walked over to him and sat down.

"Hiya Swifty, how's it goin'?"

"Oh, not bad, I think I'll be on patrol day after next."

"Yeah, well I hope you have better luck than we had."

"Yeah," I replied, trying to conceal my inner excitement, "I heard about you lot, sorry about that poor bastard that got killed, what happened?"

He dropped his voice to a whisper. "I'm not supposed to tell you this, but I don't see why not." He paused, "It's painful stuff, it's like a nightmare, can't really believe it myself. We were lying in ambush positions; we must have been there hours all lying flat on our bellies, rifles at the ready. It were pitch black, couldn't see yer bloody hand in front of yer face. Kept wondering how we'd see anything to fire at? We were

135

lying on a slope covering a jungle path about twenty feet below us. Suddenly I heard a sound, a kind of click as if a spoon had touched a plate. It were nothing more than that. We were right next to the path mind. Dave Bartman, next to me, pulled my jacket to make sure I was awake. I couldn't see him yer know. We waited tense-like. I was sure they'd heard my heart beating, it were goin' like hell!"

Listening while holding my breath, I caught another sound as if someone was brushing up against leaves. I knew then that this were it! Waiting for someone to fire, I heard a click followed by a massive explosion and all hell let loose. It were strange really 'cause I knew the explosion was at us, I felt the waft of air as it passed near me. A light went up, and we all fired at once in the direction of the path. Then I saw Teddy, who was on the other side of me, lying in a pool of blood. I couldn't see him properly 'cause the light kept flickering." He stopped obviously still shocked.

"What was he like?" I asked.

He took a drink of beer without taking his eyes off me. "He was like anyone else would look who'd been hit by a shotgun blast, a fucking mess. The bastards!"

At which point a soldier came and sat next to us, "What's this then?"

"Nothin' much, just telling him that I don't want to talk about the ambush."

The soldier just nodded. "Yeah, it's a bad do. A bloody bad do." He then looked at me and his eyes said that the subject was closed.

They buried Teddy with full military honours. The reality of warfare was suddenly in your face, in your mind and in your dreams. It was never mentioned again, except in nervous looks and sweaty brows, and the length of the sick parade, prior to operations in the jungle.

The days passed and we became more and more skilled in jungle survival, but it must have been obvious to any casual observer that our adversary was way beyond us in every aspect of jungle warfare. We knew they were there, but we never saw them. I longed to go out on patrol at first, desperate to see some action and get into fire fights; but I also liked it because it was just like camping. However, the rigours of living in the jungle soon put paid to that. After an operation, the lads would always make their way to the NAFFI at every opportunity to drink pints of Tiger beer. One night I decided not to go, but all the others in my tent went. When they returned, gone midnight, they woke me up.

"Swifty wake up," I vaguely heard someone say. "You know what's 'appened?"

I sat up wondering whether they were being serious or just being daft and full of beer.

Arnold Rushan was leaning over my bed stinking of alcohol. He couldn't speak for laughing. Every time he tried to speak; he nearly fell on top of me. Eventually, however, he managed to, "McNichols drank some of his own piss! Yeah, that dozey bloody 'scouse ghet' drank some of his own piss."

At this, I was wide awake, and noticed immediately that the others were definitely not laughing, but telling him to shut it and go to bed.

I removed the mosquito net and sat on the edge of the bed. "What you on about Arnold?" I asked.

Tommo answered me, "It's serious Swifty, and it's not funny! And if Mc hears about 'bollock brain' there," he pointed to Arnold, who by this time was wandering away towards his bed laughing, "he'll bloody well kill him!" He stopped and growled towards Arnold's retreating figure, "I'm tellin' you Arnold, it's not fucking funny."

Arnold had had too much Tiger beer, which was quite obvious to me, but not to Tommo, who'd been on it himself. Arnold staggered towards his bed before collapsing onto it in a heap. Tommo came round the edge of my bed and sat down next to me.

"Go on, tell me what happened," I encouraged.

He sighed and began, "Mc, me and Arnold were sat drinkin' and havin' a laugh, yer know how it is?"

"Yeah, go on," I said impatiently.

"Well that bastard Henfield latched on to us when we went into the NAFFI. Nobody asked him, but he came and sat with us."

"Yeah, I know him, he's in the Camp Police; from Manchester right?"

"Yeah, that's him," Tommo replied, after which he spat on the floor. "Well, we were sat talking and drinking, must have had a load, when Mc says he's going for a slash. He's hardly got out of the room before Henfied picks Mc's pint up, puts it under the table and pisses in it. Now I didn't exactly see him do it like, and what's more I couldn't really believe he would, I thought he were kidding at first."

"Hey, hang on a minute Tommo, one minute you're saying he's pissing in it; the next your saying you didn't see him do it. Make your bloody mind up!"

"Listen you stupid sod, he put it under the table, I couldn't see under that, could I?"

I could see Tommo was getting angry so I eased off. "Okay, I get you, go on."

"Mc comes back, sits down and takes a long pull on his pint. Henfield nearly falls off his seat laughin'. Mc wonders what he's laughing at, and looks at me. I get up out of me chair."

Henfield says, "Where you goin'? Sit down!"

An I says, "Get stuffed Henfield yer bastard," 'cause I know now that he's done it for certain.

By this time Mc's off his head wondering what it's all about, and he follows me out, and I tell him. Now you know what Mc's like? He were going to nut me for not telling him, until I told him that I didn't know for sure until I saw Henfield's face when Mc came back and took a drink of his pint.

"Go on," I said, getting really excited.

"Mc storms back into the NAFFI and sees Henfield still laughin', but by this time some of his mates out of the Regimental Police have joined him.

Henfield sees Mc coming and says, "What the hell do you want McNichols, some more piss?"

"Mc goes for him, but Henfield's mates pull him off and throw him out of the NAFFI. He's in bed now, but he's real mad, I'm tellin' you, I've never seen him like this before, if he had a gun he'd a shot him."

I listened, completely shocked by the turn of events, but particularly by the idea of drinking someone else's piss. Tommo sat there in morbid silence, partly out of sorrow for Mc, but more so because he was probably too drunk to move. I suggested that we should go and see Mc.

"What now?" said Tommo in dismay.

"Yes now," I answered, having no real idea what I'd say to him when I got there. I suppose I just wanted to talk to him and hear the story from his lips.

We went, but he wasn't there, so we came back and went to bed, but I had an uneasy feeling that Mc wouldn't let it rest there.

He didn't! I found out the next morning at breakfast that Mc had battered Henfield and thrown him into the stream; if two men hadn't have come back to see what all the commotion was about, he would have drowned.

I was desperate to find out more, but nobody seemed to know more than that. Eventually, after many rebuffs, I managed to find someone who actually saw Mc afterwards, who really knew everything. Apparently Mc had brooded about it in bed, and then with the help of about eight pints of Tiger beer in him, he'd gone to find Henfield again. He found him still in the NAFFI by himself, laughing and bragging about what he'd done.

This time, Mc went in and laughed with him making Henfield feel quite secure. When he saw that he was about to leave, he left quickly himself and waited by the stream between the two camps. It would seem that Mc had figured that he'd be on his own, which he was. He waited behind a small tree until Henfield made his drunken way to the middle of the bridge. Now Mc was the Battalion Light-Middleweight Boxing Champion and a fighter of no mean repute, and even though Henfield was taller and heavier, he was no match for him. Mc hit him with every punch in the book, until he was a bleeding mess, then he threw him in the river leaving him to drown.

Luckily, two soldiers heard the commotion and came back to see Henfield was floating in the river face down. They jumped in and pulled him out. It was said around camp that it was touch and go whether he'd live or die, but I don't think many cared. What we did know for sure was that Mc was in deep trouble. Discussing it with Arnie later, I found out that Henfield was recovering in hospital.

As Arnie said, "Only the good die young, in which case Henfield should live forever."

Mc was arrested and taken away to the camp prison to await a court-martial.

Life at Kota Tinggi continued with patrols going out regularly scouring the jungle for Communist terrorists. The hot season came and we baked under the tin roofs of the huts that served as shelters when we weren't out on patrol. It was generally believed that about five hundred terrorists were operating in the jungle in Johore, but we never saw one. In fact it was quite difficult to actually believe that there were any, but for the fact that one of our soldiers had been killed. Even later in Perak, the ones we killed were nearly always the result of ambushes at night, and in that kind of operation we always fired at the sound, rather than at a figure, although there were some notable exceptions. Generally speaking, nobody was ever sure who did the killing, so everybody in the patrol took the credit. Kills were always welcome because we got bounty money. This was the money any dead terrorist might have on him. It was shared out amongst the platoon that killed him. I must add that many women were fighting the terrorist cause and proved to be formidable soldiers. The bounty money provided us with a good excuse for a real binge, when accounts of the operation would be stretched and exaggerated to inordinate lengths as we played the part of true bounty hunters. I did feel some guilt about this, and in certain reflective moments I did wonder why the Army allowed it?

One day, shortly before we moved to Ipoh, rumours circulated that two patrols had met in the jungle and had fought it out thinking the other were terrorists. It was said that two soldiers were killed and four wounded. I tried to find out more, but came up against a wall of silence. I knew from my brief experience in the jungle that this was always a distinct possibility, because of the inability to see for any distance, combined with the fact that nobody wanted to break silence. If a patrol lost its way, or more significantly, misread the compass bearing, they might well end up in the path of another patrol.

The Officer commanding would march on a compass bearing, deviating only when the jungle became so thick as to be impenetrable Too many deviations often resulted in some patrols becoming hopelessly lost. Getting lost in the jungle was of little consequence provided that it was recognised immediately. On the other hand, if a leader couldn't accept that he was lost, and wouldn't contact headquarters for help, it became both serious and painful. It usually seemed to happen when a young Officer and an inexperienced NCO were leading a patrol. The Officer would be too afraid of the ribbing he'd most likely get on his return, from his brother Officers; and the NCO too timid to challenge him.

Eventually, I decided to visit my old friend Arnie to see if he knew anything. I made my way across to the Company Office, waiting until all the Officers had retired for the night. I presented myself at the door of the Company Office to be met by an irate Arnie.

"And what the hell do you want here Swifty? Don't let the C.S.M. Bullock catch you here, he'll 'ave your guts for garters. You know what he's like?"

"Yeah, I know all that shit Arnie, but what I'm here to find out is what went on with those patrols in 'A' Company that met head on and fought it out. It's said that two were killed."

Arnie was serious for a moment. "Yeah, I heard the same too, the Officers were talking about it. Bartram, Ned Ketley and Tony Justler were saying it sometimes happens in the jungle. I was listening; Tony Justler saw me and gave me the evils. I knew then that it was top secret, but don't worry we'll be the last to know officially, we always are."

"Why do they keep it a secret, I wonder?"

"Because an Officer is involved, and they can do no wrong."

Before he had time to elaborate, Corporal Mick Grantley walked into the office. "Hiya Mick, we were just talking about that latest incident in the jungle when two patrols met accidentally. They say that two guys were killed?"

Mick sat down on the edge of Arnie's bed. "Yeah, I heard too, it's true. They're trying to play it down, looks bad for the Battalion; you get no medals for killing yer own. They'll blame it on the Commies, you'll see." He paused for a moment. "No you won't see, 'cause you'll never really know."

I didn't quite understand what he meant; in fact I was completely confused. "Why? I don't really understand what you're saying. Are you saying that the Army will not report it, or hide it somehow?"

Arnie was quiet, which made me feel insecure; I glanced at him for support. He looked away. Something made me want to pursue it.

Before I could Corporal Grantley jumped in, "The Army will inform the people back home that two soldiers have been killed in action, and that will be the end of it. You get me?" He looked round enquiringly. Then he continued, "When you get back home you'll not be going round to their folks to tell them that their sons have been killed by their own men, will you? Because if you do, you ain't going to be too popular."

"Oh, I get you now," I said, "I never thought of it like that."

"No you wouldn't would you, because you're not a full Corporal are you?" And with that he smiled, got up and made to leave, but as he got to the doorway he stopped. "It's a good job you asked me and not some other bastard N.C.O. It's not a good subject just now, I'd forget it if were you."

I wasn't sure whether to believe him, so when he'd gone, I risked another look at Arnie who shook his head in disbelief.

"Don't ask me anything 'cause I don't bloody well know, and what's more, I don't want to know, alright?"

I decided there and then that in the circumstances, the best thing I could do was to forget it.

Chapter 4

THE FINAL DAYS AT KOTA TINGGI AND THE MOVE NORTH TO IPOH

"They were then transported to heavily policed 'new villages', often poverty-stricken slums, surrounded by barbed wire. Here they had no civil rights and their every move was watched by Special Branch agents. Alongside the resettlement of the squatter population was the forcible regrouping of the plantation and mine workers who were moved into guarded camps at their place of work. Once again they were closely policed."

Some days later, we were ordered to move out in the early hours of the morning. We'd been briefed about the secondary jungle we were to patrol. This type of tropical rain forest was extremely difficult to negotiate. It grew as a direct result of the virgin jungle being cut down, producing in its place, the most difficult undergrowth anyone could imagine. Such was its profusion in growth, it became almost impossible to penetrate in places. We would hack at it with machetes like maniacs, until we dropped with exhaustion, when more often than not, we gave up and made detours.

The drop off was accomplished quickly, so as to avoid informers providing information concerning troop movements. Travelling in convoy, and a Company strong, the trucks suddenly slowed down to a snail's pace allowing us to jump off. Quickly making our way to the light jungle by the side of the road, we crouched down and waited for the first signs of light. The trucks carried on with a skeleton crew, making continual detours in order to confuse the enemy.

At first light, the order came to begin the operation and we moved out in columns, weaving our way through the vegetation into ever denser jungle, leaving the bright rays of the sun for the ever deepening green gloom of the jungle, where light barely enters at all. At this time of day, the jungle is always heavy with dew, that rises as steam when the sun's heat bites through the forest canopy, shrouding the area with a forbidding hue. We moved slowly and silently, except for the occasional sound of the slash of a machete, as the leading scout hacked and cut through the undergrowth. I was second to last in the patrol. There were times when I could see neither the man in front of me nor the man behind, which always made me panic and want to hurry, but I knew from training that this was the last thing to do. The Communist terrorists would have liked the patrol to bunch up together; in this way we'd offer a better target. Suddenly, I had an uncanny feeling we were being watched, which sent instant shivers down my back. It made me feel anxious enough to ease the safety catch off my FN rifle in readiness. Continually looking from right to left I moved forward, unable to see more than a foot or so at times. We advanced warily, until the soldier in front made a hand signal to stop. I passed the signal back to the rear man, and sat down for a five-minute break and a smoke. Some time elapsed before Sergeant Conelly came back to tell us that we'd come to some open grassland, and to be extra careful as it was exposed and a most likely place for an ambush. The Lieutenant decided to space the patrol out even more, so that if an ambush should occur, some soldiers would be outside it, and would be able to do an encircling movement and trap the terrorists, at least that was the idea, although we were far from convinced that it would work.

Sergeant Conelly led the platoon through the grass. The grass was known as elephant grass as it grows up to eleven feet in height. It is dense and lethally sharp on both sides, and capable of giving serious injury to the unwary. It was almost impossible to walk through, so a method had been devised where a soldier would stand up, place his rifle in both hands above his head, one hand holding onto the butt of his rifle while the other hand held the barrel; he would then fall forward and his weight would flatten the grass, then, he'd stand up and do it again and again until he was completely exhausted, when the next soldier in line would take his place, until the whole grasslands had been negotiated. The grasses were open to the sun's rays and became as dry as cinder. Lieutenant Kartage remarked that the temperature in the grasslands could reach 150 degrees. It was so oppressively hot I could hardly breathe. Progress through the grasslands was painfully slow. Within minutes I was wet through with sweat, and rapidly losing body salts, bringing on bouts of dizziness, hallucination and fatigue. At the rear of the patrol, we had no idea what was going on up front, and correspondingly found things difficult to comprehend when the patrol stopped for no apparent reason.

A signal came down the line to take five minutes rest while our commanding officer decided which way to go. This was immediately followed by another signal indicating that we should take up defensive positions for some time. I found this hard to accept, and crawled down the line to find out more. It turned out that an elephant had confronted Sergeant Conelly as he stepped out of the grass. The elephant had been as startled as the Sergeant, and both immediately turned around and fled. Sergeant Conelly looked quite flummoxed, but after a smoke he was ready to begin again.

When I got back to my position at the back of the patrol, Shuttlecock poked me in the back, "Was he drunk Swifty?"

"No just hallucinating, that's all!" I said with a grin.

We moved slowly out of the grasslands and into deeper jungle, where the pace slowed down even further as we became even more deliberate, relentlessly searching for our elusive enemy; who just seemed to fade into the foliage like a ghost. We stopped occasionally for a smoke and a drink of water from our water bottles. At this time, I had not developed any real discipline about the consumption of water, drinking freely whenever I felt like it. Needless to say, my water supply ran out quickly; I found that consuming so much water in the heat of the day made me feel sick. Struggling with all the gear I had for five days in the jungle, and the incessant problem of insects attacking my body, I lurched on trying to keep up with the rest of the patrol.

In the late afternoon we made camp. This operation demanded we cut saplings for supports for our shelters.

We always camped near water, but never at it, for to do so would present too easy a target for the terrorists.

The light was extremely poor on the jungle floor, making for a developed sort of likeness about everything, making it easy to get lost. To tackle this, we stretched a vine from the camp to the water and the latrine. Failure to erect any of these vines often led to soldiers becoming hopelessly lost, with sometimes tragic results. Soldiers would literally hold onto the vine until they arrived at their chosen place, and do the same when they finished their various ablutions. At the water and latrine, a guard would always be posted in case of an attack. It was primitive, and took some getting used to and some found it distressing.

Like so many other soldiers, I found the virgin jungle floor claustrophobic. I felt hemmed in with no escape, like trying to surface in water when running out of breath. We all knew it was the result of poor light that enveloped everything in a dank sinister green. Secondary jungle differed in that the foliage was far more dense, and when you moved one great leaf, another took its place immediately, and then another and another, until some became frantic to find space. Some soldiers suffered silently, while others couldn't hold their emotions, and screamed and shouted hysterically, and had to be evacuated. It was like drowning in a green pond of putrid rotting leaves. Some never got used to the decaying stink of rotting vegetation. Things seemed to be either growing frantically or in a state of decay. It always seemed to me like one great fight to the death, everything furiously fighting for the light. This fight for survival was evident in the animal and insect life as well.

The soldier ants fought with no quarter given, just as the boar pigs did at night, uttering the most blood curdling screams, making sleep almost an impossibility. The insects were absolutely astounding. They came in all shapes and sizes, but the mosquitoes were the ones that caused the most discomfort, for their bites really hurt.

When on patrol, it was quite impossible to use any type of mosquito net, so a repellent was issued to those who wanted it. However, this proved ineffectual and somewhat dangerous to administer during the Malayan night when it was pitch black. I knew of one case where a soldier was subjected to so much pain and irritation by mosquitoes that in desperation, and complete darkness, he grabbed the repellent and splashed it on his face. Some of the liquid went into his eyes and blinded him. Our medical orderly said that he'd been sent back to England, his eyesight permanently damaged. It was a lesson to us all. I never liked the stuff, preferring the discomfort of the mosquitoes to the dangers of the repellent. It never really bothered me, for when I had real need of it, on the occasions when I was totally driven to distraction, I could never find it.

Lying in ambush was the worst time of all, with no movement other than the sound of rhythmic breathing and the incessant beat of the heart. It was so frustrating just waiting for something to happen, guns at the ready, being bitten by a thousand insects all night. It was hell on an unparalleled scale, and in the morning the bites showed themselves in pockmarks all over our bodies.

One morning, we were lined up on parade and told that we would shortly be going to Ipoh in the state of Perak, North Malaya. I knew little about Ipoh other than it was the biggest city in the state, and was quite near to the Thai border. The camp was situated on the outskirts of the city. We were told that our primary job was to patrol the surrounding area and kill Communist terrorists. We were also told that there would be a lot of action, as many Communist terrorists were making their way from all over Malaya towards the Thai border. I felt quite excited about going; it had an air of mystery about it somehow. We boarded the trucks with great expectancy and a little apprehension. The journey opened up to us the incredible beauty of the country, as we travelled the three hundred miles northwards. Malaya is a land that varies greatly. It has deep valleys, surrounded by jungle covered hills and mountains, and huge valley areas given over to the growing of rice. Its beaches of silver sands looked majestic, with palm trees coming down to the sea that stretched for miles. I watched the natives working in the paddy-fields, presumably getting ready for the coming monsoon. They looked strange, almost alien, dressed in ill-fitting clothes draped around their bodies. I thought the men looked dirty in an assortment of traditional dress and Western clothes. Somehow they gave the appearance of being lazy and unacceptable, being totally polarised to Army philosophy concerning tidiness and uniformity.

The houses in the villages were built on stilts and made of wood, giving them a flimsy look of no permanence. Although I had been told why they were built on stilts, it was impossible for me at that time to take in the reasoning behind their design. However, the stink of the villages really horrified me. I was told that the pungent smell came from human raw sewage, stacked up into mounds waiting to be put onto the paddy-fields. The villagers saved the sewage in order to use it as fertiliser for the growing of rice. At the time I had little understanding of the wisdom or the need for such a procedure, and immediately considered it dirty in the extreme, as did every person in the Battalion. This spontaneous interpretation led us to reducing the native people we met to being almost sub-human, or at best second-class people. Although the Army frowned upon this view officially, it was one held by most of the Officers and all of the N.C.O's I met. It went some way toward appeasing the conscience when the killings took place. In some macabre way, we were able to accept it, by believing that the terrorists were dangerously inferior human beings, and therefore superfluous.

We arrived in Colombo camp on the 21st April to begin patrolling the surrounding jungle less than a week later. It was hectic rushing around trying to organise everything. As usual there was a lot of grumbling about going into the jungle at such short notice, but we went. The terrain in North Malaya was quite different to that of Kota Tinggi. It was more extreme, with high mountains and deep valleys in between them, where deep and slow moving rivers ran into swamps and the sea. It was beautiful but forbidding. It was wild, nobody owned the jungle, it was just there for everybody and anybody, or so it seemed. Those who entered, did so knowing that danger and death lurked within it.

At first we patrolled the lower slopes of the mountains and hills. The ground was as dry as tinder; our water went quickly, but we soon found more. The first few patrols went well as far as coming to terms with the jungle, and we learned to live with some degree of comfort. This was mainly due to the influence and help of our two Iban trackers, Gendang and Igoh, who had been posted to serve with us. They held nearly all the secrets of the jungle. I struggled, much to the frustration of Tommo who found me wanting in nearly all areas of seeing to my own needs. He cooked for both of us, while I did the menial tasks, cutting the saplings, fetching the water from the water point, and doing some of his guard duties.

The jungle varied, with virgin and secondary jungle presenting different problems. The massive trees grew so high it made me feel small and insignificant; I remember twelve soldiers surrounding the trunk of a huge tree, and being unable to span it. It must have been well over two hundred feet tall. I found that I became very insecure in virgin jungle. It was gloomy with nothing much growing on the jungle floor, and it had an awful smell of decomposing vegetation. I never got used to it, and it proved extremely difficult to patrol, due to the varying degree of light filtering through the thick tree canopy as the day progressed. Secondary jungle was also forbidding, but not quite in the same sense. More light filtered through the lower tree canopy, so there didn't seem to be the same murkiness about it somehow. It was much hotter, and what light did get through was sickly green. The real problem was the dense foliage, which was always in your face. We patrolled thousands of acres of secondary jungle around Ipoh. We also patrolled the swamplands near the coastal region, which constituted the most difficult type of jungle that I encountered in Malaya.

One day 5 platoon, of which I was a member, was ordered to patrol some swamplands to the north east of Ipoh. It was the first time I'd ever been on patrol in one. It was suspected that some terrorists had retired there, due to extensive patrolling in the area they were operating in. Apparently they were desperate to find a safe haven, and considered the swamps to be a place where they wouldn't be followed. The swamplands consisted of mangrove trees, that grow to about thirty or forty feet and completely cover the floor with their enormous roots. These roots go deep into the mud of the marshland, near to the sea or the river estuary, and are washed by the incoming tide. It had all the makings of hell on earth.

Before going into the swamp I heard a row going on between a soldier who'd just joined the Battalion and our wireless operator called Dickens, known as 'Dickie'. Not surprisingly they were whispering at first, but getting louder as they got more and more agitated.

"I can carry that wireless set through anything you can, you're only a short-arsed little ghet." Dickie looked at him, then looked at me.

"Hey, Swifty, 'ave you heard, he doesn't know a bloody thing yet, does he?"

"I'm not getting involved in this, but I hope you know what you're doing Stadden?" I whispered.

Stadden sneered at me before replying, "Yes I do know what I'm doing, and I can carry anything anywhere, all right!"

Just at that moment our Corporal, Bill Langen came up to us. "Ready?" he asked.

Dickie answered him, "Hey Bill, this silly sod thinks he can carry this." He pointed to the huge wireless set on his back. "Tell him will yer!"

Bill just smiled, "If he wants to, let him." He suddenly changed his expression, "but there's no changing his mind when we get going, okay?" He then addressed us all, "Come on, get everything ready, and make sure you've got your water bottles full, we'll be needing them, ok?"

"Okay, we'll be there," replied Dickie with a grin and a quick look at Stadden.

Lieutenant Kartage was waiting, and he certainly didn't like waiting, so we hurried and lined up ready to enter the swamp. The lieutenant ran his eyes down the platoon starting with Sergeant Conelly, then Corporal Langen, before coming to the leading scout, who stood there looking like something out of a western with a Remington shot gun draped over his forearm. "You ready Leak?"

"Yes Sir, I'm ready," he replied with a quick grin.

"Good, because I'm thinking we're going to be lucky today and bag a couple."

"Thinks he's on a bloody duck shoot," remarked Dickie in a whisper.

Lieutenant Kartage must have heard something because his eyes darted down the line towards us, "You said something Dickens?"

"No Sir! Not me Sir, wouldn't dream of interrupting you Sir."

"Very well Dickens, very well," he said, his eyes moving on down the line to the Bren gunner and his number two, "You got your ammunition?"

"Sir," came the standard reply.

"Right, we're eleven strong, and from my information, the enemy in this area is eight strong; so I think we'll be more than a match for them." He looked at us for confirmation.

"Yes Sir," we all replied, but I wasn't so sure we all felt like that. I instinctively ran my hands down the wood of the F. N. rifle I was carrying, caressing it like a cat, knowing that my life may depend upon it at any time.

The day had all the makings of another blistering hot one as we moved silently forward, watching all the time for signs of an ambush. We'd all heard rumours that our enemy was a crack Communist outfit called the 13/15 Independent Platoon, which made us all a little on edge, because we knew they could fight and were well organised. The rumour also suggested that they didn't take prisoners; they tortured them before nailing them to rubber trees. I vowed there and then never to be taken prisoner. After we'd been going for some time, I saw Stadden struggling with the burden of the wireless set and all his other gear on his back.

Dickie went up to him, "Hey dog breath! You want me to take over?"

"Piss off Dickie," the reply came back. "It's a man's job."

Dickie turned and came across to me, "That stupid sod'll regret it, silly bugger doesn't know what's ahead!"

I instinctively looked towards the swamp that we were about to enter.

"You been in a swamp before then Dickie?" said Tommo with a wry smile.

"Oh listen smart arse, will you? I've bin in all types of shitty jungle, and I can carry anything right, unlike bollock brain?" he said pointing to Stadden.

"It's those short little legs isn't it? Running up and down those Pennine hills near, where is it? Todmorden!"

Dickie turned to see Mal Forler, one of the riflemen who'd joined us. "Well you know what they say, don't you?"

"Well, what do they say my little friend?" said Mal with a twinkle in his eye.

"Short legs, long dick."

We all laughed, but we laughed even more when Stadden who'd overheard the comment added, "Don't worry Dickie, you've got to be the exception."

Suddenly Lieutenant Kartage appeared, "Cut this chattering out, you can be overheard for miles."

We all instantly recognised that the Lieutenant was on edge and made all the final preparations before entering the swamp in silence. The choking smell of the swamp hit us immediately. It was a nauseating, repulsive rotting stench. At first it didn't really bother us, but after some time it became very serious business, as it became our reality, as we stumbled through the roots of one mangrove tree to another. In between one tree and another was a sea of deep slimy mud. At first I plunged into the mud with abandon, sinking up to my waist, except when my foot happened to find a mangrove root, when I'd raise my body out of the mud for a brief moment, only to plunge back into it with my next step. The mangrove roots were irritatingly difficult to stand on, as they were slimy and twisted. Being rubber, our jungle boots slid so easily off them, making for some awkward falls in the mud.

After an hour in the swamp, I had mud in my mouth, up my nose, in my ears and eyes, and perhaps worst of all, up the barrel of my FN rifle making it unfit to fire. As a fighting force, the unit was in some trouble after only two hours. I very much doubt whether any weapon in the whole group would have fired, but we pressed on. Lieutenant Kartage was determined to cover the allotted ground. Towards midday we stopped for a break and to take stock of the situation. I looked round our group of soldiers and saw the dishevelled and stinking state we were in. Mud covered most parts of our bodies enveloping us in a film of grey. This, combined with sweat that ran freely from our bodies like a river, made us a sorry looking bunch. Sitting down on a mangrove root that was sticking out of the mud, I looked around. I could only see Tommo in front of me and Shuttlecock behind.

Tommo, never a silent sufferer, cast me a glance, "What the bloody hell are we doing here? Who in their right mind would hide in shit hole like this? We should leave 'em here, not follow the silly bastards in!"

I was too tired and miserable to argue or add to it; I threw him a cigarette.

"Thanks," he said with a flicker of a smile, "but I do hope you're not thinking of me carrying you out of here?"

"Piss off!" was all I could manage to utter.

As the day grew longer, the heat of the sun began to penetrate through the mangrove foliage, and we wilted under its effect. Lieutenant Kartage ordered a rest. I'd saved some water, and debated whether to drink it, but I remembered the last time I'd drank water when overheating, and put it back in my pouch. We moved on again through the swamp, clambering and sliding through the mud near to exhaustion. The only thing that kept me going was the knowledge that everyone else must have felt the same, including Lieutenant Kartage. That thought alone spurred me on. I continually looked at Tommo, and saw that he was almost done in, but I knew he'd never give up, and that helped me keep moving in the right direction. At the rear, Shuttlecock was getting further and further behind, until I lost sight of him. By mid afternoon, we were all bickering at the back of the patrol as we voiced our general despair, when I heard what sounded like trouble up ahead, but I couldn't see clearly enough to decide what was wrong. All silence forgotten and gone, we stumbling forward in desperate hope. It was quite simply a matter of getting out, and not getting left behind, which was quite a terrifying thought. I started to feel sick and retched almost immediately, but nothing came up. It seemed that my whole life now became completely centred upon taking the next step and no more. The thought of survival etched its way into the front of my thoughts.

At that precise moment, I recognised a broken mangrove branch that I'd seen before - we were lost! We'd gone round in a full circle. I could have cried. I tried to speak to Tommo, but my voice was hoarse through the heat and lack of water, which I still daren't drink.

Tommo moved towards me, "You know what Swifty? We're bloody well lost!"

"Yes," I managed to whisper back, "we're lost in this shit hole too."

We sat there too exhausted to grumble any more. Then much to my amazement, we carried on. The heat of the day had gone by this time, but it left us with the frightening thought that night was fast approaching. It was the night that frightened me most, not the terrorists. After continuing for some time, it became quite apparent that we'd be spending the night in the swamp.

Lieutenant Kartage stopped the patrol, and came down the line with Corporal Langen to explain that we were lost, but said that there was no real problem, as we could get a fix from a spotter plane, and get out the following morning.

I found a suitable mangrove tree to lean back upon waiting for the night to come. The mangrove swamp proved to be much lighter at night than either virgin or secondary jungle, the canopy being nowhere near as dense. The moon's light filtered through the foliage to give some form to objects, while at the same time creating a ghostly scene. Everyone slept fitfully and the continual glow of cigarettes indicated our general unease. The noise of the jungle night is frightening, squeals, shrieks and wailings, intermitted with the noise of a million flying insects, that made you feel that the whole jungle was on the move. We waited for dawn, which seemed to take an eternity to come, while being plagued by countless millions of mosquitoes that really bugged us with their incessant stinging attacks. Dawn came, and with it the daunting task of getting out of the swamp. Nobody had eaten since coming into the swamp and it showed. Everyone looked dishevelled and weary and coated in grey; nothing was untouched by it. Water was running low, but experience had prevailed and we all had some left.

We moved out at first light knowing that the spotter plane would be circling around overhead. However, we also knew that Lieutenant Kartage wanted to get out without its help if he possibly could, otherwise he'd be the butt of the Officer's jokes for months. We continued at a fast pace, stumbling and cursing into the mud, very near to complete exhaustion. Quite out of the blue I heard somebody screaming and shouting, the likes of which I'd never heard before. Tommo rushed forward to find out what was wrong. I thought we were either attacking or being attacked. I waited with Shuttlecock quite undecided what to do. The screams and shouts continued, followed by demented cries for help, pursued by pleadings, as if someone was about to be shot. Quite unnerved by this time, I went forward.

The scene that met my eyes was to say the least unexpected. Lieutenant Kartage and Corporal Langen were restraining Private Stadden who had apparently gone berserk, and looked completely insane. He'd totally snapped, was frothing at the mouth, his eyes protruding like great landmarks. He was a frightening sight. The platoon just grouped together and watched. Tommo looked at me. I returned his look, then I looked at Shuttlecock, but no one spoke. We just stood and watched Stadden writhing around in the mud, while the Lieutenant and Corporal tried to tie his hands and legs together.

"We'll 'ave to get a fix now, otherwise we'll all end up like that," said Dickie quite seriously, but loud enough for everyone to hear him.

Sure enough, Lieutenant Kartage heard him and threw him a glance, but chose to ignore the remark. He must have also realised the dire situation we were in and he called everyone together. "Right, with all this racket going on, we'll never find a terrorist within miles now, so it's no use patrolling this area anymore. We'll get a fix, and should be out of here within two to three hours. Okay, now back to your positions, and keep alert just in case Johnny terrorist has heard us, and is waiting in ambush." He walked away and studied the map with Corporal Langen.

"Do you hear that?" said Shuttlecock. "He's blaming Stadden for all the noise he bloody well caused getting us lost in the first place. Stupid bloody sod."

Sergeant Conelly lifted his head after Shuttlecock had spoken. He got up slowly and came across the mangrove roots to where we were sitting, never taking his eyes off him for a moment, until he was within an inch of his face. "You watch your bloody mouth Shuttlecock, you shit heap, or I'll tell Lieutenant Kartage what you've just said, shall I?" He stood there glowering at him, while Shutts stammered out something quite incomprehensible that sounded like an apology.

When the Sergeant had gone, I looked at Shutts, I mean, I only looked at him, said nothing, did nothing.

It was enough to make him respond angrily, "What you looking at Swifty, yer bastard! Just like me ter get done wouldn't yer?"

I returned his look, I didn't like Shuttlecock, nor did I trust him. "Norman, you're not pretty at the best of times, but today you've obviously been trying very hard, because you're really ugly, so belt up."

"My name's not Norman," he said almost spitting the words out.

"No that's quite true." I said, "but it should be, because it suits you."

Mouthing obscenities, he sat down on a mangrove root and attempted to roll a cigarette.

Dicky was instructed by Lieutenant Kartage to attach an aerial to the highest branch he could find in the nearby mangrove trees. He dutifully disappeared up a tree, with everyone listening to a tirade of obscenities as he climbed. He continued to shout down to us despite a request from Lieutenant Kartage to be silent. "Bet you buggers would laugh if I fell down wouldn't you?" he stated.

Tommo could stand it no more, "No Dickie, we'd piss on the spot you disappeared into."

Lieutenant Kartage made his way over angrily, followed closely by Sergeant Conelly. "What do you men think this is, a bloody picnic or something? Thomkin you will be on orders when we get back to camp, as you will be Private Dickens." He looked up into the tree just as a lump of wood came crashing down from the upper branches where Dickie was trying to fit the aerial, it narrowly missed his head. He was quite obviously shaken, and I had no doubt that he thought it intentional.

Before he had time to speak Dickie jumped down, "Right Sir, I've put the aerial up on the highest branch I could get to."

The Lieutenant wasn't really interested in the aerial. "Did you dislodge that stick deliberately Dickens?"

Dickie looked perplexed and it saved his bacon, "What stick Sir, I didn't see a stick Sir!"

The Lieutenant lost his cool, "That stick you idiot!" The Lieutenant pointed to a stick lying in the mud near him.

"Oh I don't know anything about that Sir." Then he seemed to grasp what the Lieutenant really meant. "You mean did I throw that stick down there Sir? No Sir, it was a dead branch Sir. It must have broke off when I was climbing down. When I stepped on it, I nearly came down with it Sir."

The Lieutenant studied him for a moment then decided it was an accident, "It nearly hit me Dickens." He changed tack, "The aerial's up, is it?"

"Yes Sir, should be no problem contacting the spotter plane now Sir."

"Right let's do it then."

With that, the whole incident was forgotten, but it was a near thing for Dickie and we all knew it. Whether he actually threw it, we never really knew, Dickie was astute enough never to admit or brag about things like that. He quickly set the wireless up and attempted to contact the spotter plane. Eventually, we made contact and we were given our position. From this fixture, maps were studied and calculations made to get out of the swamp as soon as possible. Lieutenant Kartage also asked for a helicopter in order to evacuate Private Stadden quickly.

"He must be worse than I thought," I said to Bill Langen who was standing right by me.

"He's bad, can't get any sense out of him at all," he replied.

We made our way out of the jungle carrying Stadden on a home-made stretcher. He was bound hand and foot. Later in light jungle, the helicopter lifted him out. We never saw him again; some said he never recovered; others said that he had, and had been posted back to England. To my knowledge, nothing more was said about the incident. We made our way out of the jungle without contacting any terrorists. Whatever the outcome of the patrol, the terrorists knew that they could never rest.

Upon returning to camp, I went over to the Company Office to see Arnie Wilkin. He'd been made full Corporal and greeted me in his usual manner.

"Hi Swifty, everything alright out there playing bloody soldiers while I'm sweating my bollocks off working here."

"There's only one answer to that isn't there?" I said with a cheeky grin, "now that you're a full Corporal we'll all have to watch our Ps and Qs won't we? I mean no more, Piss off Wilkin. But, yes full Corporal Wilkin. What honour can I bestow upon you now, sort of thing."

"All right, shut it. Rank is given not taken." He gave me a greasy grin.

"Now tell me this thing about Stadden. I've heard a bit about it. Was it as bad as they say it was?"

"Worse!" I related the whole thing to him in great detail.

Just as I finished, Bill Bosby came in. He had become Major Coker's batman since we'd been out in the jungle. He sat down on the bed without a word. I nodded to him.

Arnie continued, "You heard about Sipputeh then?"

"What about Sipputeh? I don't know anything about that."

"Well," said Arnie, "you know that 'A' and 'C' Companies are stationed there, don't you?"

"Yes, of course I do, go on," I said impatiently wanting to know more.

"It's really funny, two Provo's, you know Camp Policemen, sat on the gate at the camp entrance, supposed to be guarding it." He stopped. "I don't think you know anything about Sipputeh camp do you? Well I'll explain. Sepputeh is not like our camp here at Colombo; it's right out on the edge of the jungle. There's nothing there, it's very basic and the gates are always guarded by Regimental Police. You get it?"

"Yes, I get I," I said, reluctant to admit that I didn't know much about it.

"Well," he continued, "these two Regimental Policemen are guarding the gates of heaven; it's hot and they've been there for hours, and they're bored to death and a little more than pissed off, get it?"

I nodded, so he continued, "That baboon Hart decides to play Russian roulette with his pistol."

"You're kidding me?"

"No, I'm not kidding, this is for real. He puts one bullet up the spout, spins the chamber and pulls the trigger. Nothing happens, so he does it again and again, and still nothing happens. In the meantime, his mate shifts his position without Hart noticing it. Hart spins the chamber again, as he has done on the previous occasions, and pulls the trigger, only this time there's a bloody great bang; his mate has stretched his leg out and the bullet goes straight through his knee."

"Right through his knee," I repeated not able to take it in.

"Yeah, right through it, smashed all the bone, it's said you could hear the bastard screaming for miles. M.O. said he'll be lucky to walk properly again."

"What was he like?" I asked without thinking.

"How do you mean? Haven't I just told you," muttered Arnie quite irritated.

"I mean didn't he pass out, like?"

"This lad from 'C' Company said he screamed like a stuffed pig, blood spurted out of his knee like a fountain."

"Serves him right, that swine had it coming to him."

"Who?" Bill queried, wondering which one I was talking about?

"Both of them, they're Regimental Police aren't they? That's enough in my book."

"But you don't know them," Arnie retorted somewhat irritated.

"I know Hart and he's a right bastard," I said with some conviction.

"Yeah, but you don't know the guy that's been shot, do you?"

"No, I suppose I don't."

"Well don't talk crap then." Arnie was getting mad and I didn't know why. He continued, "You're always over the top, you're just like a little boy at times, or is it all that boxing that's numbing your brain? Anyway Hart will be court-martialled and I wouldn't like to be in his shoes."

The incident was soon forgotten as were Arnie's remarks about my boxing, or so he thought. Camp life continued without any further reference to it, there were far too many other things going on to worry about such events for long. However, it was noticeable that regulations concerning ammunition tightened up considerably after that.

Some days later, after coming into camp from a jungle operation, I was met by Sergeant Conelly, "Private Swift, get yourself to the Company office immediately, Major Coker wants to speak to you so make it quick."

"Right Sergeant, I'll be there."

He grunted something that I didn't quite grasp, but I knew that it would be rude and quite untrue.

"Hell Swifty, what's that all about?" Tommo asked as I passed him.

I shook my head indicating that I had no idea. I walked across the spare ground to the Company office to find out.

On entering into the Company office, I was met by Arnie near the door. "Wait there Swifty, he's busy at the moment, but he'll be free in a minute."

"What's it about?" I queried.

"Oh it's an escort duty to Kinraha Barracks, you know the military prison somewhere near Kuala Lumpur, I think."

"Who's been court-martialled then?"

He paused for a moment, put his hand up to silence me; cocked his head to one side and listened intently. I wondered what the hell he was doing at first. When he'd finished, he turned and sneered at me, "It's McNichols - the boxer remember?"

"Oh, I remember. What did he get?"

"Six months hard labour in Kinraha, and I think you're taking him down."

"With who? I hope I'm not taking him down on my own."

"Don't be daft," he said before casting a quick glance at the office door. "I think he's finished now, I'll see." He knocked on the door gently and went in, reappearing almost immediately. "Right Swifty, he's coming out to see you, don't forget to salute him otherwise you might well be keeping McNichols company."

I smiled, knowing that there had been occasions when I had forgotten to salute an Officer, but I'd somehow always got away with it, much to the amazement and jealousy of my friends.

Major Coker appeared, "Private Swift, the Regimental Police are somewhat stretched at the moment, and 'B' Company have been asked to help out by providing one soldier for escort duty. I've chosen you." He paused, "How do you feel about that?"

"Yes Sir," I responded immediately, "I'll do it Sir."

"Very good, you'll be going with Corporal James out of the Regimental Police." He turned to Arnie, "Corporal Wilkin will put the details on Company orders tonight." He stared at me and waited for an answer.

"Very good Sir, is that all Sir?"

"Yes, I think that's about it, I know you'll do a good job."

With that I saluted him and made my way back to the Company lines. Major Coker seemed to like me, and I took it as a compliment that I'd been asked. I also knew that I'd miss a jungle patrol by doing it. That night, I wandered over to the Company office to read the orders for the following day. Sure enough I was to report to the guardroom at 07.00 hours the next morning. The lads gave me some stick about being the C.O.s blue-eyed boy, but I didn't let that worry me.

It was just light when I reported to the guardroom the next morning. What I didn't expect was 'Big Mick', the Regimental Sergeant to be there. He stared at me as I entered the guardroom, which immediately made me feel uneasy under his aggressive surveillance.

"What do you want?" he growled, without taking his eyes off me for a second.

"I've been told to report here to provide an escort for Private McNichols to Kinraha prison barracks Sergeant."

He looked at the floor and then at me, "And why would they be sending a little shit like you to guard a dangerous prisoner then?"

I was scared of 'Big Mick', of that there was no doubt, but I had the backing of Major Coker, and that gave me confidence. "Well Sergeant," I began. "You'll have to see Major..."

I hadn't got his name out before he interrupted me, "Stop!" he bawled, "I know all that bull shit." He then turned to the Corporal standing next to him, "Take him inside and show him the ropes."

The Corporal gestured for me to follow him, which I did knowing that the Sergeant was following my every move.

Once out of Big Mick's presence, the Corporal smiled, "You taking McNichols down to Kinraha then?"

I nodded.

"Well, you'll be going with Corporal James; he's just gone to get the passes from H.Q." We continued walking towards the cells where I presumed Mc was being held.

"You're a boxer, aren't you?" The Corporal said enquiringly.

"Yes, I got to the finals of the Battalion Light Welterweight Championships."

"Yeah," he replied, "I thought you won. He looked a lot bigger than you though."

I didn't really know how to answer that, so I left it. We stopped outside Mc's cell. Mc had been placed in solitary confinement due to some minor infringement I was told. The Corporal opened the cell door and Mc stood up immediately. I noticed he was a lot thinner than the last time I saw him; he was noticeably worried and showed it in his face, twitching as he endeavoured to speak.

"Hi Swifty," was all he managed to get out in the end.

"Okay Mc, how yer doing? I'm going to Kinraha with you."

The Corporal intervened, "Shut up McNichols, this isn't a mother's fucking tea party!" He paused for a second before bawling out, "Attention!"

Mc suddenly became as stiff as a doorpost as I did. He then walked nearer to him.

"You're just like a fucking snowball McNichols, only instead of snow they've rolled up all the shit they could find, and called it Mc fucking Nicholas haven't they?"

Mc didn't flinch, whereupon the Corporal turned and gave me a withering glance that spoke volumes. We marched out, me in front of Mc and the Corporal behind him shouting, "Left! Right! Left! Right!" Until I thought my hearing would be permanently damaged.

Eventually we came to the guardroom where Sergeant O'Shan was waiting for us.

"Detail," the Corporal shouted, "Detail halt!"

I banged my boots into the floor so hard it jarred my ankles. Standing there absolutely rock solid, hardly daring to breathe, I waited for what I knew would be a detailed inspection by 'Big Mick'.

He ambled across to us muttering under his breath as he came. Then in his broad Liverpuddlian accent, he asked question after question.

I replied, "Yes Sergeant, no Sergeant," where I thought appropriate. I knew it was a game but it had to be played well.

The Sergeant eventually, and after much silent proliferation bawled out; "Stand easy."

We stood at ease with every uncertainty in the book, while he walked away towards the door, never once taking his eyes off us, then coming back towards us until he was invading my private space. While he was there, just inches away from my face, I suddenly had a tremendous impulse to head-butt him. There I was, in total fear of this most brutal man, who had the most enormous power to inflict all sorts of misery upon me, and I was actually thinking of head-butting him. All these thoughts kept continually going round in my head as he peered into my eyes. Being so fearful of him seemed to heighten the thought of attacking him. All kinds of strange thoughts raced through my mind. I mulled over the consequences of such action, but the most disturbing thought was that in one heightened movement, I could join McNichols in Kinraha prison barracks. It would most certainly ruin my comfortable existence in the Army I reasoned, but while he remained there, inches away from my face, I couldn't get away from the thought, dare I do it?

Sergeant O'Shan couldn't possibly have read my thoughts, but he did say something that shook me, "You thinking what I'm thinking Private Swift?"

"I don't know what you're thinking Sergeant," I replied.

"I'm thinking that you don't like me Private Swift."

Now that was true, but dare I enter into the world of truth with this most dangerous man? "You have a job to do Sergeant, and you do it well."

His eyes screwed up as he summoned up enough strength to answer, "Don't fucking well give me that shit soldier. Only Officers talk to me like that."

I said nothing, but it must have been noticeable that I was scared stiff, wishing the ground would swallow me up.

"We'll have to put up with you I suppose," he said pulling himself up to his full height while shaking his finger at me. "But you come back here telling me that Mc fucking Nicholas has escaped, or any other shit like that, and I'll be squeezing your balls so hard you'd wish you were a woman."

A feeling of confidence crept back into me to some degree as I realised that his game was nearly over. "He'll not escape Sergeant, on that I'll stake my life."

"Well that's not worth a lot, is it?" he said curtly.

"No Sergeant, it's worth about as much as yours." As the last word left my mouth, I knew it was a mistake.

His face went red; his great head looked like it might burst or explode. He could hardly speak, but managed to splutter out sounds at such a volume and intensity that intermingling with his non-verbal gesticulations read something akin to, *I'm a Sergeant!* The rest was lost in pure spittle that sprayed out from his mouth.

At that moment, I caught sight of the Corporal who was stood at the back of the room shaking with silent laughter, so much so, he had to leave the room.

This made me panic into trying to explain, "All I meant Sergeant was that death is death, and life is life, that's no reflection on you personally."

"Listen to him will yer, he's now telling me how to fucking think now. Get him out of here, him and McNichols."

Corporal James appeared with the railway passes, and in no time we were on our way to the station in a Landrover. McNichols was handcuffed to Corporal James, while I walked along besides them to the platform. We had about twenty minutes to wait for the train, but waiting never mattered in the Army, we were used to it.

As we stood there on the platform, I became aware of the furtive glances being made at our prisoner and us, by the other people on the platform, and realised that there was an incredible social mix. Malays, Chinese and Indians were huddled together in tight groups around the platform, all giving us the occasional glance when they thought we weren't looking. I knew that another race of people also existed in Malaya, but they didn't really register as being worthy of recognition, the aborigines - people who lived in the jungle. I never asked any questions, just accepted things as they were. I never asked why or how the racial mix came to exist together, mainly because it might make me look stupid if I did. Anyway they all looked foreign, and we were fighting people just like them in the jungle, who was to say it wasn't them in their spare time?

The train clattered into the station, and seemingly hundreds of people clambered onto it. I couldn't quite believe how so many people could get onto one train. We waited until most of them had got on the train before boarding. Our seats were reserved, and after finding them we settled down, As the train got going, I noticed that Mc was still handcuffed to Corporal James, although there was some attempt at concealing it.

"Corporal, do you think it might be an idea to take them off?" I pointed to the handcuffs, "he's not going any place."

He listened, but never answered. I was formulating my next plea when he decided to speak.

"I'm not so sure about that," he said with a look of unease and some nervousness.

Mc jumped in, assuring him that his prime intention was to serve his time in prison, get on with his service and get out of the Army.

Corporal James listened, but still seemed unsure about it.

Mc tried again, "Look Corporal, I'm not going anywhere, there's only the bloody jungle. Look at it."

I glanced out of the window as did the Corporal. It looked formidable.

The Corporal slowly turned his head until he looked Mc straight in the eye, "If you try to escape, I'm going to have to shoot you. You know that?"

Mc knew, and I knew that he would. Corporal James then took the handcuffs off Mc and immediately changed seats with him so that Mc now sat next to the window. He was taking no chances.

I found my hand somehow caressing the butt of my rifle, only snatching it away when my conscience came alive to the fact that Mc was the prospective target. We had been issued with Mark 5 jungle rifles for escort duty. I'd never fired one in my life. They were generally given to soldiers going on leave or doing other duties in and around camp, although they were sometimes given to the Iban trackers.

We arrived at the station just outside Kuala Lumpur where two Military Policemen greeted us with curt questions and withering stares. We climbed into the back of their Landrover and sped off to the prison camp.

"Had any trouble with him?" asked the Sergeant in charge of the detail.

"Oh no he's been quiet enough," I answered.

The Sergeant stared at me for some time, "Was I talking to you soldier?"

Thinking as fast as I could, while inwardly, and possibly visibly, panicking, I replied somewhat hesitatingly, "I thought so at first Sergeant, but I now realise that you were talking to Corporal James."

"Right soldier. When I want to speak to you, I'll let *you* know, until then shut yer mouth 'cause you haven't got anything to say that interests me." He continued to stare at me intently, almost willing me to say something, but I just put my head down until he turned his attention to Corporal James again.

"Well Corporal?"

"Yes, he's been no trouble Sergeant."

"He better not have been," he said, as he glared at Mc, who immediately hung his head down.

"Look at me you fucking lump of shit."

Mc immediately looked up, "Yes Sergeant."

The Sergeant paused for some time, giving him chance to say something, but Mc looked passively at him without speaking; whereupon the Sergeant changed his attitude and became visibly less aggressive.

"You've made a mistake son; it was a big mistake that brought you here. Keep your nose clean and you'll get out without too much pain; but let me make myself quite clear, if you don't, they'll carry you out on a fucking stretcher; believe me we break more than bones in here."

Mc listened, pale, drawn and pensive as the Landrover stopped at the huge gates of the Military Prison. We drove into the penal complex. The first thing that I noticed besides the barbed wire was the huge pile of sand in the middle of the parade ground. It looked completely out of place, and at the time, I had no idea why it was there. The sun beat down on us as we waited for the Military Police Sergeant's instructions. It was airless sat there, and before long we were all wet through with sweat, which began to show on our uniforms in great damp patches. I slowly began to realise that this was all part of the procedure and was intentional. Mc got restless and made a slight movement.

"Stay where you are soldier. You fucking well move when I tell you to move. You shit when I tell you to shit. You understand me?" he boomed.

Mc nodded and mumbled, "Yes Sergeant."

Such was the intensity of the Sergeant Major's voice; I froze, and went into a state of sheer panic. With some difficulty, I gained what was left of my equilibrium, but it was not without the inner knowledge about what went on inside; rumours from regular soldiers suggested that conditions were brutal in the extreme. I even heard that soldiers died inside their walls, it seemed that they could do what they liked with you, and they were not accountable for it. Realising this, I became extremely anxious and fearful.

"Escort and prisoner will assemble at the front of the Landrover. Move!"

As I scrambled out of the vehicle, I noticed the look on Corporal James's face, and he too looked uncomfortable, and in some strange way it comforted me. We stood there ramrod still in the blistering sun.

"Prisoner and escort will double on the spot." The Sergeant yelled out as if his life depended upon it.

Doubling meant that we kept bringing our knees up to our waists in a continual running action, while staying on the same spot.

"Forward!" His command saw us making ground, while continuing the same action. We doubled round the parade ground until I thought I was about to pass out.

"Prisoner and escort will halt."

We halted, but there was no respite. "Prisoner and escort will double again."

And we were off again, running in the oppressive heat of the day until I began to feel totally shattered, dizzy and wondering how long it would be before I broke down completely. Fortunately the command came to halt, interrupting my fears. Sweat by this time, was running down my face in rivulets, making me blink as the salt ran into my eyes.

Again he told us to double, which we dutifully did. From the corner of my eye, I saw the Sergeant walk over to an Officer who had appeared on the scene.

After speaking to him for a moment, he came back to us. "The prisoner will continue to mark time at the double. The escort will halt."

We both halted, leaving McNichols still marking time at the double. That was the last I saw of Kinraha Barracks. We were driven back to the railway station, but this time without the Sergeant, leaving Mc to his fate. It was a frightening experience for me, not knowing, but slowly realising the fate of soldiers who fall foul of Army rules and regulations. I think it was the total power and control that the Army had over individuals that scared me most. My father had told me many times about soldiers in the First World War who'd gone to military prison, and some time later been reported killed in action.

"Which action?" he'd asked his friends, but he knew that there would be nothing forthcoming, principally because nobody dared to ask the right people.

I pondered upon his words on the long journey back to camp. My father always maintained that they'd died while being held in custody, although he had no proof.

The journey back to camp was uneventful. Corporal James rarely spoke, and when he did, it was mostly to himself, but loud enough for everyone to hear him. We had to share our carriage with some of the local population which consisted of Malays, Indians and Chinese people. They obviously caused him much displeasure, for I saw him continually looking at them, while mouthing silent foul obscenities. They didn't need to know any English to understand his hatred for them. I was neither brave, nor strong enough to challenge him, because I knew it would make me a possible target for some future abuse. In fact I went along with him by making grimaces at them too, then looking at him for approval, which I got. This spurred me on to make quick jerky movements towards them, from which they would recoil with fear, making all kinds of strange sounds. Their reaction sent us into peals of laughter, making me ever more aggressive in attitude. They moved as far away from us as they possibly could, giving us only furtive glances, laden with fear at what might happen next. I contented myself with the thought that we were a far superior race of people, for our Officers had never tired of telling us that we had a God-given right to govern all semi-civilised people. Unbelievable as it may seem, beneath all this, I knew that my behaviour was wrong, and I was only doing it to ingratiate myself with the Corporal. I can now rationalise what I did to some degree, but I couldn't then, it was all lost in a morass of youthful emotion in order to survive.

Chapter 5

SOME INCIDENTS IN CAMP AT IPOH

"The repression was stepped up. The police and military made increasing use of their wide powers of arrest and detention, imposing curfews, collective punishments, and food controls. Altogether, during the Emergency, 34,000 men and women were to be interned without trial and thousands more Chinese were deported from the country. More were brought to trial under the Emergency laws, receiving long prison sentences or even the death penalty. Capital punishment was introduced for a wide-range of offences, including the possession of firearms, and in the course of the war 226 rebels were hanged, a total only exceeded in postwar British campaigns by the judicial massacre carried out in Kenya."

One morning, some time after my escort duty to Kinraha, I heard someone crying. It seemed to be coming from the roadway near to the camp gates. At first I ignored it thinking it might go away, but it got louder and louder, until I could stand it no longer and went to investigate. When I arrived at the scene, the cries had reached screaming pitch. I found a group of women road workers huddled together in great distress. I had no idea what was wrong, although I tried my best to understand. That was when I saw Tommy Morton, our heavyweight boxer, dragging a Chinese man towards the group, followed by a Malayan lady who was hurrying to keep up some way behind him.

"This him, then?" shouted Tommy.

The group of ladies all nodded in agreement, although it was pretty obvious to me that most of them didn't understand a word of English. However, one of them, who obviously did, approached us, "Him not pay," said the woman, coming up to Tommy.

Whereupon Tommy flung him round until he faced him, "Right, I'll flatten yer if you don't get your money out, yer bastard!" he shouted, an inch away from his face, while tightening his grip, until the man seemed about to burst a blood vessel in his face. He then almost lifted the man off his feet as he shook him.

I laughed when I realised that he was sorting out a pay dispute, mainly because Tommy had a reputation for drunken violent behaviour and was nearly always on 'jankers' for something connected with some unruly deed, and here he was acting as judge and jury.

He made the Chinese man empty his pockets onto the floor and then shared it out among the women, who smiled at him and left.

He then turned to the Chinese man and told him to piss off.

The man looked completely perplexed and bemused. and immediately tried to communicate with Tommy in Chinese. However, the combination of noise and a total lack of comprehension, resulted in Tommy flipping his lid and hitting him so hard, he floored him. The man got up and ran off holding his nose, which was bleeding. We both laughed uproariously, thinking that he deserved it.

Our laughter was short lived however, when we saw Sergeant Major Bullock, followed by the Chinese man, striding up the road towards us some minutes later.

"Hey Tommy, what have we done?" I asked with more than a little apprehension.

"We've sorted this thing out 'aven't we?"

"What do you think Bullock wants then?" I replied.

He looked too worried to answer.

I wanted to laugh, but I daren't, but I did consider just trying to wander off, but quickly realised that such action might show some guilt. In the end, I just waited with Tommy.

"What the bloody hell 'ave you two been up to then?" the Sergeant Major shouted at the top of his voice, when he got closer.

Tommy tried to explain what had happened, "He wasn't going to pay 'em Sergeant Major," said Tommy in all innocence.

"So you gave them all his money, is that it? Besides giving him a bloody good hiding? Do you know who this man is?"

"Yes Sir, he's the foreman isn't he Sir?" answered Tommy with some confidence:

"Well," shouted the Sergeant Major, "he's fucking well not, he just happens to be the man in charge of all road mending in this area of Ipoh, and he's come to sort this dispute out!"

"What dispute?" asked Tommy.

"Oh nothing really. Just the fact that the guy who usually pays them has pissed off with all their money. That's all!"

"Oh heck," replied Tommy, as the blood drained from his face.

I smiled in direct response to the look on Tommy's face, which was the picture of utter dejection.

"And you can take that grin off you face Swift, or I'll bloody well knock it off!" he said, before turning his attention again to Tommy. "Morton you can consider yourself under arrest." Then he turned to me, "You too Swift." After which he addressed us both, "The two of you can go back to your quarters and wait for further instructions from me."

Later that day, I was called up to the Company office to explain the incident to Major Coker. I said that I'd heard some women crying and wailing and had gone to investigate what was wrong, and found Tommy Morton already there, trying to sort it out.

A sardonic smile came onto Major Coker's face, "Morton can't sort his own problems out, never mind someone else's." He looked at me more intensely, "and you never did a thing?"

"No Sir," I answered truthfully.

"You're always on the edge of trouble Swift. Be careful, you are consorting with soldiers who are never out of trouble in the Battalion, and believe me, it rubs off." He paused, sighed whilst fiddling with his pen, almost daring me to say something.

I knew his game, I'd learned it at school. You never interrupted a senior when being told off. You always allowed them to deliberate, to show their power. I waited submissively.

After a long silence, he eventually spoke, "You should know better, but I think you'll have to learn the hard way." His piercing eyes sought mine and he stared at me until I lowered my eyes in submissive obedience. "Mull over my words Private Swift; ignore them at your peril." He dismissed me before lowering his eyes onto some papers on his desk.

Before I was allowed to go, Sergeant Major Bullock gave me some advice. "If you as much as breathe heavy Private Swift I'll have yer bloody guts for garters. You got off lightly this time, but then Major Coker likes you, don't he? But it'll do to remember that I don't, and you'd be fucking wise to remember that."

I marched out of his office at the double. I never bothered to find out how Tommy went on, thinking it would be better to lie low for a while until the whole thing had blown over. However, it didn't stop me from chuckling now and then when I thought about Tommy Morton's justice, hitting the wrong man.

When I got back to the Company lines, I heard rumours that the boxing team were going to get together for the Regimental and Divisional Championships. Pop Quint, the Captain of the team, came round to see me. I was keen to box again, seeing it as a way out of patrolling the jungle. Pop talked to me for some time, telling me all about the special conditions I'd get if I decided to join the team. I listened, and when he'd finished, I agreed to join. About a week later, I was called into the Company office to see Major Coker again, only this time I had no idea what it was for. Sergeant Major Bullock marched me into his office and I stood there at attention and waited.

"Right Private Swift," he said without looking at me. "I'm glad to see that you've volunteered to represent the Company again in the Battalion Championships, I just know that you'll do well." He paused as he always did, but this time he never took his eyes off me for a second. "By the way, Private Swift you'll be pleased to know that you've been promoted to Lance Corporal," he leaned back on his chair and waited for my response.

"Thank you Sir," I murmured, wondering whether I had permission to speak.

He hadn't finished. "You'll be excused jungle patrol duties for the time being, I have some interesting jobs around camp for you to do. The first that comes to mind is Company Operations Clerk. Never heard of it I'll bet." He paused, smiled and continued, "Well, you shouldn't have, it's only just come into being."

I listened as he explained to me in great detail what he wanted me to do; after which he leaned back in his chair only this time I knew that he was open to questions; but I remained silent, not wanting to put my foot in it by asking a stupid question.

He carried on, "Do you think you can do it?" It wasn't really a question; it was a way of telling me how lucky I was.

"Yes Sir, thank you Sir," I answered beaming, "I'm sure that I can do a good job."

"Right Corporal Swift that'll do for now."

"Very good Sir, thank you Sir." I saluted and marched out of his office.

Sergeant Major Bullock was there to greet me as I came out. "We'll 'ave to be on our bloody toes now that you've got yourself an important position Corporal, won't we?"

The mention of my new rank pleased me, but the way he addressed me brought some confusion, it was as if he hadn't taken it seriously until he added that if my rank wasn't sewn onto my shirt by the following morning, I'd be demoted before I was officially promoted. I smiled, assuring him that it would be done, but I went away thinking that in the Amy you couldn't even get promoted without a threat.

The weeks followed each other with the unbroken pattern of boxing training in the morning, Company Operations Clerk in the afternoon, and sparring in the gym at night. This was organised so that it coincided with the hot and the cooler periods of the day. The job of Operations Clerk never really got off the ground, for after setting up the maps and plotting the routes of the various patrols operating in the jungle, the job was largely done, and only took a few minutes. The rest of the time I hung around the Company office and irritated Arnie. He had been promoted to full Corporal and was very pleased with himself. One day, after making sure the Operations Office was up to date with all the information available, I made my way over to the Company office. Arnie was busy typing, so I sat down near to him waiting for him to finish what he had to do; when through the open eaves of the hut, I saw a soldier making his way towards our office. This was quite unusual as 'B' Company lines were empty, everyone being out on jungle patrol except Major Coker and the Company office staff. I got up from my seat immediately to meet him as he arrived at the entrance. I saw, to my utter amazement, that it was Max Beamer out of 5 platoon.

"What the bloody hell are you doing here Max, aren't you supposed to be out on patrol?"

"Ah yes," he replied, "but I got lost."

"Got lost," repeated Arnie who'd come out of the office and was now standing behind me. "You're kidding me Beamer, you couldn't have got out of the jungle by yourself it's bloody well unheard of."

Max looked sheepishly at us both.

"You'd better come into the office Beamer," said Arnie after we'd stood there for some time.

Max entered the office and sat down, whilst Arnie went to inform Major Coker, who upon hearing, came scurrying out of office.

"I'm very surprised to see you here Beamer. Come into my office and tell me all about it."

They disappeared into his office leaving Arnie and myself to contemplate what would happen next. After a moment or two, I couldn't resist going over to the door of Major Coker's office and listening. Max told the Major that he'd gone down to the water point on the first night in the jungle, just before dark. When he'd finished washing, he turned round to find that everyone had left.

At that point the Major stopped him. "Where was the sentry on the water point?"

After a long pause Max answered, "I don't know Sir. I just don't know anything except that no one was there except me."

"That's odd," commented the Major. "What did you do then?"

"Well Sir, ah didn't really know what ter do, it were going dark quickly. I felt like calling out and shouting you know, 'cause I were scared, but I knew it would give my position away if any of the Commies were around like."

"Good man Beamer, you did the right thing. Anyway continue."

"Yes Sir, I tried to remember which way to go, but it all looked the same to me." He stopped, coughed, then carried on speaking, "When it were dark, I felt scared, I suppose I were a bit frightened really when I knew I were there for the night. I propped myself up against a tree. That way Sir, nobody could get me from the back and I could see everything in front of me." He laughed, "If I could see anything at all that is. When it came light…"

Major Coker interrupted him at that point, "Not so fast Beamer. What did you do in the night?"

"I slept with my back to a tree Sir."

"Right Beamer, I want Corporal Wilkin and Corporal Swift to hear this story."

The Major came bursting out of his office, "Have you heard Beamer's story you two?"

"Yes Sir," I said without thinking.

Arnie turned to me with utter dejection written all over his face.

Major Coker's face furrowed into a frown, "What I meant was for you to come into my office to hear Beamer's story, but it would seem that you've already heard it."

"Not everything Sir, just that…"

"Yes Corporal Swift, I'll have to remember that for future reference." Again he looked deeply concerned, but decided to leave whatever he had in mind for some future occasion. "Well come on, I want you to hear it again, it's certainly worth the telling."

We both walked into the office followed by Major Coker. "I want you to hear a most remarkable story," the Major said, completely ignoring the fact that we'd, or should I say I'd, heard most of it through the thin door of the office.

"Beamer has walked the best part of eighteen miles today. No mean feat, I can tell you. By my reckoning about eight miles through the jungle and twelve miles along the road, never mind spending one night in the jungle."

I thought that's twenty miles, and was about to correct the Major, but managed to stop myself at the last moment. Corporals do not correct Majors at *any* time. We stood there in silence and listened.

The Major continued to extol Beamer's bravery. "He spent one night by himself on the jungle floor; now I'd say that was as far from the light as any one can get in this world. Not even able to see your hand in front of your face, not forgetting that he was also lost; and here he is in front of us, having walked out himself without any help or any fuss. My mind boggles. He had no compass, no map no food, nothing but what he stood up in. How the hell did you know which way to go?"

"Oh I followed the stream Sir."

"But streams run into swamps, not rivers around here," said the Major enquiringly.

Beamer didn't answer him; he just stared vacantly to the front.

By this time the Major was getting quite excited. "How did you get out then; follow a path or something?"

"Yes Sir, the path by the stream came to a logging track; I followed that until it came to another pathway that were bigger. I took that, and it eventually came out at the main road."

"Were you at all worried?"

"Yes Sir, but I had me gun."

The Major looked at him and then at us. "Right Beamer, you can dismiss now, go to your quarters and we'll find you something to do until your platoon returns to camp."

When he'd gone, the Major turned to us again. "Do you appreciate his extraordinary luck? He could have gone in the wrong direction and been eighteen miles into the jungle you know instead of being here."

Yes, I thought, if me auntie had balls she'd be me uncle. It was a saying that I'd learned off the Liverpuddlian lads, and it seemed to fit the occasion.

The Major stroked his chin and continued to speak, although he was really only speaking to himself. "We'll have to have an enquiry, too many unanswered questions. Anyway we'll see when they get back." He immediately looked at Arnie, "When do they get back Corporal Wilkin?"

"Day after tomorrow Sir," Arnie replied almost before he'd finished asking the question.

The Major agreed, "Yes, yes. Did you know about the R.A.F. helicopter pilot shot down in the jungle? No, I don't mean shot down; you know engine trouble, had to come down in the jungle while on a reconnaissance mission. The aborigines brought the pilot back into Seputi camp a fortnight ago, completely off his head, doubt he'll ever recover."

"What was he like Sir?" I asked.

"Oh in a terrible state, frothing at the mouth, eyes protruding, staring, but seeing nothing, quite frightening. I really can't quite believe Beamer's story, it's beyond anything I've heard out here. In fact it's comparable to S.A.S. stuff really. Anyway keep me informed, both of you, of any developments, and that includes anything that Beamer might say to you." We saluted and he left.

As soon as he'd gone Arnie looked at me in utter dismay. "Well, you big gobshite Swifty. What did you say that for?"

"Yes, I know, I never thought," I said, realising that Arnie would never let it go until he'd had a good moan.

"That's your trouble, you never bloody well think!"

"Don't go on about it Arnie, it was a mistake, he'll get over it."

"Yeah, he'll get over it just in time for the next one. You know him, there'll be repercussions, you'll see, and what's more, he now thinks that I'm bloody well involved in eavesdropping at his door." He fiddled around his desk pretending to tidy it. "Right, I've got some work to do, not like some other buggers around here."

I took the hint and left.

.

Chapter 6

JUNGLE PATROLS

"By the end of 1949 the MRLA had managed to seize the initiative. The guerrillas carried out hit and run attacks, striking and then disappearing into the jungle. The British responded with large-scale cordon and search operations, combing the jungle with hundreds of troops and police, hunting for an elusive enemy that had long since slipped away. Unable to find the guerrillas, the British became increasingly brutal towards the local Chinese civilian population. Suspects were beaten and on occasion killed (the worst known incident was the massacre of twenty-four civilians at Batang Kali in December 1949) and their homes, sometimes whole villages, were destroyed. Far from intimidating the people, these methods only increased their support for the MRLA."

The arranged boxing match was cancelled, so all the boxers went back to their units to engage in patrolling the jungle again. I was sorry to lose my cushy job as operations clerk, but as Arnie said, it was too good to last.

Tommo welcomed me back in his usual style. "Bloody hell, why should we all tremble, he's back. The emergency will be cancelled tomorrow."

"That'll do from you Tommo, don't forget that I'm a Corporal now."

"No you're not, you've reached the pinnacle of your Army career, you're a Lance Corporal, and a bloody good one at that."

Everybody laughed, although I knew he was taking the Mickey, but I didn't mind, it was good to be back.

Tommy suddenly became very serious. "We've just got back from patrol, right?"

I nodded.

"You heard about Slim Morris then?"

"What do you mean, I don't know what you're on about?"

"You know Slim, he's that boy soldier, came to the Battalion at Kota Tinngi?"

"I think so," I said.

"You must know him, he's the one that told us about his dad, who was a Major in the Loyal, got killed at Anzio in the last war."

Suddenly it clicked, I knew him, "He's a Lance-jack, right?"

"Yes, that's him, tall skinny guy. Well, last patrol we were resting during the day ready to go on ambush at night. When Slim gets awful pains in his side. I'm about ten feet away from him, but his winces and groans upset me like, so I crawled over to him to see if I can do something for him, 'cause I carry the first aid kit, right?"

"Yes, go on," I said becoming suddenly very interested.

"I asked him how bad it was, but he couldn't answer me 'cause he's in so much pain. Then Lieutenant Kutchen crawls over to him to have a look, followed by Sergeant Conelly, and to my bloody amazement Kutchen tells him not to be so soft and to shut up. Well by midday

Slim's making enough noise to wake the dead. Everyone has his gun at the ready 'cause I'm sure you could hear him for miles, groaning and crying. It were terrible." He paused for breath then continued, "By the time Sergeant Conelly had persuaded Lieutenant Kutchen ter get the chopper in to evacuate him, it were too late. Chopper can't come in when it's bloody dark, can it? Kutchen's real mad 'cause there's no use going on ambush now, he's making too much noise. He moaned and cried all night. There was nothing we could do except listen to the poor bastard. By morning he were unconscious. When Kutchen saw him the next morning he nearly shit himself, an ex Major's son an all, dying on the jungle floor. He should have got him out sooner, and he knew it."

"When did this happen?"

"Day before yesterday."

"How's Slim now then?"

"Nobody really knows, took him out by chopper the next day, I think he's in Singapore hospital now, Kutchen says that he's got appendicitis."

I left Tommo and made my way back to the Company office to see if Arnie knew anything more about Slim, but he knew little more than we did. The Army is very secretive about such matters. Some time later, I learned that Slim had almost died, having developed peritonitis due to an unnecessary night on the jungle floor. Shortly after this event, Lieutenant Kutchen was transferred to Signals; some said it was a punishment, others said it was promotion, Sergeant Conelly only smiled, which meant that we'd never really know. Five Platoons did not greet the news of his move with any joy, for Lieutenant Kutchen was a popular leader with the men, even though we all knew he'd made some serious mistakes. He was a good man to be with in a tight corner. However, we all knew that he was never too popular with his fellow officers. It would seem that they never really accepted him as equal, due to his promotion through the ranks, together with his pronounced Lancastrian accent.

The next morning, walking across to the canteen, I ran into Arnie again.

"Hey Swifty what's this I've been hearing about you getting a bloody medal?"

"What are you on about Arnie, just taking the piss?"

"No Swifty, I'm serious," he said, a grin beginning to emerge onto his face. "I heard Major Coker talking to Captain Whitford, saying that you'd got a medal for being best recruit in basic training."

"Yes, he did," said Tommo who'd joined us without me noticing. "It were wrong, bloody hell Swifty getting a medal. He were always in trouble fighting and that. It were an inside job, all to do with that posh school he went to. Officers fell over themselves when it came to him. He were in all sorts of trouble and never did a day's 'jankers'."

I felt very embarrassed by Arnie's revelation, although nobody had mentioned it until then, some must have known about it as Tommo did. I also recognised that there was some truth in what Tommo said.

They both stood there looking to me for an answer.

"Yes, well, I couldn't help it, could I? I mean if they give you the best recruit. You must be doing something right."

"Yes, I wonder what that was?"

I turned to Arnie unable to ignore the implications of the remark, "Meaning what exactly?"

"Meaning that you have all their airs and bloody graces at times, you know," he said turning away from me and addressing Tommo. "All the confidence and arrogance in the world and none of the bloody brains to go with it." After which they both fell about laughing.

When he'd recovered Arnie said, "I don't think you know what you're like when you speak to the Officers Swifty, so I'll tell you."

I listened passively, somehow unable to extricate myself from this unwarranted attack on my character. "You get an 'A' for arseholing. Yes Major Coker. No Major Coker. can I wash your underpants Major Coker."

Arnie saw me move and sensed that he'd gone too far. "Okay Swifty; come on, a bit of truth and a joke won't hurt you"

I walked away unable to refute any of the insinuations which I knew were to some extent true. I'd always thought that Arnie and Tommo were my friends, but I wasn't too sure now.

As I walked away Tommo shouted after me, "How do you feel about me then? I should have won the medal for the best sportsman and you got it instead, didn't you?"

I knew that there was some truth in what he said, "Yes, well I don't give the medals out do I?" I shouted back angrily.

"No but your mates do," he replied as quick as a flash.

I didn't answer him, although I knew that he was referring to the competition we'd had in basic training which involved the hundred yards, long jump, high jump and the hop step and jump. He'd actually won the competition by one mark, but Captain Whitford had explained at the time that he'd decided to give it to me because I'd played cricket and rugby for the depot in the short time I'd been there. I'd never had any problems at the time, and nobody had bothered to even mention it except Tommo.

Things were pretty cool with Arnie and Tommo for some time after that, but one day as I was walking over to read Company Orders, I saw Arnie and he came over to me. "Hey, Swifty, your new Officer's called O'Silvan, and he's a real idiot."

"Why do you say that?" I enquired:

'Cause he bloody well is," said Arnie getting irritated.

"Where's he from?"

"Straight from the bloody university."

When I got back to the Company lines, I was immediately summoned to meet my new platoon commander. "Oh, you're Corporal Swift, or should I say Lance Corporal Swift to be more precise; I've heard a lot about you. You're a boxer, aren't you?"

"Yes Sir," I said wondering where this might lead.

"Well, we'll see whether you're as good an N.C.O. as you are a boxer shall we? What!"

I stood there at attention waiting for him to finish, knowing that life was going to be more difficult from now on.

"You'll be joining us the day after tomorrow, no time for anything else now except killing terrorists. Right?" After which he looked at me for a response.

I could see the lads smiling at him behind his back. At that point, I couldn't understand who they were smiling at, him or me; I was later to understand the many meanings of a smile.

"Very good Sir," I eventually responded.

"You know of course that Sergeant Conelly is your platoon Sergeant?"

"Yes Sir," I answered puzzled as to why he should deem it necessary to tell me something that he must have known I already knew.

Two days later, at about four o'clock in the afternoon, we boarded trucks and made for the jungle somewhere to the north of Ipoh. Upon arriving at the point where the trucks dropped us off, the drill was always the same. The trucks would slow down to a snail's pace, and we would jump for it. When everyone had got off the trucks, we'd space out, and kneel down in the ditch by the side of the road, so as not to provide an easy target, should the terrorists attack. We waited there until the sun began to splash its rays of light all around. It was never anything but magic to me, to watch the dawn, and see the sun rise on the jungle edge, and witness the clouds of steam rising in response to its sudden heat, never to see its rays again until we returned. It was through this cloud of steam that we entered into the jungle.

It was like another world, a world within a world with different rules and different ways. A place that was largely alien to us, for we only knew a few of its rules and ways, which made for nervous twitches and nightmares later. We marched in single file threading our way through the outer lighter foliage to the ever-denser jungle, gradually losing sight of any signs of the sky and the sun. We normally marched for five or six miles before establishing a base camp. Being a Corporal, I now had the privilege of using a hammock. However, I'd never put up a hammock in my life, but I was utterly convinced that it presented no problem. Immediately dispensing with the idea of stakes or supports, I attached two ropes to two saplings that seemed to be the right distance apart, and looked strong enough to bear my weight. The job done, I stood back and surveyed my efforts.

"I'm bloody glad that you're sleeping in that and not me," said Tommo.

"What's the matter with it then?"

"Well everything really."

"What do you mean, everything?"

He screwed his face up, contorting it into grotesque shapes, while moving it up and down in jerky movements. "What's to stop a snake crawling up the tree then?"

"Don't be daft, I've never seen a snake yet."

"You might tonight," he said with a grin.

"C'mon Tommo, what else is wrong with it? Nothing right?"

"Okay, if you say so."

Stand-to at dusk was always a difficult time. We were told that if the terrorists attacked, they would most likely attack at dawn or dusk. It never happened while I was there, but it became a vigil of watching and waiting for the coming and going of the light. Dusk stand-to for me was a particularly traumatic experience; we stood there waiting for its going; and we were never quite ready for it when it went, plunging us into total blackness. I saw fear on the faces of all my friends, as they waited for the engulfening blackness, where shadows reared occasionally in response to the filtering light of the moon, or a piercing flash of lightning. It sent some soldiers crazy.

After stand-to, we'd have one or two minutes to get ready for the numbing effect of total blackness. From the perimeter vine that encircled the camp, I made my way back to my hammock and attempted to climb in, only to fall out on the other side. I felt such a fool, but it was no good giving up, and as far as I knew nobody had seen me, being too busy getting ready for the coming night themselves. I tried again, only this time I carefully placed my leg onto the edge of the hammock while holding onto a rope that was secured to one of the saplings. In this way I intended to roll gently into the thing. Not wanting to provide too much thrust off my other leg, I practised, with just enough power to enable me to balance once there. I rolled and pulled with my arms steadying myself with the leg already in the hammock - I've made it I thought, and stretched out in order to acquire a more comfortable position, only to topple out of it onto the jungle floor to hear Tommo's voice quietly commentating on the event.

"It's bloody amazing this. It's a circus act. Do it again Swifty; only just what are you trying to do?"

"Piss off Tommo, will you. It's not easy getting in it."

"Oh, is that what yer trying to do, I thought it was some kind of religious ritual yer know, tribal."

By this time I was quite worried, "C'mon, give us a lift will you."

So with his help, I eventually got in and lay there, in the hammock, balancing with ever-greater skill.

However, Danny wasn't convinced, "Hey, Swifty, what yer going to do if yer want a piss in the middle of the night?"

"I might just piss on you!" I said with a laugh.

"You bloody well would, but then you might fall out and end up pissing yourself."

They all grinned at the thought. They eventually left me, and I settled down feeling very confident and comfortable in the hammock, to the point when I decided to turn over, which I accomplished without any misfortune. I felt extremely pleased with myself, if somewhat apprehensive. When it rained, the rain became heavier and heavier making the saplings bend slowly until my body was almost doubled up like a 'U' shape. I abandoned it with great reluctance, knowing that I'd be in for some stick in the morning off the lads. However, the immediate problem was the coming night. With only a glimmer of light, I made my way over to Tommo's 'basha'.

"Piss off Swifty, you're not kipping up here, look there's no room." He swept his hand round the 'basha' to show me.

It was then that I saw Gendang and Igoh's 'basha', our Iban trackers. These men from Borneo could put up a 'basha' in minutes.

I went across to them and asked if I could join them for the night, telling them that they could have my food rations and some of my cigarettes, as long as they fed me. They laughed and laughed calling me a crazy white man, not like the others. It never really occurred to me that most Officers and men saw them as good guys, being on our side, but with a difference. That difference was that they weren't quite equal, not being European. I moved in with them. They took my food and cooked it with theirs, and it was good. They were astounded at my friendship, although they continued to call me a crazy white man. I felt really happy and very well cared for until Lieutenant O'Silvan heard about it.

He came across after a couple of days, "This moving in with the Ibans is highly unusual Corporal Swift." His face twisted and turned as he tried to overcome his habitual stutter.

I felt like telling him to spit it out. His stutter had such an effect upon me that I was actually helping him to finish sentences, knowing by then the next few words that he was going to be saying.

It never seemed to bother him at that stage and he carried on, "The fact is Corporal Swift you should know that you shouldn't be in there." He sneered with a gesticulation that indicated non-verbally that they were dirty, and how could I do such a thing?

I immediately responded by telling him about the hammock; but he didn't listen to what I was saying.

He stopped short of telling me to get out of their 'basha'.

I stayed, but there was a noticeable brand of disapproval in his manner towards me afterwards. The

Ibans heard everything he'd said, but how much they understood I never knew, but they understood enough to know that the Officer wanted me out of their 'basha'. When I returned, determined to stay, they laughed and laughed even more. While I stayed with them, I spoke to them about their homes and families and their way of life. They seemed intrigued by me asking, and readily gave me information in broken English. From their general conversation, I learned that their primary motive for coming to Malaya, was to earn enough cash in order to buy a boat with an out-board motor when they returned. I questioned them about everything, including the rumour of cannibalism among the tribes in Borneo.

They readily admitted that both their grandfathers had eaten human flesh, usually of enemies that had been taken prisoners in tribal wars, then they'd say, "Hey Corporal Keet, we eat Communist terrorists yeah?" Then they'd be totally convulsed with laughter until they shook, which would normally bring Tommo over, followed by Dickie the wireless operator.

"Don't worry you two, he has that affect on all of us, even Lieutenant O'Silvan creased a bloody grin, and he's never been known to smile, except when a dead terrorist once farted."

"Shut up Dickie," I said, "they were only saying they'd eat a terrorist, so why not eat you? Mind you, they'd have to be hard pressed to eat a little turd like you."

"Oh listen to him will you? Bloody Corporal now, it's gone to his head."

"Hey up," said Tommo, O'Silvan's coming over. Watch it!"

Lieutenant O'Silvan appeared. "Cut the noise down will you, we can hear you quite clearly over there." He glared at me before he left.

After he'd gone, Dickie turned to me, "You'll have to watch it Swifty, he's got it in for you."

"Yes," was all I could manage to say, being inwardly too worried about what the Lieutenant had actually heard. I just stood there staring at the mass of green foliage, gradually realising just how much I hated it. The abominable stink of rotting decaying vegetation, the dingy greenness of the light that somehow managed to penetrate through the thick canopy of trees that shrouded everything in mystery and fear. It was a place that frightened me. The terrorists had chosen hell to hide in. We chased them, they fired at us, then ran, retreating into ever-deeper jungle in order to shake us off, but we never stopped searching.

Some time later, we were on patrol about two to three miles from our base camp. It was late morning, the sun was beating down on the canopy of green that covered us, making it as hot as a sauna on the jungle floor. I was drenched with sweat, and feeling very uncomfortable, when suddenly we came to much lighter jungle. I thought that we must have come to the edge of a rubber plantation, when I got a signal to halt. This procedure was quite normal when coming to lighter jungle, due to the obvious danger of being ambushed. We rested for some time for a smoke; the Lieutenant consulted his map, making absolutely sure about our exact location.

After some time, the signal came to us down the line to continue. So we pressed onwards, ever searching for our elusive enemy. I noticed that we were going up a slight incline and that visibility was becoming much better, when Norman Scot, a loud mouthed Liverpuddlian in front of me, stopped and looked to one side. I naturally followed his gaze, but saw nothing except another rise, but he kept on looking which immediately made me think that I'd missed something. By this time, Bobby Cort, the soldier in front of him, had turned back and joined him, and both seemed to be looking at the same thing; when Norman raised his rifle into the firing position ready to press the trigger.

"Go on fire!" I heard Bobby say quite loudly.

Eager to see what was going on, I caught up with them, and looking across in the same direction where I saw a bandit silhouetted on a mound against the trees, his red headband clearly visible, although he had his back to us. I turned instinctively wondering why Norman hadn't fired and saw great tears begin to run down his face.

"I can't fucking do it, " he moaned. "I can't do it, I can't kill him." After which he sank to his knees sobbing.

Bobby Cort, the soldier with him lifted his rifle, took aim and the explosion wrecked the stillness of the day. I watched in horror as the bandit's body leapt in the air with the impact. The next thing that I remember was the sound of shots followed by shouts and screams. I thought that it must be members of the platoon up ahead, who'd now joined the fire fight, and were firing at other bandits that I couldn't see, until a large disturbance near my face made me suddenly realise that someone was firing at me. I threw myself to the ground and pressed my face into it as hard as I could. Shouts continued to rent the air, combined with intermittent screams and then silence; my heart froze. For some seconds I thought we'd been wiped out and I was the only one left. Bobby and Norman were nowhere to be seen. Eventually, I heard English voices. Standing up, I saw some of the platoon peering at the corpse of a dead terrorist on the floor. Although I had no desire to see it, some inner force took me there. The terrorist was Chinese and quite young. He had a hole in his back where the bullet had entered the size of a tennis ball; but when they turned him over, we saw that his whole chest had been blown away where the bullet had left. I just stared at him transfixed with the dreadfulness of violence and death. The bravado would come later in the telling of the deed, with the help of gallons of Tiger beer, paid for with the money the dead terrorist had on him. The horrific scene left its scar on me, as I saw the mass of twitching malfunctioning flesh struggling to come to terms with a life that had gone. The whole platoon gathered round him. Some recovered quickly and spat on him while others turned away in disgust.

"Well, come on, he's fucking dead. What are you all looking at?" Sergeant Conelly's voice brought us back to earth.

I could see that Lieutenant O'Silvan looked distinctly unhappy, so I went across to see what was wrong, as did Sergeant Conelly. "I'm very concerned about Private Scot Sergeant," he said.

"Oh bloody hell," I thought, here he goes again, nothing is ever right.

Sergeant Conelly waited patiently before saying somewhat indifferently, "What seems to be bothering you Sir?"

Lieutenant O'Silvan looked immediately perplexed as if Sergeant Conelly should have known all about it. He didn't, nor it would seem, would he answer the question for some reason.

Whereupon the Sergeant tried again. "Do you mean Scot not firing Sir?"

"Is that cowardice Sergeant or what? Bloody hell Sergeant, he could have got away, or worse still, he could have killed before being killed."

"Not with that bloody thing," pointed out Sergeant Conelly looking at the dead terrorist's weapon lying on the ground.

I said nothing, there was nothing to say, but I thought, how could they charge anyone for not killing an enemy that had already been killed? It seemed stupid to me.

The lads went through the dead terrorist's pockets, finding money, papers and some photographs. I knew that they were only interested in the money, which we could keep. It was bounty money, a kind of incentive to kill as many terrorists as we could. It turned out that the bandit hadn't much money on him, which didn't worry me too much as the procedure always left me feeling uneasy somehow.

The conversation between Lieutenant O'Silvan and Sergeant Conelly began to heat up, and made me shelve any further thoughts I had. I could see that the Lieutenant was getting very irate and giving the Sergeant a hard time. I moved towards them again and listened.

"If I say he's a coward Sergeant, then I damn well mean he..."

"Is," the Sergeant, finished off the sentence for him.

"Don't finish off my sentences for me Sergeant."

"Y-y-yes S-s-Sir," said the Sergeant as if he was taking the 'Mickey' out of the Lieutenant's slight stutter. I knew that he wasn't, but did the Lieutenant, I wondered?

The Lieutenant was beside himself with rage. He stormed off shouting instructions to everyone.

I walked across to the Sergeant who was stood there looking into space.

"What's going on Mick?" I asked.

"Fucking Sergeant to you Corporal bloody Swift."

I ignored the remark and waited until he could no longer contain himself, "I'll die for that bastard yet. I bloody well will Swift, I'll die for that bastard." He stared at the back of the Lieutenant as he walked away from us.

We stood there for ages without speaking whilst the lads tied the dead terrorist up to a pole with his hands and legs. Occasionally the Sergeant's eyes would dart from the dead terrorist to the Lieutenant. I made a connection and it really disturbed me.

"Is it as bad as that Sergeant?"

He jumped instantly back to reality. "Is it as bad as what?" He shouted at me with a venom that knocked me back instantly. He didn't want an answer and neither did I attempt to give him one. He began to give orders, getting the platoon ready to move out with the dead terrorist.

Before we moved off, Shuttlecock, who was standing passively at the back, suddenly decided that he wanted to smack the dead terrorist in the face with his rifle butt. "C'mon, let me give him a bloody smack will yer?"

Barny Liddle, our full Corporal grabbed hold of him, watched by Sergeant Conelly and myself. "Leave him Shutts, the dead's dead. Leave him be."

Sergeant Conelly had heard clearly what Shuttlecock had said and came across. "You wouldn't do that if he were alive Shuttlecock; you'd be bloody well hiding in the sodding grass, wouldn't you? You dog's bastard! Get into fucking line before I deal with you."

His language made me cringe, not because it was bad or anything like that, but because of the way he used his voice, and the emphasis he placed on some of the letters. There was something about it that hurt. It was truly offensive, with enough poison to wipe a smile off anyone's face, even if they were behind him.

Shutts never said a word in protest because he knew that the Sergeant would have hit him. As we made our way back to base camp, with the dead terrorist swinging from side to side as the soldiers walked, making blood ooze out of him onto the jungle floor; I noticed the Sergeant move to catch up with Corporal Liddle. As I continued to watch, I saw the bottle of rum, which every platoon carried in order to ease the jungle night, change hands. I could see enough to know that the Corporal was unhappy about it, but he had no option.

This done, the Sergeant gradually allowed most of the patrol to pass him until he came to me, "What you fucking looking at Swift, you dog's bastard?" After which he sneered at me in his usual manner, eyes screwed up, and nose puckered in the most obnoxious fashion.

I never took him up and refused him eye contact, which I knew he wanted. We walked on towards the jungle edge; I noticed the Sergeant dropping further and further behind until he was out of sight. I had a duty to know exactly what was going on with the Sergeant.

I allowed Shuttlecock to pass me. "You going to help him sup the rum Swifty?"

"No I'm not. And it's Corporal to you Norman, Corporal remember."

He laughed. "Yer going ter get some rum Swifty, I'm not daft, I know! And my name's not Norman right?"

By this time I could see the Sergeant swaying about swearing softly to himself. Some bloody Army, I thought. Here we are in the middle of the jungle after a fire fight in which a terrorist had been killed, and our Sergeant was drunk. I really didn't know what to do. If I told Lieutenant O'Silvan, I'd be blackballed by every N.C.O. in the Regiment, if I didn't, the Sergeant might well let off a round accidentally and kill someone in the patrol, in either case, I'd be in trouble. After much consideration, I decided to stick with the dishonourable way of things and simply ignore it.

I caught up with Barny Liddle. "Hey, Barny, Mick's as pissed as a fart."

"I knew as much," he replied.

"Well what are you going to do about it then?"

"What do you mean. What am *I* going to do about it? What you really mean is what are *you* going to do, because I haven't seen him as yet." Barny never as much as looked at me when he spoke, he just kept looking ahead.

I couldn't leave it. "What shall we do then?"

"Leave him, when we get to the logging track O'Silvan's bound to see him then, okay?"

I nodded and made my way back to my position near the back of the patrol, but not before I saw Tommo casting worried glances towards us, obviously wondering what was going on. After what seemed like an eternity, we stopped.

Lieutenant O'Silvan came down the line and asked Barny something, and then he came to me, "Corporal Swift," he said with some irritation in his voice.

I went over to him.

"Where is Sergeant Conelly?"

"He was behind me Sir, taking up the rear, I think."

He gave me a look of disbelief that suggested that I knew more than I was prepared to say. He then went down the track until he was almost out of sight.

"Corporal Swift. Here at once!"

I went and saw the Lieutenant with Sergeant Conelly, who was hopelessly drunk by this time. Lieutenant O'Silvan asked Sergeant Conelly for the rum. The Sergeant disclaimed any knowledge of any rum, stating that it was a lie.

"What are you talking about Sergeant, a lie. What lie?"

The Sergeant was quite gone and just leered at the Lieutenant, which made me want to laugh.

The Lieutenant was beside himself with rage, "You are drunk Sergeant."

"Oh no I'm not Sir, it's the jungle air, it doesn't suit me."

The Lieutenant turned to me. "He's bloody well drunk Corporal. I'll have to report this when we get back to camp."

After some considerable time, the patrol set off again for the base camp. As we neared, the Sergeant slowed down until he was hardly moving, then sat down on a clump of vegetation and refused to budge. Nothing I said, or anything that anybody else said for that matter, would make him move. Lieutenant O'Silvan was completely flabbergasted. After all else had failed, two of us manhandled him the rest of the way. The next day we broke camp and made for the road to be picked up by our trucks. The Sergeant had recovered to some degree, when we arrived at the picking up point, but he was being closely watched under the Lieutenant's instructions. As he passed me, I smiled at him.

"What you looking at Swift? Kick a man when he's down will yer?"

"What's going to happen to you Sergeant?"

"What about?"

"About you," I said with some amazement.

"What about me?"

Here we go again," I thought, "Forget it Sergeant?"

"Forget what Swift?"

He either couldn't remember, or he didn't want to talk to me. I walked off, inwardly wishing that I could curb my natural desire to communicate with people that quite openly disliked me.

We arrived back at camp victorious with our kill. Amid the jubilation and relief at getting out of the jungle in one piece, I completely forgot about our drunken Sergeant. Some days later, I realised that he wasn't around, so I went across to the Company office to ask Arnie about him, thinking that he might well be in prison.

"Sergeant Conelly," said Arnie, "he's on leave in Singapore."

"But Arnie," I protested, "he was as drunk as a skunk in the jungle. How come he was allowed to go on leave?"

"Don't ask me, I'm only a bloody Company Clerk. Ask Major Coker, he okayed it." He thought for a minute, "I'm very surprised they never informed you. Bloody hell, a soldier of your importance."

I ignored his reply, "Arnie, he was really bad. O'Silvan was hopping mad, I'm telling you."

"Maybe, but O'Silvan doesn't count for much, he's only a National Service Officer. We're talking about regular soldiers here."

I began to understand. I stood in the doorway of his office for some time trying to take it all in, until Arnie disturbed my thoughts again.

"I do believe that you're going to Singapore next week, if my memory serves me right."

"Bloody hell, you're right, I'd forgotten. Shit! That's all I need, Mick Conelly on the piss in Singy." I left Arnie highly amused at my misfortune.

"Join the Army as a regular soldier Swifty it'll solve all your problems. Ask Mick Conelly when you get to Singy," he shouted after me as I walked away from the office.

I didn't answer; I just gave him the 'Vs'.

One day, we were sat on our beds talking and speculating about how long it would be to the next stint in the jungle, when out of the corner of my eye, I saw Sergeant Major Bullock walking towards Company lines with all the platoon Sergeants. Before I had time to speak, Danny, having seen them too, jumped up off his bed.

"Watch out lads Bollock's on the warpath."

We all instinctively jumped up and waited for him and his entourage to enter out hut.

"Right, attention!" he shouted at the top of his voice.

We stood there waiting to hear what he had to say.

"We are going on operations tonight. It's going to be a joint effort, so I don't want any of you bloody well letting our Company down, got it? I mean going on sick parade tonight or any other excuse."

"I'm going on leave tomorrow Sergeant Major," interjected Private Green somewhere further down the hut.

"Like hell yer going on fucking leave soldier, 'cause all leave's bin cancelled," he shouted back.

"But Sergeant Major, "I've got me passes and everything."

"Will yer listen to him, he doesn't fuckin' well get it, does he? He thinks we're on a Sunday school fuckin' outing."

By this time he was working up to one of his rages. We all stood there waiting for his next breath.

"Yer not going on leave soldier, 'cause yer going out into the jungle to do some killing. That's if you've got any balls! And that's what you're here for. You understand soldier?"

217

"Yes Sir," replied Green, sounding very peeved.

"Right," continued the Sergeant Major, "I don't have a clue where we are going, and I don't know at what time; it's all top secret. But what I can tell you is that it's big, and we'll be seeing some action. All right?"

He paused and looked around at the assembled men before continuing. 'B' Company is confined to Company lines, so get all your kit ready, and be sure you've got enough ammunition and water. Don't forget that!" He then left as abruptly as he came.

Whilst waiting to go, we speculated as to where it was most likely to be, and what we would be called upon to do. Nothing happened and we all ended up thinking that it was just another ruse to keep us on our toes.

I went to bed at about one o'clock thinking that it would be cancelled, but sure enough, at about three o'clock our platoon Sergeant came through shouting for everyone to get on their feet and be prepared to move out. I hated these early morning starts, it was so cold and stark at that time in the morning. I also knew we'd be on trucks for a couple of hours before we got there.

Rumours began to circulate that we were going to a village that had helped some Communist soldiers. What was expected of us, I had no idea! Many rumours circulated until I became totally disinterested. I just sat there on the back of the truck and waited.

About two hours later the convoy began to slow down considerably; we all knew we were near the dropping place. The Sergeant stood up, struggling to keep his balance as the lorry bumped around as it made its way down a logging track.

"When I give the order, I want the two people nearest the tailboard to jump for it, and the rest to follow. Got it? Make it snappy!"

We all nodded, as we'd done it a hundred times before.

The lorry slowed down to almost walking pace before a slight knock on the window gave the Sergeant the signal to begin.

"That's it, let's get off this fuckin' thing," the Sergeant whispered.

We all jumped off and scrambled into the ditch by the side of the track, awaiting the next command. As I looked around I could see the whole Company by the side of the road waiting at the ready.

Dawn came in a wonderful and mystical way, with the sun's heat bringing steam clouds, that spiralled in beautiful waves, curving and corkscrewing up from the jungle around us. We fanned out and walked away from the jungle edge, before entering a rubber plantation. At this time we still had no clue when or where we were going, or what we were to do when we got there.

"Bloody hell Swifty, I bloody well hate walking through rubber plantations. Seems like I'm being fuckin' watched all the time," whispered Tommo, who was slightly behind me.

"I know what you mean," I whispered back. "It sends shivers down my back too. Anybody could be peering at you, couldn't they?"

"Did you need to tell me that?" muttered Tommo sullenly.

Suddenly we were told to halt; at which point the Captain informed us we were near the village. We then slowly moved out of the rubber and saw the village. It was one of the new villages that had been specially built by the Government to re-house people whose former villages were considered to be too near the jungle edge, and an obvious target of subterfuge for any would be Communist sympathisers. Their removal had been done forcibly and ruthlessly, and these people could have come from anywhere in Malaya.

The village had a wire fence that completely encircled it, with an official entrance that was guarded by soldiers of the Malayan Army. Electric lights were placed at regular intervals around the perimeter wire, in order to make the village safe at night.

"Its like a bloody concentration camp," Tommo commented in my ear.

"I think I'd be a bit careful with that kind of language Tommo. Wouldn't go down well here."

He didn't answer me for a minute. "Well, they're caged in like bloody chickens, aren't they?"

Sergeant Connelly led us in a movement around the village, until the whole of 'B' Company encircled it.

The Major then addressed us, "These villagers have been co-operating with the terrorists. That's why we are here. At least two terrorists have come to the village. The dog handlers followed them here. We also know that one of them is badly wounded, because of the amount of blood left on the track. The Special Police are in there now interrogating the villagers, in order to find out their whereabouts. However, so far without success. One thing is sure though, the blighters are still here hiding somewhere in this village. We're here to make sure that if they make a run for it, we'll blast them to hell, what!

In the meantime stay in position until you're told to move; it could be a long job. And by the way, the Ghurka's usually do this kind of job, so think yourselves privileged."

Tommo gave me a wistful look. "I bloody well 'ope we're not here long; there's no shade from the sun, and I'm sweating me bollocks off already."

I laughed quietly, whilst facing the village with my rifle at the ready.

Sweat began to run down my face as the morning went slowly by and the sun climbed to its height. It must have been 140 degrees. At one stage I wondered how much heat the human body could take before hallucinations began. I took my water bottle out, but put it back quickly as I realised that it was warm.

As the afternoon wore on I began to cheer up, thinking that before long we'd be on our way back to camp. However nothing happened, and we continued to face the village and waited for the coming night. After kneeling and sitting for hours I began to feel extremely uncomfortable, which made me irritable and edgy.

"How much longer do we have to wait for them to decide what to do Sergeant?"

The Sergeant turned his eyes to me for a second, before turning them back to the wire surrounding the village. "You'll be told when the Major's good and ready. You're in the bloody Army now, not in that…"

Before he had time to finish, a faint tormented cry came from somewhere in the village. We all listened in horror as continuing cries were heard for some time, before silence enveloped the scene again.

"They're torturing the poor bastards," Tommo stated softly.

"Where's all the animals and things?" I asked, without really thinking what the implications might be.

"Yeh, where are they?" Tommo said realising that none were about.

"They'll have shot 'em all; teach the little bastards a lesson," remarked someone further down the line, before our Lieutenant got up and came across to us.

"What's all this gossiping about? Shut up and keep your eyes on the wire. Remember these are desperate men we're waiting for. It's your life or theirs!"

We waited as the sun slipped down in the sky, knowing that we'd soon be shrouded in the blackness of the Malayan night. It came with all the noises that night brings, as every living creature sought to make its presence felt. However the lights on the perimeter wire suddenly came on, which was small comfort, due to the light casting ghostly shadows. We waited, not daring to move, not daring to speak, just praying for the dawn. Darkness always came as a shock, one minute it was light and we could see, then within a couple of minutes all the sun's light had gone, which always sent goose pimples down everyone's back.

It suddenly became very cold; we shivered as we held our position. It didn't take long before I felt really tired and longed to close my eyes. I looked all around me at the others, and saw that they too were experiencing the same exhaustion. The Sergeant continually made his rounds, warning that anybody caught sleeping would be court-martialled. It made me worse, as my eyelids closed even though I tried my hardest to keep them open. For the first time in my life I felt like screaming because I was so tired. I tried to think of something that would keep me awake, but after a few moments it passed, and I ended up thinking of nothing but sleep. The night moved on slowly, and I thought of death, but quickly dismissed it as an impossibility, because as most young soldiers think, I really thought that I would live forever. Dawn came with great relief, and some distinct apprehension, as we all realised we'd been there for nearly twenty-four hours.

"They can't be much longer now," whispered Tommo next to me, with anxiety in his voice. "I can't keep awake much longer."

"How much water have you left?" I asked him.

"Not so much; what about you?"

"I've got enough."

We watched and waited as again the sun began to heat us up. By this time my throat was so sore and swollen. I drank all my water in an effort to alleviate the pain. It didn't go away, and before long my tongue began to swell until it didn't seem small enough to fit into my mouth. It felt like a great big cucumber.

"When are they going to finish; we've been sat here for bloody hours?" I asked myself out loud in desperation.

Tommo thought I was asking him. "I don't know, but I bet those bastard Special Police are working in shifts, while we silly buggers sit here sweating our bollocks off!"

It was then that I started to hallucinate; my mind started to drift into a morass of thoughts which brought panic. I looked across at Tommo, partly to speak, partly to relieve the psychological stress that was beginning to take over. After some scrutiny I noticed that his eyes were almost red raw from continuous rubbing, in order to keep awake, and I wondered what mine looked like.

Hey Tommo, are my eyes like yours?

Initially Tommo looked mystified by my question, "Oh, he answered eventually, "you mean are they like yours? Yours are like a couple of over-ripe tomatoes."

I was about to respond when the Sergeant moved towards us. "I think we'll get out tonight lads, but it could be late. So keep watch!"

Some time towards midnight, I saw that some soldiers were standing up, and obviously getting ready to move out.

"At last!" I thought.

"Not before fuckin' time," came from somewhere. "It's nearly midnight."

We all got on our feet and filed out to the trucks that were waiting for us just outside the village. There by the side of each vehicle was a full canister of water. The whole platoon fell upon the ones beside our truck, and we drank greedily until we were sick.

I can't say I felt any better on the way back to camp where, after handing in my rifle I collapsed onto my bed and succumbed to an irresistible desire to sleep.

When I awoke it was light, and that was enough to make me nervous. I sat up and looked around. Everybody in the hut was sleeping. I lay back and tried to sleep some more, but I couldn't. In the end I got up, dressed, and made my way over to the Company office.

Arnie greeted me with his usual style. "Well go on, tell me which picnic you have been on this time?"

"Arnie you know it was no bloody picnic," I answered, "but tell me, what are we supposed to be doing today?"

Arnie laughed, "Bloody hell Swifty, don't you know it's your day off?"

"But our day off's tomorrow," I replied almost angrily.

"Oh no it's not, you slept right through yesterday, don't you remember?"

"I slept right through yesterday," I repeated incredulously. "I don't bloody well believe you Arnie."

"Right," he said, "you went out on Saturday morning at three a.m. and now it's two p.m. Tuesday, so work that one out!"

I went back to Company lines and found out that what he said was true. I'd slept through a night and a day. There was no one to tell this to as everyone was still asleep.

Chapter 7

ON LEAVE

"In June 1950 an ambitious resettlement program was launched. It was carried out with considerable determination and ruthlessness, so that by the beginning of 1952 over 400,000 Chinese squatters had been compulsorily reset fled in some 400 "new villages". This was accomplished by force. Troops and police would raid the squatter settlements in the early hours, round up the inhabitants and then destroy their homes, burn their crops, and slaughter their livestock. A Gurkha officer described the human suffering and the emotions of the squatters as they faced the combined forces of police and soldiers who had descended on their homes without warning, during the hours of darkness."

"A few cursed, some wept, but the majority of the squatters moved like automata in a dream, without visibly expressing their emotions'. For those who watched as part of the cordon force it was a very moving experience; the flotsam of humanity being carried away by the government as a step, a vital step, in this struggle against Chin Peng and his followers."

I'd been due some leave, and had decided to go to Singapore, where, it was rumoured, all the action was to be found. I wasn't quite sure what all this action amounted to; I just assumed it was good. I'd considered Penang, but the lads said it was just booze, beach and bed. It turned out that everyone that I knew was going to Singapore, which meant we'd be in for an interesting, if riotous time.

The train journey to Singapore was always difficult, principally because the terrorists continually caused as much disruption as they possibly could. They felled trees across the track, or they placed large heavy objects onto it. The train would have to stop, heavy lifting gear would have to brought up the line from the nearest depot, which took hours, whilst those soldiers on the train took up defensive positions in order to ward off any attack that might come. In the event of the terrorists continuing to fire at the train, soldiers would put into effect an encircling movement, which entailed going into the jungle after them, and trying to cut them off by coming round the back of them. Of course the terrorists had long gone by the time we'd got everything organised; it was a pure waste of time. However, it did cause delays and much discomfort to the troops and people on board the train, which I assumed was their intention, for by the time we arrived in Singapore, we were all tired and weary.

I'd decided to stay at the Union Jack Club. It proved to be a large Victorian building, with ornate stone balustrades at the front, while sporting beautiful wooden banister rails on the staircases inside. What impressed me most were the marble floors, which made it look so cool and so clean. It reminded me a little of the Bull and Royal in Preston, in that you couldn't quite see how big it was from the front. Quite obviously it wasn't run like a hotel, but more like a Salvation Army Hostel, only catering for soldiers and other non-commissioned ranks. We were housed in large dormitories and there was a curfew. It was spotlessly clean, and we were waited on hand and foot by servants. It was situated in the centre of the city, which proved both comfortable and convenient. After settling in, we went out to see the sights of the city before getting down to the main pastime that occupies all troops worldwide, drinking. Prior to my enlistment in the Army, I'd never really touched alcohol. In my father's household it was considered the drink of the devil. This idea was to some extent endorsed by the sights I'd seen in the poorer parts of Preston as a boy. It was also apparent that Friday and Saturday nights were drinking nights, when a large proportion of the town came alive, and went out drinking in the town centre. I'd seen them rolling around singing and fighting, and generally acting very strangely. I'd built up the idea that when people wanted to escape from their surroundings, or from themselves, they went out and got thoroughly drunk. I developed a strange fascination for it, and always inwardly longed to try it for myself.

This inward desire, together with the fact that I was far from home, made me more determined to experience it for myself. My initial attempts at drinking were amusing for everyone except myself. I'd take one or two drinks of Tiger beer, and they would have a warming effect upon me. It was as if I had a warm blanket over my body. After more drinks, I felt a tremendous exhilaration, as if I was capable of doing anything. It made me feel extremely confident in my own ability. If I then went on to drink more, it was all quickly replaced by a numbing sensation, which affected my speech, making me slur my words. This was quickly followed by bouts of effusive disclosure, bordering on the manic. By then I'd nearly lost all control and drank with real abandon. It saw me staggering round the N.A.A.F.I. in a drunken stupor, bumping into tables and chairs, before falling over into a heap on the floor. Fortunately, most people found it amusing, and my friends were nearly always on hand to guide me back to the Company lines, but not before I'd usually had some difficult encounters. Singapore was to be no exception.

The second night on leave I was at on my bed contemplating what to do, while looking through the pages of a magazine, when Pop Quint walked into the room, "Hey Swifty, yer coming down town for a bevy?"

I looked up from the magazine feeling quite privileged at being asked, for Pop was held in almost reverential awe in the Regiment. He was in his late twenties, had a wealth of experience behind him as a whaler in the Antarctic, and as a formidable Welterweight boxer, which was rewarded with him being made Battalion Boxing Team Captain.

"Sure," I replied, "Just let me get changed and I'll be with you."

Before I had time to think about changing, two of Pop's friends appeared and sat on the end of my bed. I recognised Tony Robins immediately. He was a small skinny guy with a crew cut. He boxed Lightweight; I'd sparred with him a couple of times, although I was a Light Welterweight. The other soldier was an old friend of mine called Bobby Cort. Bobby came from Dingle in Liverpool, and he too was skinny but tall, but what made him most distinctive was his nose, which seemed to jut out like it had been stuck on. He boxed Middleweight, and was noted for his lethal body punching. However, Pop had told me that he'd never do much at boxing because of his nose, which would take too much damage.

"C'mon let's get down to the waterfront," urged Bobby with a big grin on his face.

I smiled knowing full well what he had in mind, but dangerous as I knew it to be, the excitement attracted me. So full of expectation and a little money, we made our way towards down town Singapore calling into many of the bars en route. By the time we arrived on the waterfront, I was well gone. I ended up sitting next to a prostitute near the bar. I looked at the woman, it seemed a natural thing to do.

Before I had time to collect my thoughts properly, she spoke to me, "You want woman Johnny?"

To suggest that I was shocked would be an understatement; to suggest that I wasn't interested would be a lie. In truth, I was totally confused. My body wanted the woman; I could feel myself bulging in places affected by sheer lust. However, I was completely inexperienced with women and hadn't a clue what to do. I found myself smiling at her, and purposely running my eyes up and down her legs. Her long skirt was split right up to the top of her thighs; as she moved her leg, I thought I saw something move. Instinctively I pointed to it, thinking that something was crawling up her legs. She, by this time had noticed and understood my concern.

She laughed, "You see snake Johnny? You wanna see where it goes?" She quickly lifted her dress up to reveal the tattoo of a snake on the inside of her thigh, disappearing, presumably into her vagina.

I'd never seen a woman expose herself like that before and gave way to an involuntary gasp of excitement.

"Hey Swifty! You going for it then?" Pop Quint hit the right spot.

I was certainly going for it until his next remark brought me back to reality.

He egged me on, "Go on Swifty give it a do! You'll only get a dose at the worst."

The thought of venereal disease brought a whole new emphasis to my semi-drunken state. Fears of getting this sexually transmitted disease held special horrors for me, although I'd never disclosed them to anybody. I'd decided that suffering from this, was the worst affliction anyone could endure. It was beyond the pale, and most certainly beyond any discussion. The Army was very specific about how it dealt with would be sufferers; we were lectured to at great length to take adequate precautions many times.

On one occasion, C.S.M. Fitzgerald assembled the whole Battalion on parade in order to speak to them about the unacceptable level of V.D. in the Battalion. "Listen you men! We have what you might call a crisis on our hands at this moment."

I wondered what he was on about.

He paused and waved his cane at us until everyone was looking at him, "That crisis, as most of you know, or should know, is V.D. - Venereal Disease, and I say that because most of you have got it, and the rest of you have had it at some stage."

I thought," "Well I haven't had it, and as far as I knew none of my close friends had either.

He continued, "I want to tell you that we will be the first Regiment to be sent home in disgrace if this trend continues. Seventy percent of the Battalion have either got it, had it, or are, at this present time recovering from it. So, it's no bloody use saying it has nothing to do with me, because it has. The Army regulations are quite clear. They state that the time suffering from it, and the time recuperating from it, will be added onto your service; but that's not the real issue is it?" He paused for a moment glaring, as his eyes swept across the parade ground daring anyone to answer the question.

Nobody spoke.

"It's the fact that you're not fulfilling your duties, you're letting your Regiment down." He stopped, took a deep breath, his eyes bulging until I thought they might pop, before he shouted, "Do you understand me?"

"Yes Sergeant Major," we shouted back with one accord.

Again he waited before reiterating what he'd just said.

Again we shouted, "Yes Sergeant Major."

"Right," he continued, "Well, how can we avoid getting a dose then? Does anyone know?"

Nobody said a thing.

"Right, well I'll tell you. You go to the bloody clinic **before** you go with the ladies, not bloody well afterwards like some of you 'gobshites' do. Then they give you ointment to rub on it, and a rubber to pull over it."

By this time everyone on the parade ground was in stitches laughing at the Sergeant Major's attempted description of minimising the chance of contracting V.D.

He saw the whole Battalion falling about laughing, and he laughed as well. He finished with a phrase that we were all familiar with, "Remember," he bawled at the top of his voice, "A blobby knob stops demob."

An empty glass stuck right in my face brought me quickly back to the present. Instinctively I took it, and placed it on top of the bar to be refilled. In doing so, I glanced at the Chinese girl next to me. My look must have betrayed my thoughts, for the next minute she was screaming abuse at me in broken English. I moved backwards while she continued to hurl obscenities. Her words meant little though; I was too relieved to be making a good escape.

Pushing past the crush of people, I made my way somewhat uncertainly to the back of the bar, where I found an empty chair. Propping myself up against the wall, I tried to sober up. The noise was deafening, everybody seemed to be talking at once. The place was a fever of emotion, a whirlpool of hysteria, as soldiers gave vent to pent up anxieties. It was strange sat there feeling quite detached, yet in some strange way part of the scene while knowing, at the same time, I was quite drunk. All these thoughts kept coming into my mind when I noticed Tony Robins making his way towards me with a pint of Tiger beer in his hand.

"Here you are Swifty; get that down yer neck! It'll do more good than starin' into space."

"Thanks Tony," I muttered, as he smiled at my drunken state. Desperately needing to look the part, I downed two thirds of the pint and waited for the effect, while surveying the scene. It was then that things started to move, I knew that shouldn't and couldn't. I stood up and pretended I'd seen someone at the other side of the room, just to see if I could stand, only to shake the table in front of me making the beer spill over the tops of the glasses, much to the annoyance of the two Australian soldiers sat opposite me. I tried focusing on the ceiling, then on the soldiers at the bar whom I knew, believing that this would help me lose the worst effects of the alcohol. All it did was to make me eventually lurch sideways and fall off the chair in comic style, making the two Aussies laugh. I got up immediately and apologised profusely, which made them laugh even more. By this time I was beginning to feel really drunk, and the noise around me seemed to be getting louder; when out of the corner of my eye, I saw Pop in a heated argument with a Scottish soldier.

The next second Pop punched him in the face. I watched, as nearly everybody else did; blood spurted out all over his face. Undeterred by the blood, or maybe spurred on by it, Pop hit him again so hard that it knocked him off his stool and onto the floor. Silence came over the place as everybody became almost hypnotised by the violence. However, it was broken as quickly as it came, when all hell let loose.

An Australian soldier, who was sat near to the incident, grabbed a stool and raised it above his head intent upon burying it in Pop's skull, but a bottle hit him on the back of his head, and he slowly collapsed into a heap on the floor groaning. Another Aussie grabbed Pop, who was in the act of raising his pint glass to his lips, and threw him bodily across the floor. Pop was thrown so hard he broke the glass, but was still clutching the handle. I got to my feet with the intention of going to help him, but the sheer size of the soldier, who was now striding across to where Pop was lying on the floor, put me off, so I just watched. At the precise moment the soldier arrived at where he was lying, a bar stool, presumably thrown from somewhere at the back of the bar, hurtled through the air and hit him on the side of his head. It felled him like an ox, and he lay there next to Pop looking as if he were dead. Although I still felt decidedly dizzy and sick, I knew that we had to get out of there fast before the Military Police arrived. So I made my way over to where Pop was lying. He sat up as I got there and smiled through glazed eyes.

"C'mon, let's get out of here."

He didn't or couldn't answer, but just looked at me with glassy vacant eyes and grinned. I grabbed and dragged him towards the back exit, while evading missiles that were being thrown at us. As we got to the back exit, I saw that a number of soldiers had begun fighting right in front of the door. Not knowing what to do, I waited until I heard whistles being blown which sobered me up considerably more, for I knew that the M.P.s had arrived. However, it didn't seem to have any effect upon anyone else, for the uproar continued unabated.

Eventually, I managed to get him to the exit door only to find that it was locked. The soldiers fighting near the door thought that Pop and myself were after them and promptly turned on us. I tried to explain that we were only trying to get out and received a fist in the face for my troubles. The blow made me feel numb, but I managed to avoid the next one and got a good solid left hand into his face, which stopped him momentarily. Pop, by this time was fighting like a tiger. I managed to get to the door, but try as I may, it wouldn't open. I ran at it with my shoulder and thankfully it burst open. As it opened I fell flat on the floor in an untidy heap. Pop didn't follow me out, which meant that I had to go back inside again. I was now really sober and frightened, but for some strange reason quite undeterred. The sheer raw violence of the scene both shocked and excited me simultaneously. Pop was on the floor with two soldiers kicking him continuously in the head and body.

"Leave him!" I shouted hysterically, "You bloody well trying to kill him?"

The soldiers stopped momentarily, and in that moment Pop jumped up, as if from the dead, and threw a massive right hand at one of them catching him flush on the jaw. He dropped like a stone, leaving just one assailant, who immediately backed off and fled into the heaving mass of bodies behind him. I grabbed hold of Pop and guided him towards the door, where we made our exit through a dimly lit passageway into a back alleyway. Pop was a mess, with a bloody nose, mouth and small cuts and scrapes on his face, that were bleeding profusely making him look hideous. Once in the passageway, I saw a faint glimmer of light in the distance and ran towards it, thinking that it must be the main road.

Pop was struggling, so I stopped and waited for him, "Come on Pop, shit; they'll get us if you can't run any faster than that."

"Piss of Swifty! I'm running as fast as you," was all I got by way of reply.

I laughed, but didn't argue, knowing that he could easily punch me if I pushed it any further. Even though it was really dark, I could see the extent of the bruising around his eyes and nose, and it made me feel quite uncomfortable as I began to realise the serious situation we were in. "Let's get out of here, see if we can get a rickshaw okay?"

He nodded and lit a cigarette.

At that precise moment a squeal of brakes rent the night air and a jeep appeared as if from nowhere blocking our exit. We became involuntarily transfixed for a moment by the unexpectedness of it all, but the sight of two enormous M.P.s climbing out of the jeep made me run immediately in the opposite direction.

"C'mon Pop, run for it," I shouted.

We both ran as fast as we could back up the alleyway. I thought we could escape onto the main road at the other end. By this time, I was more aware of the darkness, and saw people watching us from the shadows as we passed the many passageways leading off it. With goose pimples beginning to surface down the back of my neck, I ran faster, abandoning Pop to the darkness. I could hear him shouting for me to wait, which meant that he was sobering up to some degree, but such was my fear I just ignored him and kept on running as fast as I could.

Coming to a bend in the alleyway, I rounded it, only to freeze as I saw a couple of M.P.s slowly walking towards me. They seemed to fill the whole alleyway, and I stopped walking and waited for Pop to catch up. Immediately I saw them I knew there was no escape, for while watching them slowly coming towards us, I could also hear the sound of boots scrunching on the floor as the other M.P.s came up behind. I admit that I was terrified, sheer panic-stricken when the two M.P.s facing us got nearer. They were closing the net; we'd had it!

When they got to within a few yards of me instinct made me give myself up. I simply put my hands in air and walked towards them. "I give in okay?" I said with a grimace of fear.

One of the M.P.s grabbed me roughly.

"Hey, I'm giving myself up alright," I protested somewhat aggrieved.

"Yeah, I've heard that one before," he said, as he held me in a neck hold.

By this time the other two M.P.s began to move in towards Pop, who began to growl like a dog. As I was being taken to the vehicle, I could clearly hear one of them speaking to him.

"You're not going to fight me, are you soldier?"

"Fuck you!" was all I heard Pop continually saying back to him.

As the M.P.s got me to the vehicle, shouts and screams echoed through the alleyway, as they arrested him. The M.P. holding me instinctively tightened his grip when he heard the screams, as he somehow expected me to start struggling.

I gasped, "Don't bloody well squeeze, I can't breathe!"

Fortunately for me, he must have realised that he was throttling me and slackened his grip. Another M.P, who, presumably, had stayed with the vehicle, came over to us. Together, they grabbed me, and in the same movement threw me into the back of the truck. I crashed onto the floor and lay there hurting all over, wondering what might happen next?

"Hey," I managed to stutter, "I wasn't doing anything wrong you know."

They didn't answer me, even though they'd heard, they just continued talking to each other as if it was all in a night's work.

"If you don't stop bloody struggling, I'll break your arm soldier."

I knew Pop was on his way to the truck. I watched them grab him by his legs and shoulders, before throwing him in the truck. He landed on top of me so I softened his fall to some extent. We lay there a sorry sight. I was scared stiff, wondering whether we'd be court-martialled, and I tried to share my anxiety with Pop, but he couldn't or wouldn't answer me. As the truck came to the Military Police Depot, he began to recover a little. The lights shining into the truck as we came to the Depot entrance revealed the extent of his injuries. He looked an awful mess, both his eyes were nearly shut, his nose was swollen to about twice its normal size, and cuts and abrasions, together with congealed blood made him look distinctly gruesome.

"Hey Pop, what did you hit that Scottish lad for?" I asked.

Pop just looked at me for a moment, before he spat out, "because he looked at me right queer."

"He looked at you," I almost shouted, "is that all he did? Is that why you hit him?"

"Yeah," he replied, "he looked at me real queer."

"Shit Pop," was all I could say, "we're in this mess because he looked at you?"

"Shut your bloody face Swifty."

This was all I got by way of an explanation, and he never spoke another word until the following morning, not even when they threw us in the cells for the night. The next morning, very, very sober, we both nervously waited to see what would happen. We didn't have to wait long.

At about seven o'clock, the Sergeant stormed into our cell. "Right you two bastards! We're going to deal with you first thing, right? Drunk as bloody skunks last night you were, making it unsafe for decent people to have a quiet drink, right?" He shouted so loud, I thought my eardrums would burst.

"Yes, I remember," I replied, only to be silenced by his booming voice.

"You haven't a bloody clue what went on last night, so don't give me that bullshit."

"I have Sergeant," I said quietly.

"Don't bloody well argue with me you little shit!" He boomed an inch away from my face. "If I say that you haven't a clue about what went on last night, that's exactly what I mean, got it?" He waited for me to answer, his hot breath entering my nasal intake, making me instantly nauseous.

"Right Sergeant," I said not wanting to antagonise him any further.

We waited in silence until about ten o'clock, when we were brought before the Commanding Officer. Pop went in first, while I waited under escort outside. He was ages, and I could hear stern voices being raised, which sent involuntary shivers down my spine.

After what seemed like an eternity, I was eventually called into the office. As I marched in at the double, all I could think about was what had happened to Pop, mainly because I expected him to come out the way he'd gone in. After much thought, I reasoned that they must have taken him out another way so as to avoid me. I felt petrified and knew that I showed it. I marched in, flanked on both sides by two enormous M.P.s, and stood to attention before a large table, behind which sat a Major who never seemed to have noticed that I was there.

After some considerable time he looked up, "You're Lance Corporal Swift, I believe?"

"Yes Sir," I replied dutifully.

"You admit that you were in an affray last night?" He paused and sighed as if he was bored with the whole thing. "A fight in a bar on the water front?" Again he waited.

I was unsure how to explain. Before I had time to begin…

He began again, "Do you understand? Answer me."

"Sir," I stammered. "The truth is, I was there when the fight started, but I had nothing to do with it."

He stopped me, "Well you must explain to me why you were running away from the scene with Private Quint, who has already admitted to fighting in the bar, and afterwards with my Military Policemen, who had been called to restore order."

By this time I was quite panicky; it sounded so bad coming from him. I knew that I had to say something.

"Sir, I was sat by myself in the bar when the fight started…"

"Yes," he interrupted me, "but wasn't the bar full to capacity, wasn't it crowded?"

"Yes Sir, that is true but…"

Again he interrupted me, "Well how could you possibly be sat by yourself?"

"I mean that, I Sir…"

I hadn't time to explain before he came at me again. "You mean," he interjected, "that you were part of the scene, that you were with Private Quint, intent upon causing a disturbance. That's the truth of the matter isn't it?"

"No Sir!" I said quietly and adamantly. "As I said before, I was sat by myself, not with my friends, I wasn't feeling too well, so I went to the back of the bar and sat at a table there, opposite two Australian soldiers when all the trouble started."

"Well how in heaven's name, did you end up with Private Quint then?"

"You see Sir an Australian soldier had thrown Pop, sorry Private Quint Sir, across the floor near to me, so I went to help him and got him out of the bar by the back entrance."

"Well, well, we have a little hero, rescuing Private Quint then, have we?" He shook his head in mock amazement. "Private Quint is the last person in the Army that needs rescuing, I would have thought, according to my understanding of last night's debacle. But give you your due, you felt it your duty to go to his rescue, did you?" His piercing eyes searched for immediate contact with mine.

"Yes Sir, I answered quickly.

"I don't believe you."

"Well it's the truth Sir."

"But you were drunk, what would you know about the truth?"

"I'd been drinking Sir, but I was in control of myself, and I gave myself…"

"Yes, yes, I know all that about you surrendering, but doesn't that tell me, and anybody around, that in a word you were disgustingly drunk and out of your tiny mind, and that you hadn't a clue what you were doing?"

I thought for a moment before I answered the question, "I have to admit that I was drunk Sir, but I wasn't fighting Sir."

He considered what I'd said for some time, while I stood rigidly to attention before him, not daring to move a muscle. Occasionally he threw furtive glances in my direction as if he couldn't quite make up his mind what to do.

The heat of the day combined with fear was making me sweat profusely until I was wet through. I could feel my uniform sticking to my skin.

Eventually, he addressed me, "Right, I'm going to send you back to your Regiment Corporal and your Commanding Officer can deal with you there."

"Thank you Sir," I said, feeling incredibly relieved.

"Don't thank me Corporal, if it were up to me, I'd have you horse whipped!"

The shout of, "Attention!" instinctively made me stiffen up before I was marched out of the office, where I was given a pass with which to board the train back to camp. I was both frightened and bemused by the suddenness of the decision.

"No escort back to camp then?" I asked the M.P. nearest to me.

"No, but you should be relieved about that, because if there were, you'd be still in the nick."

"Yes, I suppose I would be, wouldn't I?"

He grinned at me then looked away, before turning his head back again quickly, "You will collect your gear from the Union Jack Club?"

"Yes that's right, I will," I answered, somewhat bewildered by his question.

"And you will be on the first train to Ipoh, otherwise we could be meeting again, couldn't we?" He then walked into the building without waiting for a response and closed the door behind him.

I was still very unsure and wondered whether it was all a game and continued to stand there for some considerable time. In due course, I regained enough confidence to realise that I was free to go, so I made my way, somewhat apprehensively past the sentry box to the main gate, expecting to be stopped with every step. The M.P. on duty there never took his eyes off me for a second. When I got outside the camp, I realised that I had no idea where I was, nor had I any idea where the Union Jack Club was situated in Singapore, but no matter what, I wasn't going to ask him, or anyone there.

Once outside, I felt relieved, followed immediately by pangs of guilt at leaving Pop there. I also started to think about my other friends, and wondered how they'd managed to get away without being caught? However, I soon dismissed these thoughts and proceeded in what I thought was the right direction. After a nightmare of wrong turns and misdirections, I eventually found it. Not one of my friends could be found, and I presumed they were out in the city. Without wanting to hang around, I gathered my belongings, hailed a rickshaw, and made for the railway station, where I boarded the first train for Ipoh.

It was always a dreadful journey at the best of times; I prayed that the terrorists would give us some peace, and not disrupt it as they usually did, by fouling up the railway line. As it happened, the journey was uneventful, I arrived back at camp in the early hours of the following morning.

As I walked past the guardroom, the Guard Commander met me, "Lance Corporal Swift, I believe?"

"Yes Sir," I answered wondering how he knew me?

"You're to report to 'B' Company office first thing in the morning, got it?"

I saluted the Lieutenant before replying, "Very good Sir."

He then came closer to me. I'd seen him before, but I didn't know his name, but his face was familiar.

"What the bloody hell have you been up to Corporal Swift? The whole Regiment's talking about you and Private Quint taking on a whole detachment of M.P.s in Singapore. You're an absolute disgrace to the Regiment, aren't you?" He didn't wait for an answer before he launched into another tirade, "You're a bloody loony, never mind a disgrace. I sincerely hope they deal with you severely." He paused for breath, then shouted at the top of his voice, "Do you hear me?"

"Yes Sir!" I answered, wondering why all people in authority seemed to ask the same question about being heard.

He was about to walk away.

'Sir!"

He stopped, turned and folded his arms, "Yes Corporal?"

"Sir, it's not what it seems you know! I mean, I didn't fight or anything like that. Although I admit that I was drunk, but I wasn't drunk enough not to know what I was doing."

"Being drunk is bad enough, don't you think? I mean what is it coming to when you can't go on leave without getting into trouble?"

"The trouble started without me being involved Sir!"

"Yes, yes, but weren't you with Private Quint?"

"Yes Sir."

"Well tell me that he wasn't involved? From what I've heard already, he started the affray."

Now that was a question that hit a chord and really hurt, was I to admit that Pop had hit that Scottish soldier in the bar or not? I only had the M.P. Commander's word that Pop had admitted to it, and I wasn't entirely sure he wasn't just winding me up. The truth was, I didn't know for certain. The Lieutenant waited for me to answer.

"I don't really know what exactly happened Sir, I don't know who hit who, it happened so fast."

"And you were so drunk you didn't see a thing? Or is the truth something else and you're just lying?"

"I didn't see who started it Sir," I repeated.

"Yes you bloody did, but you're not prepared to say who it was, although we all know it was Private Quint because he's admitted to it. This is what is called misguided loyalty Corporal Swift. I hope you know that?"

"No Sir, it's the truth," I knew that I could never retract my statement and I'd have to stick to it, no matter what. At first, I couldn't understand why he kept on at me to name Pop, until I suddenly realised that if I did, he could then point to my possible involvement in the fight. I already knew that I'd convinced the M.P. Commander that I was partly innocent; otherwise I'd have been returning under escort. This made me more confident, and I tried to show him that I was relaxed and unworried by his suspicions and accusations, but I also knew that I was treading on dangerous ground and I'd have to be careful.

After staring at me for some time, he walked away disgruntled and quite obviously annoyed. I saluted him as he left and made my way to 'B' Company lines and my bed.

The next morning at the appropriate time, I went over to report to the Company office as ordered.

When I arrived Arnie was there to greet me, "Well what have we been up to then?"

I tried to explain, but he wouldn't let me.

"You're in the shit. I hope you know that Major Coker's hopping mad."

I waited around until I was eventually called into his office. I felt terrible, and very worried standing there in front of him. I managed to explain, in faltering tones, my part in the disturbances in Singapore. He listened to me without interrupting, and I began to feel quite confident. When I'd finished, he pondered upon what I'd said, which immediately made me feel nervous again. I wanted a quick response, but he kept fiddling with his pen while giving me occasional glances followed by prolonged sighs. I hardly dare breathe when he began to speak.

"I have spoken to M.P. Commander in Singapore about the incident, and he informs me that you were violently drunk." He waited for me to respond.

"Sir, I was drunk, that I admit, but I wasn't violent. Nobody hit me and I didn't hit anybody, and that's the truth."

"Pardon me for interrupting Corporal but you were drunk weren't you? So how would you know what really went on?" A long pause followed when he just stared at me, making me feel absolutely awful. I felt like I just wanted to disappear.

"Quite frankly, I'm disappointed with your behaviour, and I have no qualms whatsoever in confining you to camp for two weeks." He stopped, wrote something on a piece of paper in front of him before telling me to dismiss. I was marched out of his office where Sergeant Major Bullock gave me a knowing look, which interpreted, meant be careful.

As I made my way back to the Company lines, Arnie came running after me, "You lucky sod Swifty, he must bloody well like you pal."

"Friends in high places Arnie. That's what you need boy."

"Piss off, you can buy me a beer for that."

"Beer Arnie? I don't touch the filthy stuff. You're talking to a teetotaller now my boy."

"Yeah, yeah, a man of iron will, some bloody hope. See you in the N.A.A.F.I. tonight, and bring some money with you."

I laughed as I made my way to my bed and some well earned rest.

The next morning, I learned that Pop had been transferred from Singapore to the Regimental Guardroom in Ipoh. It seemed that most of the charges had been dropped against him. However, he was to be charged with being drunk and disorderly, and it was generally believed he'd get fourteen days inside. This prediction came true and Pop served his time in the camp jail. During his time inside, I managed to keep him supplied with cigarettes and sweets and some of his mail that came to 'B' Company office. I took a chance, because all prisoners' mail was opened and read by their Commanding Officer before being given to them. It was usually placed on the office table in the morning before the Officers arrived, so I'd look through it, then take what I thought I could get away with. I always took it down to the guardroom before mounting the guard in the evening, and slipped it to him when I went near the cells afterwards.

However, one night a friendly Provo Corporal saw me walking down to the guardroom. "Hey Swifty," he shouted.

I immediately started wondering what he wanted, "Hi! How yer doing?"

"I'm okay, it's you I'm worried about."

"What's the problem then?"

"The problem my son is 'Big Mick!' he thinks you're slipping stuff to Pop Quint, and he's out to get you, right?"

I must have paled visibly, because he laughed, "Just be careful, and I'm doing it for Pop, not you. Right?"

I nodded, "I will be, don't worry."

He looked at me intently, "So you have been slipping him stuff?" We've been wondering where it's been coming from."

"Me?" I pointed a finger at my chest. "Me? You must be joking; you must be crazy to think that I'd take a risk like that; it's against Army regulations."

Yeah," he said, with a sardonic grin, "you'd better believe it pal!"

All my forays to the guardroom ceased from that day on when I had to go there, I always made sure everything was above board, especially when I knew 'Big Mick's eyes were on me.

Chapter 8

A Visit to Ipoh

"Templer admitted to the use of "killer squads", though as he told the Colonial Secretary, Oliver Lyttelton, "I won't call them that, with a view to the questions you might have to answer."
"Later, as the MRLA retreated deeper into the jungle, suspected jungle gardens were sprayed from the air with trichlorophenoxyacetic acid (245T), something which the British have remained rather shy about."

The next day I went over to Bernie's 'Basha'.

"Bernie!"

He stopped what he was doing. "Hi Swifty lad, what do you want?"

"Oh nothing much," I replied, "except maybe about this woman you got in Ipoh then."

Instantly a big grin came onto his face, "Where did you hear that?"

"Oh around," I said, becoming increasingly embarrassed and uneasy.

"What if I have?" he replied, pausing before looking away, and increasing my apprehension.

I knew his game, but somehow I couldn't help myself. I knew exactly what he was doing, but I didn't have the nerve, or the words, to tell him. It was as if I'd given into him somehow. He'd been the focus of my thoughts for a long time, and I'd have done anything to get to know precisely what he was up to.

He turned to me after a long pause, "You want woman Johnny?" He spoke imitating the pimps in Ipoh. "You can have woman; you want me to arrange it for you? She's clean, no disease, and willing to do anything you wanna do Johnny." After which he roared with laughter, and said, "Well?"

Blood rushed through my body, until every nerve tingled and I thought I might burst. However this feeling was immediately countered with every feeling of guilt I'd ever experienced. Confused and embarrassed, I stuttered and stammered, which made me feel annoyed and humiliated, annoyed that is because I'd allowed myself to get into such a position.

"Well," said Bernie, still laughing, "If you're shit scared of getting V.D., get some cream from the medics, rub it on yer 'dick' and Bob's your uncle, yer away."

I looked around to see if anyone was listening, but we were on our own. "Okay, but don't let me down, right?"

"Listen," said Bernie, "it's better than parachute jumping, you'll be in heaven."

"But I've never parachuted," I blurted.

"What innocence, never parachuted, never had a jump, and what's more you admit it. Pure as the driven snow," he laughed outrageously, "Wait till Leila gets her hands on yer, you'll have more experience in one minute, than you've had in all yer life so far."

"Yer think?" I said somewhat confused.

"Listen to him will yer," he said as if he was talking to someone else.

"Bernie?"

"Yeah, what is it now?"

"Oh forget it," I muttered, "it doesn't matter."

Bernie's face puckered into a frown, "If you're worried about it being your first time, don't worry. There has always got to be a first time for everything, right?"

I turned to walk away, but he stopped me.

"Swifty, here a minute."

I turned round to face him. "Remember Jack Walker?"

"Yeah, I know him, plays for the Battalion Cricket Team."

He nodded, "Yeah, that's him. Well I took him to see Leila and it was really funny." He laughed again, but never took his eyes off me.

"It must have been funny," I replied, feeling a bit annoyed, and more than a little apprehensive.

"I took him to see Leila for a session, it was *his* first time, and mind you he'd had a few drinks. I waited at the door while Leila did her business. After about ten minutes, I could hear them still going at it, when Jack, for some reason, tells her that it's his first time. To which Leila replies, it's hers as well! I nearly pissed myself laughing; half the British Army must have shagged her."

That statement did something to me that I couldn't explain to Bernie. I wasn't familiar with the term abuse then, but that's how I felt for her, I knew that she was being used. I walked away from him without coming to terms with the thoughts I'd had, because something else inside of me kept surging over everything else. It made me tingle with excitement; it made me want to jump with glee, it even made me want to tell everybody I met that I was alive. This was all because Bernie had spoken about a possible meeting with Leila.

Some time towards evening on the following Sunday, I was contemplating going to the NAFFI with Bobby and Danny, when Bernie walked into the 'Basha'.

"Hello, hello, are you ready to hit town then Swifty?"

I'd completely forgotten about the promise he'd made about fixing me up with Leila. I was quite happy to just hold it as a possibility. From that premise I could fund all kinds of imaginative things; but now it was here, I hesitated. "Hell Bernie, I'd forgotten all about you!" I exclaimed somewhat taken aback.

"How could you, knowing that it's going to be your birthday party and all?"

"What's this then?" Bobby queried, combing his hair, while walking towards us.

"I've just fixed Swifty up with Leila, and an experience that he'll never forget."

"Why will he never forget? Let's hope there'll be no permanent reminder," Bobby said with a sneer.

"What do you mean?" rejoined Bernie, beginning to look ill at ease.

"Shall we say a small dose of syphilis for a start." All this time Bobby continued to comb his hair while he was speaking.

Bernie listened, but his facial expression hardened noticeably, indicating that he was very irritated by the way things were going.

"You got any smart replies, Mr. Smart Arse?"

Bernie could contain himself no longer. "What you on about, Swifty knows the score."

"Well Mr. Cool, tell him that you've had a dose, then."

This visibly stung Bernie, "Okay, right. But that was some time ago; I know what I'm doing now, alright?"

Bobby ignored his reply and turned to me, 'Swiftly, if you trust this guy, you're daft. I wouldn't trust him with me underpants."

Bobby had never said anything like this before, his concern for me was unsettling to say the least. "What's all this concern for my health Bobby?"

"Swifty, I come from Liverpool remember? He's a pimp, and pimps are all the same; they don't alter, they just dress differently that's all. What I mean is they're still bloody pimps, dangerous and full of shit, got it?"

Bernie had heard enough and began to walk away. I followed after him without saying anything, but I could hear Bobby when he shouted after me.

"You remember what I've said Swifty, you wait, see if I'm right."

I walked with Bernie for some time in silence; when we were a safe distance away he stopped. "You'd think he was yer mother Swifty, he's so bloody well interested in yer. Don't suppose he has any money, otherwise he'd be with us, eh? That's probably the truth, them Scousers are all the same."

I nodded in agreement, whilst wishing he'd left the mother bit out. We got a rickshaw and headed towards Kampong Java, the notorious red light district of Ipoh. The streets of Ipoh were crowded with people seemingly just wandering around. It reminded me of a football crowd loosing after the match. Eastern cities always seemed that way, with one difference, they never went away. The streets were crowded for most of the night, and all of the day, with thousands of people, or so it seemed. To add to the crush, rickshaws plied their way through the mass of people, as ours did. The driver shouted abuse, while continually ringing his bell. We sat there behind him, while people ran alongside the rickshaw staring at us with enquiring eyes.

At last we arrived at Kampong Java, which was some way from the centre of the city. Waves of guilt started to wash over me as I contemplated the reality of the visit. Some short time after entering the Kampong, the driver turned down a side road, stopping outside a building, that presumably was the one that housed Leila and the other ladies of the night. I got out of the rickshaw, and waited while Bernie paid the driver then joined me.

"Listen my boy, always pay the driver well."

"Give him what he asks for?" I asked enquiringly.

"Oh no, give him that plus a good tip."

We walked over to the door and Bernie knocked on it. In the dim light it looked sordid and in need of repair, but then most things off the main street looked like that to me. Instinctively we looked at each other as we heard the clatter of feet coming down the stairs. I'd sensed that Bernie was uncomfortable from his previous comments about the rickshaw waller, but his face now reflected his nervousness, which in turn, put my mouth in my heart as we waited. No matter, it didn't stop him acting as super organiser and man in charge.

"Always give a good tip to the rickshaw waller," repeated Bernie, before staring at me with a new intensity in his eyes. "You know why?"

"No, but I think I can guess."

He completely ignored my attempt at sarcasm and continued, "Because if you don't they just might inform on you. You know, tell the Military Police of your whereabouts off limits in Kampong Java, and if they do, you've shit it."

"We've shit it, you mean?"

Before he had time to answer, the door of the house opened to reveal a most beautiful woman, who, I was quick to notice, was quite young. "Bernie, we bin expecting you."

He smiled at her, and then at me, and we went inside. The room was very dimly lit, yet there was light enough to illuminate ornaments and figures which looked like gods and animals. They cast strange shadows around the room. This gave a kind of expectant atmosphere, together with an eerie feeling that we were being observed. Beautifully woven carpets lined the floor; while in one corner I saw what I thought might be a bar.

"You wait here," the girl instructed, before proceeding to return upstairs.

We waited in silence. I kept glancing at Bernie for a sign. I had no idea what I was looking for, except that I wanted something that would reassure me, and put me at ease; but all I got was his usual grin.

"Is that Leila?" I asked with a sheepish grin.

Bernie laughed, "Well she won't know, but it's what I call her."

"Oh, you don't know her name?"

"No!"

I could sense from the way he responded that he was getting irritated by my probing questions, so I remained silent. Leila eventually came downstairs, but this time she moved slowly, purposely, until near the bottom of the stairs she opened her skirt right up to her navel. My heart responded by missing a beat. Transfixed, unable to move, I waited, watching in total wonder at the infinite beauty of her legs, and her breasts. Just as my heart was about to burst with the adrenaline rush, she spoke.

"You come wiv me Johnny, I make you very happy."

I suddenly wished that the floor would swallow me up, as my mind was in such a whirl.

"Well go on then," urged Bernie in my ear. "Give it all you've got Swifty lad."

Leila turned round and began walking upstairs, presumably hoping that I'd follow. I turned to Bernie for help, but he only grinned.

"I can't do it Bernie," I pleaded.

He was most accommodating, "Okay Ill have a do first, and when I get down you'll have changed yer mind." He proceeded to go upstairs, whilst I stood at the bottom in a state of shock.

Halfway up the stairs he stopped, "You want to watch then? Maybe it'll turn you on."

I was too shocked by the suggestion to answer. I'd just turned down my big chance to break my duck, and I felt that I'd been shown up to be a chicken. My mind was in turmoil. Some part of me wanted sex at any price, the other carried feelings of guilt, that I'd never

258

experienced before. Thoughts flashed through my mind in a continual carousel; but something inside me was kind of stronger, and ever present, ready to override anything else. I felt that I didn't want to go through with it, but deep within, an excitement surged uncontrollably throughout my entire being, saturating it with the need to satisfy the desire. I felt helpless against it, yet I couldn't stop the arguments that kept coming into my head. How would I feel if I got a dose? What would my mother say if she knew? The deep respect I held for her ran counter to my presence here. I knew it was morally wrong, yet I knew I had to go through with it, otherwise Bernie might well make me the laughing stock of the whole Battalion, and the thought of Arnie and Tommo getting hold of it sent shivers down my spine. It would be unmerciful. I began to imagine what they would say.

"And you know what? Swifty's there with his pants down, pissed as a fart, and finds he can't get started. You see he had this apparition, you know one of them things when you get all religious."

Bernie says, "Hey Swifty this is the wrong time for all that; yer out to shag her, not convert her."

I didn't know what to do when Bernie started to come down the stairs, looking like a Cheshire cat.

"Let's go for it Swifty."

Before I could answer him, there was a loud banging on the door.

"Who the bloody hell can that be?" Bernie said looking very worried about the way the door was being banged.

No sooner had he spit out the last word, then the door burst open; two extremely large Military Policemen stood before us in the hallway. "Bin dipping yer dirty little wicks boys?"

I cast a quick glance at Bernie, and realised that he was ready to try to make a run for it given half a chance.

The policeman nearest me, noticed the same thing at the same time. "Don't even think about it son, you'll never make it."

Bernie immediately looked sheepishly at him, but kept silent.

"Go get the others out Benny; flush the rats out of the nest."

Benny, the smaller of the two disappeared up the stairs. Shortly afterwards cries and squeals of surprise could be heard as the M.P's burst into the upstairs room. I looked at Benny in utter belief, mistakenly thinking we were on our own. I'd somehow come around to the idea that we were visiting one lady who had a working relationship with a regular number of soldiers, Bernie being one of that number. The truth became a stark reality, as I realised that we were in a brothel. Some might say that I should have known it all along, but that was not the truth. I'd certainly known that Leila charged for sex, but somehow I got it into my head that she was Bernie's personal woman, and as such he not only got her favours, but he also gave others her favours, at a price. All these things were going through my brain when a commotion at the top of the stairs caught my attention. The M. P. who'd gone upstairs was struggling trying to drag our Cook Sergeant down them, followed by an Officer who seemed to be following quite amiably, which jolted me instantly into the present.

"Shit Bernie," and I thought…"

"Now is not the time to think," he said, before I could finish the sentence.

I stood there silently watching them come down the stairs, wondering in my innocence, whether I should salute the Officer, when he tripped up on the second to the bottom step, pitching forward into a heap on the floor. Instinctively I went to help him.

The M. P. nearest me stopped me in my tracks, "Stay where you are soldier, let the bastard get up himself."

Now this was another world, a world where Officers became just men. I immediately recognised Captain Taunton, and he was very drunk.

He addressed the M.P's, "I say, who the devil's in charge here? And what are you doing speaking to an Officer like this, hey?" He lurched forward uncontrollably.

The M. P. nearest to him laughed, "To a drunken Officer Sir. That's who I'm speaking to; and by the way that drunken Officer will be accompanying us back to camp before going in front of his C.O."

"Me Corporal?"

"Yes you Sir."

"Good god Corporal, can't we, well come to some arrangement or something? Oh dear me, I think I'm in the shit as they say. Can't you see?" He looked pleadingly at the Corporal.

"Yes Sir, I can see, and what's more I'm bloody well responsible for you being in the shit, as you've put it. Now Captain are you coming back with us, or are we going to throw you in the back of the truck? The choice is yours."

The Captain became extremely agitated at the Corporal's words. "I do hope that you realise that I'm an Officer boy?"

"I do Sir, and might I remind you that I'm not a boy, and you're drunk, and you're in a brothel which is off limits to troops, and that is a very serious offence for an Officer of the Queen."

I smiled as I listened to the conversation; I'd never heard anything like this before coming from a non commissioned Officer.

"And what are you smiling about soldier, I haven't said anything funny yet, have I?"

The smile disappeared as I realised that I was in serious trouble. "Sergeant!" I said, "I do hope that you are aware that I..."

He cut me short, "I know exactly everything I want to know about you sonny, so shut your mouth and get in the fuckin' truck."

We waited for the Captain to get into some acceptable state before we made our way to the truck parked outside the building. The journey back to camp was hilarious, as the Captain was sick all over the M. P. sitting beside him; while the Cook Sergeant, who was in a drunken stupor, was totally concerned about the whereabouts of his underpants, which he quite wrongly thought he'd lost in the truck. The M. P. tried to tell him that he'd most probably left them in the room in the brothel, but he wouldn't listen and began to cry. Eventually he fell silent, but only after the M. P. lost his temper and began to threaten him, but he continued to mutter occasional, almost inaudible remarks until we came near the camp gates.

Suddenly he looked at me and shouted at the top of his voice, "I can't find me underpants yer know."

I laughed, only to be told to shut up by the M. P. who said that it was no laughing matter, and that I really was in the shit.

Arriving back at camp, we were bundled out of the truck and placed in the cells, except that is for the Captain, who disappeared to his quarters, I presumed.

"You watch," said Bernie, "we'll get bloody hammered, and that bastard'll get off with it."

Now this kind of outburst wasn't at all like Bernie and it disturbed me. "Be careful Bernie," I warned, "we're on holy ground, I'd shut up if I were you." It was the first piece of advice I'd ever given Bernie.

He mulled it over for a minute before replying, "Yeah, I suppose you're right, but it stinks don't it? We in here, and him in his bed."

The night passed slowly. It was difficult to sleep due to the lights being on, together with the thought of what morning was going to bring. The Sergeant sobered up, and became very remorseful; he wept continually after Bernie asked him which girl he'd had? He was silent for some time, when suddenly, and quite out of the blue, he stood up and screamed at Bernie to shut up, which brought the guards running to the cell. Bernie was bewildered, because he hadn't said a word.

"What's going on?" asked Big Mick, the Provo Sergeant, looking round the cell, his eyes finally resting on the pitiful figure of the Cook Sergeant, who was sat on the floor crying. "Someone worrying you Harry?"

The Cook Sergeant raised his head up until he met Big Mick's gaze, "Mick I've bin a fool, what can I do?"

"You'll be alright Harry, just see it through, then take it up where you left off. Okay?" He then turned to us, "And you bloody lot better leave Harry alone, or you'll be seeing more of Michael O'Shan than what's good for yer."

"Yes Sergeant," I said, trying my best to please him, but it was like trying to stroke a tiger.

He turned to give me his full attention. "Haven't we met before somewhere?" He stroked his chin and stared at me intently.

I certainly wasn't going to remind him.

"Michael O'Shan never forgets a face," he said with a sneer, that was as near to a grin as you could get. Then he remembered, "Yes, you were on escort duty, Kinraha Barracks with McNichols, am I right?"

"Yes Sergeant," I agreed somewhat apprehensively.

He grinned at me in a sickly manner before his reply caused me to shiver. "You just might be going there again sonny; only this time you might well be stopping."

The sudden involuntary start I made at the suggestion of going to Kinraha Detention Centre, was enough to make him roar with laughter, which quickly reduced into a sneer.

"You like the thought Corporal?" He waited for an answer.

"No I don't Sergeant, but it's not that serious a crime is it?" I said this in the hope that he would confirm it.

"You never know, do you?" he replied, before walking away.

They left us in the guardroom over the weekend, as was their normal practice. On Monday morning, we were taken to our respective Company offices to be formally charged, and in my case, hopefully sentenced, because if we weren't we would be court-martialled. I waited outside whilst Bernie went in. I knew that he could talk and argue better than anyone else I knew, and that included Arnie. You can imagine my surprise and disbelief when he came out half an hour later having been sent for a court-martial.

I went in immediately afterwards. Sergeant Major Bullock marched me in at the double, halting in front of the Commanding Officer's desk.

Major Coker stared at me for some time without saying a word. Then he looked at the Sergeant Major. "At ease Sergeant Major."

The Sergeant Major roared for the party to be at ease.

Major Coker continued, "Corporal Swift, you get yourself into some scrapes, don't you?" Without waiting for an answer he asked, "Tell me what you were doing in that brothel?" He suddenly realised what he'd said, and a rueful smile came onto his face. "Yes, well I know what you were doing, but…"

At this point I interrupted him, 'Sir…"

But the Sergeant Major bawled in my ear, "Don't interrupt the Major when he's speaking to you Corporal."

The Major glanced up at the Sergeant Major in approval. "Yes, well as I was saying, whatever possessed you to risk such a thing, especially when you know the terrible consequences of V. D. not to mention stopped pay, cancelled leave, and of course you know that you'd lose your place in the Battalion Boxing and Rugger

Teams?" He paused for breath. "Dear me! Quite stupid, I don't know what you were thinking about." Whereupon he looked at me intently until I lowered my eyes, then he carried on, "I really don't know what to do with you. What do you have to say?"

"It was the most stupid thing I've ever done Sir. I must say that I thought twice about going with one of the girls, then decided not to for the very reasons that you have just stated Sir."

What I said had an immediate effect upon him. His facial expression changed. It was as if he'd allowed a hint of a smile to enter the interrogation. "You mean to tell me that you didn't get up to any hanky panky?"

"No Sir, I just sat there and waited."

"Yes," he said, "waited for Private Rend to satisfy his carnal desires." He fiddled with his pen, looked up at me, glanced at the roof, then at the Sergeant Major, before coming back to me.

I must admit that I thought I'd had it.

Eventually he spoke again in a low voice, "I think I believe you. Private Rend took you, that much we know already. You are easily led, that much we know too, and we know that by the friends you keep in the Company." He stopped for a moment, glancing at the Sergeant Major for approval, before continuing in a much sterner voice, "You should be very wary of people like Private Rend, he's in grave trouble. You know what he's been up to?"

"No Sir, he just asked me if I wanted to see the girls in Ipoh Sir."

Before I had time to finish the last word, he'd jumped out of his chair, and was standing right before me. "Now I don't believe you Corporal Swift, I'm afraid it's just not plausible."

I hadn't a clue what he meant, but something inside of me told me to keep quiet. Silence ensued, while he contemplated what to do with me. All this time I stood bolt upright to attention, until I was wet through with perspiration. Great balls of sweat had begun to form on my forehead before cascading down my face, then tickling and irritating my skin, before crashing down onto my shirt and the floor.

The Major began to speak again, "You know nothing about Private Rend's activities in Ipoh? Like hell you don't. He was a drug runner in Ipoh to that tart, who goes by the name of Leila, for which I presume she gave him her favours, and some money no doubt. We all know about Private Rend except you it would seem, and yet you insist that you still don't know anything?" He waited for me to answer.

"No Sir," I said quietly, "I had no idea he was up to anything like that."

Again there was an awkward silence, I knew that it was important to show a new found conformity and intention, so I stood absolutely still, looking directly ahead without moving anything, including my eyes.

The Major leaned forward, "Did you by any chance see an Officer in that brothel?"

The question immediately confused me, because he knew that I'd seen one, so I reasoned why he was asking such a question? My brain felt like it was bursting as I tried to understand why he might be asking the question? I could of course answer the question truthfully, but a sixth sense told me that was not what they were looking for. Then it came to me, "No Sir, I never saw any Officer there."

Major Coker stiffened up, "Are you absolutely sure?" He spoke softly leaning back into his chair again, "only Private Rend has just stated categorically that an Officer out of 'A' Company was in there."

"I'm absolutely certain Sir, I couldn't make a mistake like that."

He twiddled with his pen, rolling it round in the palm of his hand before placing it down carefully on the table in front of him. After which he looked at me, "Right, I'm going to take a chance with you Corporal Swift, I'm going to sentence you to being confined to camp for a month. Now you know what that means, don't you?"

Before I had time to speak he began to tell me. "You will stay within the camp, which means that you will be unable to go on leave should you have booked. You will also be barred from wearing civilian clothes, and you will be available for camp duties at all times during that stipulated period." He waited to see my reaction before continuing, "I do hope that you are aware that I have been extremely lenient with you. Now dismiss, and if I have the misfortune to see you again in these circumstances, you will be sorry, I can assure you."

Immediately the Major had finished speaking, the Sergeant Major roared into action, and we marched out of the office in quick time, and halted some yards from it. I stood rigidly to attention knowing that the Sergeant Major would now have his say.

"Corporal Swift," he began, "you're the luckiest man alive, you're like bloody Houdini. In all my life I've never known anybody get away with so much. I'm beginning to wonder about you boy. You amaze me. Caught in a brothel, and you plead bloody innocent, and get away with it. Well you fool some, but you can't fool me. You're a bloody lucky sod, and I hope you know it."

"Yes Sir," I replied, unable to fully grasp the extent of my luck, but what I couldn't quite understand was why Bernie had got court-martialled and not me? However, I now felt reasonably safe, although I was aware of my incredible luck. I'd needed to play the game, and somehow I'd managed to do it, but it had been a close call, and I knew it. I'd given the right answers at the right time, which was a new experience for me.

Sergeant Major Bullock continued, "And you didn't know what Rend was up to then? Like hell you didn't."

"No Sir, I didn't, I had no idea that he was involved in drugs." I answered with a new found confidence.

"No, no, you didn't!" He spat out as if it hurt his mouth to say it. "Well I don't believe you, although the Major does. Count yourself lucky, but remember Corporal Swift your luck won't last forever, but it's a waste of time telling you, you're such a clever little sod. But you'll get caught, your sort always do." He paused for breath before he bawled out at the top of his voice, "Detail dismiss!"

I've got away with it I thought, as I walked towards the Company lines, but I knew that I'd have to watch my step closely now, and made sure that my back was directly turned against his gaze, as an involuntary grin began to form.

Upon entering my 'Basha', I was met by a barrage of questions. I managed to ignore most of them, but one question arose from their general enquiries, and that was who'd grassed on Bernie Rend? I made it quite plain that I hadn't, and I had no idea who had. Gradually things returned to normal, and we all settled down to the usual routine of patrolling the jungle at regular intervals.

One day, after returning from a jungle patrol, Bobby had his say about the warning he'd given me concerning Bernie. I wondered why he'd taken so long.

After he'd finished he said, "What made you say that you'd never seen an Officer Swifty?"

"I really don't know. I suppose it was a daft question to ask really. I mean, he knew that I'd seen him, so why ask? They already knew. I suspected something, so I said what I thought they wanted me to say."

Bobby lay back on his bed and contemplated this for a minute, "You bloody well amaze me Swifty, you do somethin' stark ravin' bloody mad one minute, then the very next, you come out with a blinder that I'd be proud of myself; and what's more bloody amazin', you hadn't a bloody clue."

"Go on," I encouraged wanting him to carry on. "Well think about it. He asked you questions that he already knew the answer to, so that leaves you with the question of why ask it? He wanted you to say no, you hadn't seen an Officer, which you did right?"

"Yes, but why would he want me to say I never saw him?"

Bobby suddenly became exasperated, "Because he's a bloody Officer. That's why, and Officers don't go to brothels, especially the ones that other ranks use anyway."

"Oh, I see," I said.

"Oh no you don't. You only think that you see." He sighed loudly in order to show his irritation, before continuing, "Don't you understand, if you didn't see an Officer there, then only Bernie did see him. Get it?"

"What about the Cook Sergeant and the M. P's?" I asked.

"Yeah, what about them? They'll have worked somethin' out, you see. And what's more you said earlier that the Officer had gone straight to his quarters, right?"

I nodded.

"Well nobody saw him that mattered did they? And if they did, he wouldn't have been seen to be in any trouble would he? It was only you and Bernie Rend that knew about that, and the M. P's."

"Yes, but I heard the way the M. P's talked to the Officer, and they said he was going to be in a lot of trouble; and anyway what about the Cook Sergeant?"

Bobby looked at me for a moment. "Mark my words Swifty, they'll have worked somethin' out I'm tellin' you."

That conversation gave me a lot to think about in the months ahead, as I realised that what Bobby had predicted, did in fact come true. I saw the Officer around the camp, mainly because he did more duties than his brother Officers, while Bernie did time in Kinraha Military Prison; but as Bobby said, Bernie was selling drugs, and was a known pimp, before being caught in a brothel off limits.

Chapter 9

My final days at Ipoh

"This repression was carried out by a huge security apparatus. Eventually over 40,000 regular police, 40,000 auxiliary police, 100,000 special police, and 250,000 home guards were raised to fight the MRLA, which never numbered more than 8,000. The police were supported by over 40,000 troops (British, African, Gurkha, Australian, Fijian and Malay) together with squadrons of heavy bombers and fighter bombers. The MRLA's protracted resistance in the face of this overwhelming force was a remarkable epic of courage and endurance."

Towards the end of 1957, I heard from Pop Quint, the Battalion Boxing Team Captain, that we were entering the Army Boxing Team Championships, and that they wanted me to fight First String Light-Welterweight. This was good news for me, as it meant keeping out of the jungle. It also countered the fact that I was not doing too well with my new Platoon Commander, Lt. O'Silvan, who seemed to dislike me intensely. He always targeted me if anything went wrong. I reasoned that he did this because he considered himself to be efficient by nature, or so he thought, and I by contrast, was totally the opposite, and therefore presented a continual source of irritation to him. I might add that although he demanded great efficiency from all those around him, he was incredibly careless himself. He was always falling foul of his superior Officers, by making the most stupid mistakes. For instance, he made continual accidental discharges on the rifle range. He regularly got lost in the jungle, and perhaps worst of all, he openly despised regular N.C.O's, and incessantly argued with them, causing bad feeling in the section.

I always read detail every morning. One particular morning, I read that I was to report to the gym to train with the Battalion Boxing Team for the forthcoming Championships. Unfortunately nobody had informed Lt. O'Silvan, who was expecting me to attend a briefing in order to be on a patrol on a jungle operation.

He met me on my return from training. "Where in hell's name have you been Corporal Swift?"

I smiled knowing that he'd got it wrong again.

"And you can take that bloody grin off your face as well. And stand to attention when I'm speaking to you."

I immediately stood still, looked straight ahead, and waited.

"Now answer me in words that I can understand. Where were you this morning? I gave you direct orders to be here, and you deliberately disobeyed me. I want to know why?"

"I read detail Sir, and on the Company board, it read that I should report to the Boxing Team Headquarters Sir. I can't be in two places at once, can I?"

When I'd finished, his face turned crimson. "Don't be so bloody impudent. I shall see about this, and you won't be in the Boxing Team very long, I can assure you. You'll be in the jungle, where you should be."

He continued to stare at me whilst I stood rooted to attention, looking straight ahead.

"Now dismiss!"

I saluted and made my way across the open ground towards the Company lines, knowing that he was watching me all the way.

Arriving back at the 'basha', I was met by Danny. "Have you been getting up O'Silvan's nose again Swifty?"

"I think he's been getting up mine," I retorted. "I can't be in two places at once, can I?"

Danny didn't answer, he just laughed and walked off.

I really didn't know what to do on the following morning, when Captain Whitford came striding towards me as I was making my way to the Company Office to read detail.

"Corporal Swift," he shouted.

I stopped immediately, saluted, and stood to attention.

"At ease Corporal, you're to report to the gym for Boxing training, and never mind what anybody else tells you, and that's an order from me, right?"

"Yes Sir," I replied with a smile.

He winked at me as I left, which I interpreted to mean that he knew all about my Platoon Commander's threats.

Training was anything but easy due to the heat. It started at six o'clock in the morning with running through the suburbs of Ipoh, much to the amazement of the few locals who had risen. This was followed by exercises in the gym, which lasted until about ten o'clock, when the heat prevented any further training. We came back to the gym after sunset to spar in the ring. This routine continued for a month, during which time I hardly saw anything of my friends, who were continually coming and going out of the camp patrolling the jungle. I felt very privileged, particularly when I came into contact with Lieutenant O'Silvan, who generally returned my salute with a stare that spoke volumes.

One day, shortly after training, I was walking back from the canteen when I saw some of my friends returning from a jungle patrol. I walked across to speak. As I approached, I told them that I sensed that something was wrong. Mick Lanton was nearest to me. "Hi Mick", I began, wanting to know what was wrong?

He acknowledged my greeting with a nod of his head, before continuing towards his quarters without another word. The others followed, giving nothing but cursory glances, indicating that all was not well, but they didn't want to talk about it. Undeterred, I went after them, but as I got near them, the stench became almost unbearable, which I might add was quite normal when returning from a stint in the jungle. Obnoxious as the smell was, I couldn't for the life of me miss any news first hand, so I followed them.

"Well go on, tell me all about it then."

Mick just looked at me as though I wasn't there, but Tommo, who had drifted towards me, spoke after a big sigh! "You will never believe this when I tell you Swifty. I can't believe it myself." He paused to collect his breath. "We got in the jungle as normal, and settled down after making camp. Next day we sent patrols out, which as usual, never saw a thing."

"Well get on with it," I said, unable to contain my suspense.

"You want me to tell yer, or don't you?" He gave me a look that suggested he'd be true to his word.

"Okay, I'm sorry, just desperate to know, alright?"

He smiled ruefully, as some of the others crowded round to listen.

"Yeah, tell Swifty about the ambush," shouted Danny from the back.

"I will, I will," Tommo shouted back, "but don't rush me."

"Don't worry, there's no rush in yer," interjected Bobby.

"Right, shut up you lot while I tell him. Tommo was getting angry, which was an indication in itself that it was a serious matter. He continued, "When we arrived at the right place in the jungle, we made a camp as usual, and settled down for the night. Next day O'Silvan sends out patrols in the usual way. One patrol comes back with all sorts of spare parts for weapons, yer know Bren and Sten gun parts, and things like that. I'm tellin' yer, I've never seen so many parts in me life. It doesn't take a bloody genius to know that there must be some Commies around looking after the stuff. Next day O'Silvan sends out patrols again, knowing that we'd mostly make contact. I was in base camp, waiting with 5 Platoon, and I can tell yer we were all on edge. We waited and listened, and about halfway through the afternoon, we heard the chatter of machine gun fire, together with the crack of F.N. rifles, coming from the ridge to the east of us. We all sat there in a state of bloody shock, wondering what was going on?

O'Silvan decides to set up an ambush on the track that the patrol has gone out on. Well, Sergeant Conelly tells O'Silvan that the track is the one that the patrol is most likely to come back on, and if this happened we'd be in danger of killing our own men. O'Silvan thinks for some reason, that the Commies will come first, and insists that we get into ambush positions. We all got together and talked about it, and decided that there was no way that we could risk it. Lieutenant O'Silvan goes mad and threatens everyone with a court-martial for mutiny. Sergeant Conelly tells him that we're right. The Sergeant's with Major Coker now, and I don't know what'll happen." Tommo stopped and began coughing uncontrollably.

I spent the next few minutes trying to glean what had happened after that, as he succumbed to incessant coughing bouts that saw great tears flowing down his face as he tried to speak, while trying to relieve something in his throat at the same time.

The gist of what he said seemed to be about the level of argument that took place between Sergeant Conelly and Lieutenant O'Silvan.

At this point I thought Tommo was going to break a blood vessel, as again he became totally engulfed in a coughing bout.

After recovering he told us again how the lads had refused to set an ambush on the track, which sent O'Silvan nearly crackers, shouting out that they were cowards, and should be shot.

"What did Sergeant Conelly do?" I asked.

He ignored my question. "Mutiny, I mean mutiny; can you believe it?"

I was stuck for words, because I couldn't believe it either. It was like something on the films, it didn't happen to you. We stood staring at each other.

Eventually he broke the silence, "I suppose they can shoot us, can't they?"

"I suppose they can," I said walking away.

I heard him running after me, "I was only bloody well kidding Swifty; don't get funny with me. This is serious business."

"You bet it's serious, they shot people in the First World War, for much less than that."

Tommo's face became a picture of intermittent rage and fear, as he alternated between thinking about me, and the potential problem of mutiny. One half of him wanted to have a go at me for taking the piss, but the sudden thought of serious trouble prevented him doing so. "What do yer think'll happen then Swifty?"

"I don't know, but it's bloody serious. I hope you know that?" I stopped to think whilst Tommo visibly paled at the thought of all the possible options.

"Look," I began, "if Major Coker was gunning for you, you'd be in the guardroom right now, not standing around talking to me, right? Sergeant Conelly's in there now giving the Major the low down on what went on, and I think that Mr. bloody O'Silvan will be in the shit, you watch."

Tommo just nodded his head before turning round and heading towards his quarters.

"You want to know something else Tommo?" I shouted after him. "You stink! Try having a shower before you talk to anyone else, otherwise they'll find you guilty just to get rid of you."

"Piss off Swifty. You can never take anything seriously," he muttered angrily as he walked away.

I felt quite relieved and thankful that I wasn't in his shoes, but I also felt quite guilty about the excitement I had experienced when listening to the tale, which made me a little depressed, but I soon forgot it as I made my way over to the gym for the usual pep talk, prior to the nightly sparring session.

Some days later, I heard that Lieutenant O'Silvan had been sent home in disgrace. The chance to pursue my natural curiosity was thwarted by the demands of the Boxing Team, as training became more intensive, and the fact that 5 Platoon were always out in the jungle on patrol when I had the opportunity to go down to their lines. Arnie was always available, being 'B' Company clerk, but he'd become less communicative, and his lips remained sealed. However I did glean from him that Major Coker had bollocked the whole Platoon publicly, and described them as being a dastardly low bunch of men, none of whom he'd want to be with in a tight corner. Of course Arnie and myself had a great laugh about the Major's choice of words, which seemed to come straight out of 'Boy's Own'. Whatever happened to Lieutenant O'Silvan nobody really knew in the ordinary ranks, although rumours continually circulated. But one thing was for sure; we never saw him again.

Several days went by before I saw Arnie again; he was walking across to the NAFFI as I was making my way to the Company lines for a training session.

"Hey Arnie, how's it going then? I shouted.

He stopped and turned towards me, raising his hand to his eyes in order to see in the light of the sun, "Hello, what are you up to then?"

"On my way to one of Lieutenant Rose's pep talks."

Arnie smiled, which suggested that he knew all about the Lieutenant's talks. "You know I'm going to leave you to fight this war on your own Swifty?"

"What do you mean?" I asked.

"What do I mean," he repeated. "I mean that I'm going where they speak properly, where they live properly, and what's more important, where they think properly! I'm going back to Kendal. This shit hole," he waved his arms around in a half circle, "has seen enough of my superior culture; and what's more Kendal is missing me."

"When do you go?" I asked him.

"Tomorrow," he replied quickly.

"You never told me," I said feeling quite hurt.

Arnie just smiled.

At that precise moment I noticed someone frantically gesticulating to me, "If I don't see you again Arnie; all the best."

He just grinned before he answered, "This time next week Swifty, I'll spare you a thought. I'll be sat in a pub with a glass of beer in one hand, a fag in the other, and the bloody jungle 12,000 miles away!"

"But Arnie," I said, "you've hardly been in the jungle. What are you on about?"

"Yeah, well I didn't have to volunteer for the Boxing Team, and get me lights knocked out in order to get out of it, did I?"

I ignored the insult, "See you Arnie."

"See you Swifty, don't suppose you'll ever get up to Kendal, we eat buggers like you for breakfast." With that he turned away.

I watched him go, realising that something within me was going too. I loved being in the boxing team, although it isolated me from my friends in 'B' Company. As with all contact sports, boxing attracts tough, and sometimes very needy people, and I was becoming aware of that need in my own life. They were usually soldiers who had a history of being in trouble in the Battalion, although that didn't apply to everyone. However, they were always great to be with, and none could ever accuse them of being boring. In some strange way, I found fighting thrilling and invigorating. It was as if someone had presented me with a dare. Being chosen, meant becoming part of an elite, which made me feel very special.

One day after sparring with a Liverpudlian called Tony Robins, I experienced amnesia again. He caught me with a cracking left hook as I came in, which put me down, but I got up immediately and carried on boxing, but I suffered as I made my way back to my quarters. I never told anyone, being too scared of losing my place in the Team, and having to return to jungle patrols. The amnesia affected me in a strange way, by making unconnected thoughts come into my mind. It wasn't that the thoughts were nasty or anything like that, but they came without any bidding. They came from nowhere, sending shivers down my spine, and making me sweat profusely, as I remembered my problems in Catterick Military Hospital.

The next day Lieutenant Rose called me over to him. "Do you think that you can beat Robins, Corporal Swift?" he asked.

"Yes Sir," I replied, believing it to be true.

"You're a strange one Swift, he puts you on the seat of your pants, and you really believe that you can beat him, don't you?"

I didn't answer him, there didn't seem to be any point.

He continued, "I believe that you could, without any problem, do you know that?"

I nodded and smiled. He'd given me two messages here. One was that he thought I could beat Tony Robins, which I already knew; the other was that he hated Tony for some reason. I never mentioned to him the strange sensations that I'd experienced after sparring, I was too frightened of what the repercussions might bring.

Shortly after this episode, McNichols joined us after being released from Kinraha Military Prison. When I heard about his release, I couldn't wait to see and hear about his experiences inside. When we did eventually meet, I was completely stunned by his appearance, as he'd lost so much weight. He looked terribly thin and gaunt. I was waiting to spar with Tony when he put his head round the door of the gym and addressed Lieutenant Rose.

"Sir, I've been told to report to you," he said saluting.

Everyone stopped what they were doing and turned towards him.

The Lieutenant knew all about McNichols, "Are you alright after your holiday then?" he said with a cynical smile.

"I haven't been on holiday Sir; I've been in prison," he replied quietly, and without flinching.

"Yes I know all about that. You won't be going there again, will you?"

Mc laughed, "No Sir, not if I can help it, wouldn't recommend it to anybody."

He joined us, and over the next month I badgered him for information about the Military Prison at Kinraha. At first, he wouldn't say anything at all. It was as if he was terrified that something might get back. I couldn't help think that prior to his release, he'd been threatened about disclosing any information about what was going on in the prison. Some time later, I managed to get him to speak about his first day there. Mc was a quiet man at the best of times, and I could hardly hear him when he did speak.

It ended up with him whispering in my ear, his lips almost touching my ear. It must have looked funny, but nobody said a thing. "You know Swifty, after you dropped me off, I never stopped running for two hours round and round the parade ground. I stopped then only because I couldn't run any more." He stopped speaking and stared at the floor before continuing, "Two M. P's, just walked over to me. I could hardly stand up, and didn't think anything was wrong. I mean all I'd done was stop running after two hours in the stinking hot sun."

When they got to about two yards away, one of 'em said, "You had enough soldier?"

"Before I had time to answer he punched me in the belly so hard, I sank into a heap on the floor. His mate laughed, lifted his truncheon up, and the next thing I remember was waking up in a cell."

I knew that terrible things went on in Military Prisons, but this was difficult to believe. "Go on what happened next?"

Mc just looked at me with total dejection, "You wouldn't understand if I told you."

"Well try me," I said getting exasperated.

"I saw an Australian soldier hit a M.P. You know what they did? Two of the bastards grabbed him, got him down on the ground, while another stamped on his arm and broke it. Then one of 'em said, "Come on soldier hit me again, and we'll break the other one too."

"And you know what? They would have done."

Later, I tried to get some more information out of him, but he wouldn't say anything more on the subject, except to say that I shouldn't go near the place. He was scared stiff of being sent back, and didn't mind anybody knowing it.

Chapter 10

Demob looms

"Much the same point was made by General Sir Walter Walker, another veteran of the Emergency, who offensively contrasted American defeat in Vietnam at the hands of "the puny men of a puny nation" with British success in Malaya. He argued that the Malayan Communists were every bit as formidable as the Vietcong had been in the early 1960s and that if the campaign against them had been similarly mismanaged, "we too could have had a Vietnam on our hands."

As my time in the Army came to a close, the reality of another life started to filter through. It came with the departure of some of my friends. I saw them waving madly as the trucks roared away, never realising that I'd probably never see them again. The day came when I too left Columbo Camp.

Upon reaching Singapore, I heard some disturbing news about an air crash in Europe. It turned out to be the Munich disaster, where many of the Manchester United Football Team died. After many false calls, that saw us trooping around from one runway to another, and some hours waiting in the airport lounge, we eventually climbed on board a Hermes plane, fervently hoping that we'd have more luck than the footballers.

We set off in torrential rain that threatened to engulf everything in its wake. The sky lit up, followed almost immediately by an enormous clap of thunder, that sent shivers of concern, followed by rueful smiles, as we recognised the beginnings of a tropical thunderstorm. Our first stop was to be Bangkok in Thailand. As we began the flight, I noticed some tremors, but thought nothing more about it until the descent at Bangkok airport. Through the window of the plane, I saw what I presumed to be the airport, a speckle of lights in the distance. I remember thinking that it looked like some giant board game, with lights marking the runway with huge symmetrical lines. As we got ever lower, I noticed that the runway was lined on each side with vehicles of all shapes and sizes. When we touched down, vehicles that previously looked like matchbox cars, became suddenly recognisable as ambulances, fire engines, Police and Army personnel cars. I assumed in my innocence, that some dignitary of high rank was expected. We landed on the runway in between them; all the vehicles flashed past on either side during a very rough landing. No sooner had we stopped, than all the emergency lights came on in the plane and the Captain spoke to us over the intercom.

"We made it," he began.

I hadn't a clue what he was on about, being completely unaware that there was anything wrong.

He continued, "During our flight, one of our port engines set on fire, so I closed down the other as well; we have been flying on two engines since. Some short distance from this airport one of the remaining engines decided it had had enough as well and promptly packed in; hence the reception party gentlemen."

Upon hearing this we all cheered and clapped.

He quickly silenced us and told us to remove our boots.

This we did and emerged bootless out of the plane as firemen sprayed foam over it.

Vinny Preston, a soldier out 'B' Company walked over to me, "You in charge of this party Swifty?"

"I suppose I am," I answered casually.

"You'd have thought they'd have told us something was wrong wouldn't you?"

I smiled at the thought before I answered, "Yeah, we're not very important, are we?"

He looked a bit confused, but I didn't pursue it, I couldn't be bothered trying to explain what I meant.

The airport bus ferried us to the central lounge where we waited while 'Airwork', the charter flight Company decided what to do with us. There we were in Bangkok Airport, twenty-eight soldiers returning to the United Kingdom for demob, with me a Lance Corporal in charge. The Officers who were with us on the plane had long since gone to some luxurious hotel, no doubt. It wasn't long before tempers began to wear thin. Of the twenty-eight soldiers only ten came from my Battalion, the others coming from other units in Malaya. It proved extremely difficult when a soldier I didn't know made his way over to me.

"I thought I heard you say that you were in charge of this party," he said aggressively.

"Yes, whatever that means!"

"Well do something about it will you. You've been sitting on your fat arse for hours."

"Like what for instance?" I asked, looking him straight between the eyes.

"Like going to the office and complaining, instead of fingering your bloody stripes."

"Sit down and shut it," I responded. "You're still in the Army sunshine, not in civvy street yet. And what's more, if I tell you to wait; you'll bloody well wait! Got it? And if you don't, believe me you'll be spending some time explaining why not when we get back. Understand?"

He muttered some garbled obscenities at me before sitting down, which I chose to ignore.

Eventually, and not before time, we were told to assemble outside the lounge in order to be taken into the city.

Bangkok proved to be a stereotypical eastern city, teeming with people. I remember thinking that the whole of Asia must have come to town; there seemed to be so many people. As the bus neared the centre of the city, it slowed down almost to walking pace, stopping and starting as it entered the congestion of traffic. At one point when the bus was stationary for some time, the lads started to gesticulate at the Thai girls passing the bus. Before long they were banging on the windows and the side of the bus, either in annoyance or in friendly communication. The situation got more serious when some of the girls tried to climb onto the bus.

The driver stopped the bus and shoved them off roughly, which the lads thought was highly amusing for a while, but quickly found that what they'd started they couldn't stop. A certain number of the girls began to follow the bus as it slowly made its way through the city centre. I naturally thought they'd disappear in the general melée of the city bustle, but they were made of far sterner stuff, running when we moved faster, walking when we slowed down, and banging on the windows when we stopped.

As we neared the hotel, which was some way from the city centre, the driver slowed down to a crawling pace in the heavy traffic. One of the lads had just asked the driver to point out the hotel to him, when a Thai lady ran up to the vehicle and started shouting.

"Johnny! This your child, you give money."

The lads went quiet immediately, waiting, almost transfixed at what might come next. Other girls followed suit banging on the windows and demanding money.

Others shouted, "You want jig a jig Johnny? Very cheap!"

If that had been all, we wouldn't have bothered, but behind the girls, I noticed another more sinister side of things, middle aged men had now appeared, and were watching the scene intently. It didn't take a genius to see the link between them and the girls.

Upon arriving at the hotel, we all piled out of the bus into a sea of people. With hardly room to move, we shoved and pushed our way into the hotel, where we were met by the proprietor and his staff. They laughed when we greeted them, they laughed when they helped us with our luggage. They even laughed when we tried to speak to them. However, it wasn't long before their laughter and noise were drowned by our protests. Some of the crowd decided to follow us into the hotel where they stood, stared and giggled at the top of their voices. It became quite unnerving when the proprietor led us upstairs and some of the young girls and their minders followed.

I decided that as leader of the party, I must do something about it, so I confronted the manager. "Can you get these people out of here?" I demanded.

He looked at me, stuck a finger in his chest and began to laugh. "You want? Okay!"

It was patently obvious that he didn't understand a word I'd said; so I pretended to push imaginary people out of the hotel, in a desperate attempt to show him what I meant. He smiled.

At that point I gave up and went into my room, and found to my horror that the rooms had no locks on the doors. Slowly realising that the situation was serious and quite beyond me; I lay down on the bed feeling helpless, when the room door began to open slowly. I sat up and stared in some amazement when two young Thai girls entered and stood in the doorway. I couldn't help notice the men standing behind them. I was sharing a room with Danny who'd gone out for some reason.

He returned, "What's this bloody lot doing here then Swifty? Is it some sort of joke or what? Tell 'em to piss off."

"I already have, but they don't seem to understand."

For some time the young girls stood in the doorway laughing and giggling. Suddenly and without warning, one of the girls went over to a suitcase and tried to open it.

I jumped up from my bed immediately and roughly pushed her away, "Right Danny," I shouted, "Let's get this shitty lot out of here."

As we moved towards them, the girls began to scream and spit at us; but they backed off and went into the corridor; but it was noticeable that their laughter had gone and been replaced by sullen and angry looks. I was just about to shut the door, when one of the girls spoke.

"You wanna woman Johnny?"

"So you do speak some English," I responded.

"Little bit that all," she answered.

"Well bugger off then all of you, and don't bloody well come back."

At this, they gave up, but we could hear the men shouting threats and obscenities at us as they left.

"You wouldn't bloody well believe it would you!" Danny exclaimed.

"Believe what?" I asked.

"Believe that the British Army would abandon us in a shit hole like this."

The heat was oppressive, we lay back on our beds and succumbed to sleep. The next thing I remember was awaking feeling uncomfortable, and hearing something scratching on the floor near my bed. Lying there, with my mind swirling around in a morass of discomforting thoughts, I heard a distinct movement. There was someone else in the room. I tried to get up, only to fall back with my eyes closed. The need to enter into the conscious world wouldn't go way, and eventually I sat up. Two girls were rummaging through our baggage.

Seeing this, I jumped out of bed making the intruders flee in a flurry of cries and screams which awoke Danny.

"What the bloody hell's going on?" he shouted at the top of his voice.

"They were going through our gear," I explained as I ran towards the door, knowing that they'd long gone.

"That's it," said Danny. "I'm fed up with all this shit."

We looked at each other realising that something had to be done to halt this intrusion.

"Okay Swifty we're going to shift the beds so the bottom is against the door; that way the bastards can't get in."

We did this, before telling the others to do the same.

Two days past, and still we had no word from the Army or anyone else for that matter. I decided to go to the British Embassy in the city and find out exactly what was going on. The lads told me to complain about almost everything from the food to the furniture; but I decided that the only things that really mattered were the location of the accommodation, and the fact that we had no money.

As I set off, some sixth sense told me that I was in danger just walking the streets of Bangkok, even in daylight; but I ignored it, reasoning that my British uniform would act as a deterrent, and who could say that it didn't, for I was only accosted once by a woman who insisted that I was the father of her child. I threw some loose change onto the pavement which kept her busy, giving me time for a quick getaway. I made my way to the Embassy and walked in after being scrutinised thoroughly by the doorman.

I rang the bell at what I thought was the appropriate desk and waited. After an inordinate length of time, a clerk appeared. He looked just like he'd stepped out of a solicitor's office in Manchester, suspicious, arrogant and supremely confident. I saw a flicker of an acerbic smile pass over his face as he realised the impression he'd made.

"Yes, what can I do for you?" he asked me as if British soldiers turned up every day.

I just couldn't believe it. I hadn't seen another British person in Bangkok, apart from the soldiers I was with, and he asks me what I want? I thought about saying "Oh I've come to see how you're doing," but I didn't, I just ignored his question, "Do you know about us?"

"No, should we?" he answered, the smile reappearing only much larger.

"Do you think the Army does?"

This time he laughed openly before answering. "I have a funny feeling that you're in trouble; tell me about it."

I told him in great detail about our plane breaking down, and about our poor accommodation. I also said in terms that he couldn't misinterpret, that if nothing was done quickly, then I couldn't be held responsible for what might happen.

At this, he became more interested, especially when I mentioned the young girls and their minders who were continually harassing us.

"Wait here," he said, after some contemplative thought, and immediately scurried off, presumably to get someone senior.

After what seemed like an eternity, he reappeared with a senior official, who looked and sounded very important. Arriving at the desk he whispered something to the clerk who immediately left, whereupon the senior official addressed me.

"I'm quite aware of your situation, but there's not a lot I can do for you. You are staying in what I think is a reasonable hotel for this country, you know. And I might add, that we were lucky to get you in that at such short notice." After he'd finished he placed his elbow slowly on the desk in front of him, and rested his hand under his chin before staring at me.

I felt like I was still at school., only I wasn't at school, I'd just returned from a theatre of war; it instantly annoyed me. He wasn't an Officer I thought, he hasn't any power over me, and that gave me enough confidence to challenge him.

"I don't think you understand me at all," I began somewhat hesitatingly.

His expression changed dramatically at hearing this unexpected rebuttal.

I didn't let it deter me, "I don't think that you are aware that young prostitutes are coming into the hotel and into our rooms. Also, the food is generally inedible, and the men are sick of it."

"Well lock your rooms, it's quite simple, isn't it?"

"Well we would if there were any locks on the doors," I replied. "We are unable to leave our rooms for a moment due to the fact that people will go in them during our absence."

At this outburst, he became very irritated, and mumbled something about soldier's demands being met by the Army, and not by the Embassy. He turned and conferred with the clerk for a moment.

Whereupon I tested the water again. "Another problem is that we have no money. You see we all expected to be in England by now, not stuck in this God forsaken hole."

"Yes, yes, I understand your point, but you must understand that we are limited in what we can do, and please curb your language about the country that you are presently in thank you."

"Well, I'm telling you now, in front of him," I pointed to the clerk who was standing behind him, "If there's an accident, a serious accident that is, you can't hold me responsible, I'm only a Lance Corporal in charge of twenty-eight men; normally a Captain's job, don't you think?"

A look of complete surprise came onto his face. "You're in charge of the party? Is that correct?"

I smiled at the question when I thought about their sudden departure at the airport, and realised that they must be in the city somewhere, or gone back to Britain in drips and drabs on other planes. This unexpected consideration presented the distinct possibility that we had indeed been forgotten.

"But you told me that you knew all about our party, so shouldn't you know all about that?" I said on impulse.

His face hardened as he realised that there was some logic in what I'd said.

This gave me enough confidence to carry on, "You must be aware that a Brigadier was on our plane, where's he staying?"

"Don't be so impudent, I'll be having a word with your superiors if you continue in that vein," he retorted angrily.

"If you can find them, that is," I said quietly, which made the clerk standing behind him turn away in order to hide the smile on his face.

Much to my amazement, he suddenly changed his attitude and replaced his anger with one of resignation. "We'll see what we can do. Come back tomorrow at about this time and I might have something for you, but..." he emphasised, "don't count on it, this is a foreign country and we're a long way from home." Without as much as a goodbye, he turned and departed through a side door.

The junior clerk raised his eyebrows and grinned, "We'll be seeing you tomorrow then?"

"You bet you will," I replied, as I left before making my way back to the hotel.

The next day, I made my way to the Embassy, and was informed that no money would be forthcoming, but a change of hotels was in hand. Sure enough, we moved to what was said to be the second best hotel in Bangkok the following day. The hotel proved to be the height of luxury, with marble floors and ornate carvings in stone and wood, which were placed in all the little alcoves of the large rooms. Waiters dressed in splendid white apparel, hovered about continually greeting guests while carrying out all the demands that were made upon them.

Our party was at first completely overawed by the scene, and walked round in almost total silence. The other guests seemed to be confused and mystified, and the looks they gave us made for general unease. Dinner on the first night proved to be highly embarrassing. The sound of the gong boomed through the air summoning all to enter the dining room.

Soldiers ran, as they normally would have done in the Army, out of a mixture of hunger and desire to get the best seat. It was immediately apparent that most of them had never been in a hotel before. However upon mentioning this to Bobby Cort, he quickly assured me that they had such things in Liverpool. I couldn't help smile when I thought about the Liverpuddlian slums I'd gone through on my way to boarding school, but I made no comment, not wanting to start an argument. Everybody was so excited.

"What's this for?" someone shouted.

"Bloody hell we must be getting a load of grub." Another one answered hysterically, as he viewed the various knives and forks displayed in every set place.

Waiters appeared and politely began asking what each individual soldier would like to start the meal?

"Just bring it all on; I'll eat the fucking lot," another shouted with glee.

The waiters were patient at first, but it quickly became noticeable that their attitude changed dramatically. They didn't ask anymore, they just brought the food out, placed it down in front of each soldier before making a quick exit. The other guests were dumbstruck by our presence; the English ones amongst them voicing great disapproval at our bad language and lack of manners. The highlight of the meal was, without a shadow of a doubt, when an ensemble set up in front of us.

"What's this then?" shouted one Luverpuddlian, "yer going to play for us while we eat, hey? Play some boogy, an I'll fart to the beat."

The leader of the ensemble gave him a look that could kill, followed by a watery smile, as they burst into sound.

That night after dinner, I decided to see some of the sights in the city rather than stay in the hotel. I knew it was dangerous, but I thought I could look after myself. I'd sensed that something was brewing when some of the lads were allowed to book drinks on the hotel bill. I did ask the manager or the under manager about it, but he assured me that everything was in order. I was concerned, because nobody from the Embassy had informed me about it, and I was pretty sure they would have done.

I left the hotel to be immediately met by a wall of hot air, that held the most repugnant smells imaginable. Spurning a natural impulse to retreat back inside the hotel, I joined the crowd going towards the city centre. As I walked, I quickly became aware that I stood out among the crowd. The Thai people are generally very small and slightly built, while I by comparison, seemed quite tall and stocky and towered over them. It wasn't long before they started to gesticulate to each other, laughing while pointing at me.

It became immediately obvious that they found my presence interesting and exciting. I presumed that it was the colour of my skin and the length of my nose, for they kept pointing to their own noses while laughing and shouting hysterically. I don't think any of them had seen a white man so close up before, and one man touched my face with his fingers. He seemed to have no idea of private space, coming within inches of me while peering right into my eyes. I felt immediately scared and threatened, but somehow managed to keep my composure.

The heat became unbearable, while the smells developed a new source of power. Sweating profusely I began to feel insecure and self conscious, which brought about a desperate need to get out of the crowd quickly. Looking to one side I noticed a billboard which advertised an Elvis Presley film. Desperately, I tried to get nearer to it, but such was the crush of the crowd, I couldn't get there. However I did manage to see where it was being shown. In due course we emerged from the narrow street into a much larger one, where I was able to breathe a little easier. The crowd thinned out, and my pursuers drifted off, making me wonder where they had gone? At this point, I began to mull over whether it was worthwhile going on, realising that I would have to make the journey back. I dismissed that thought, thinking that the uniform of the British Army would put most people off.

Arriving at the cinema, I enquired whether they would take Malayan dollars, and was told that they did. I counted out the correct amount whilst the cashier watched, in order to eliminate any possibility of the sharp practise that I'd experienced in Malaya.

Upon entering I felt cold and uncomfortable, realising that it was the sudden change from the street temperature to the air conditioning of the cinema. The cinema was brand new, filled with plush seats with acres of space between them. The film had already started, but as I began to pick up the story line, I became suddenly aware that hardly anybody else in the place had. Slowly it dawned on me that not only could they not understand English, but they couldn't read the subtitles either. They laughed in all the wrong places, which made everything else seem quite bizarre.

When the film finished, I made my way out into the street where I stood watching the bustle for some time. Street vendors were plying their trade with their noisy techniques, selling all types of goods, whilst other people were hurrying to some unknown destination in an almost demented fashion, while continually shouting in high pitched voices at people who were apparently getting in their way. I contemplated what to do for a moment, feeling lonely yet strangely unique. I felt like an alien for the first time in my life. Every now and then someone would touch me, whilst others just stared and laughed hysterically.

As I looked around, I saw a large strange looking building. The lights that lit it up gave it a mystical look, almost like it had been plucked out of a child's fairy tale. Its roof denied sensible construction to my Western mind, with excessive ornate curves and elaborate edifices. But after some thought, I began to understand that its elaboration was intended, and that its construction was to excite the mind with its splendour. The thoughts that followed really transcended my cultural understanding, but it did prompt me to begin asking questions. It made me feel small and insignificant, a nobody in the passage of time. How long I stood there, I don't know, but my whole Malayan experience flashed through my mind, leaving me feeling exposed and thoroughly confused.

"Bloody hell," I thought, "I'm going nuts," but it came again. It was as if the culture before me had spoken, revealing something else besides the poverty and oppression before my eyes.

Strangely confused and quite unable to really understand what had happened, I made my way back towards the hotel. It was late, the back streets were empty, which brought its own eeriness as I hurried, instinctively knowing that it was dangerous to be alone. I felt quite relieved upon arriving back at the hotel safely. I opened the door and entered.

My lofty thoughts vanished when I saw that things were not as they should be. The main hall was a mess with smashed glasses and furniture upside down. Some of the hotel staff were busily trying to clean it up. I tried to creep past unnoticed to my room, but it wasn't to be.

"You in charge of these soldiers?" The manager approached me.

I nodded at him and continued walking towards my room. My escape route was cut off when he positioned himself in the middle of the doorway.

"They were stinkin' drunk, fight and cause great trouble!"

"Look I'm really sorry, but you provided them with the booze, what do you expect? Anyway where are they now?" I answered defensively.

He ignored the first question and answered the second one. "We take them to their rooms."

"Oh that's good. Then everything's okay?" I responded, trying to look for a way around him.

"No," he shouted, "we not okay!"

"I'm very sorry," I apologised, "but there's nothing I can do." And with that I pushed past him and made for my room.

The manager came scurrying after me mumbling incoherently about who was responsible, but I simply ignored him and went into my room, leaving him outside. He continued to try to speak to me for some time, even though the door was locked. Eventually he went away, but I knew that the problem would be there in the morning.

I was first down for breakfast, longing to hear about the previous night's events. A little while later, some of the lads appeared, looking distinctly sheepish and very much the worse for wear.

"I've heard what a smashing time you had last night," I said, the beginnings of a grin coming on my face.

"Shut it Swifty; trying to be funny?" said one of them.

Gradually, they all came down except three, who were still feeling too sick to face breakfast.

"Well, tell me what went on then?" I asked, helping myself to more toast.

"It were that bloody whiskey that sent everybody crackers," explained the soldier opposite me, whom I didn't know.

"Where did you get the whisky from?" I asked, unsure where he could have got it from in Bangkok.

He saw and interpreted my perplexed look, "Oh some of the lads went out for some, got it real cheap, cheaper than beer in the hotel."

"Really!' I exclaimed, "I thought you were getting drinks on the house?"

"We did," he responded, "until they stopped us; must have thought we'd drink 'em dry. They went out for that stuff that passes for whiskey. You know that stuff can send you blind?"

The soldier sat next to him joined in, "When you're on the binge it doesn't bloody well matter, does it?"

"It does to me," I answered, taking an instant dislike to him. "Anyway, I understood that you were penniless."

"Oh, we are really, but you know how it is? We managed to scrape enough up between us."

I turned to Danny Baston, who was listening, "Come on Danny, tell me what went on?"

Danny's cup momentarily stopped on the way to his mouth as he began to speak, "It was a mess, everyone was stinkin' drunk, and don't fuckin' tell me that a piss artist like you doesn't understand that."

"Alright you've made your point, don't get funny with me. I just need to know."

"Okay Swifty, but it just sounds like you're trying to be like one of them bastards." At which, he looked at the other guests in the dining area to illustrate the point.

After breakfast, I got all the party together and told them that the manager was extremely unhappy, and was going to complain to the Embassy about our behaviour.

"Well if that means we're going to get kicked out of this hotel and Bangkok, it'll make me bloody well 'appy," stated a soldier out of 'A' Company.

"Back to Malaya, you mean?"

It shut him up, as he began to think about the alternatives to going home.

Finally I gave them a warning, "The manager has told me that he has given strict instructions that none of his staff are to serve you with alcohol. It can't happen again, but if it does, I'll know that you are bringing in that shit that passes for whiskey, okay? If that happens, I can assure you the soldier responsible will not be accompanying us any further, right?" I knew that I had no power to do anything whatsoever, but it sounded a good threat.

A mumbled response greeted it, which didn't give me much confidence, because in my heart I knew that given half a chance they'd do it again and what's more who's to say I wouldn't be with them!

Two days later, we left the hotel and boarded a Hermes plane and headed for Heathrow and the ice and snow. Shortly after arrival, we all got off the plane, thankful to be back in England, but shivering profusely, as the wind blew snow in our faces as we made our way across the tarmac to the airport lounge.

"It's bloody cold, but it's good to be back."

I recognised Danny's Bolton accent as he continued to make comments about the weather from the back of the group; it still grated on me, although I'd become used to it over the past two years.

Somehow, I couldn't make a reply; it was all too much like a dream. Walking into the airport lounge, I looked around naively expecting some kind of recognition. At that moment, I wouldn't have been too surprised if some people had offered to shake hands with us. It never happened of course. They simply turned away and ignored us.

I felt like shouting, "We've been to Malaya you know," but I didn't, instead I became conscious of the orderliness of the place, before noticing that all the people waiting there were dressed in expensive clothes. I quickly became very conscious of how I might look by comparison.

Danny saw me looking. "Different world Swifty; we were kings out there, but we're pure shit here."

I just nodded, realising that we were simply being ignored. It was so different in Malaya where we had been treated with awe and respect. I felt like going back, but immediately replaced the idea with thoughts of seeing my family and friends.

The journey back to Preston was largely uneventful and cold, apart from one of the lads forgetting his tie, and being cautioned by M.P.s on Waterloo station. Upon arriving in Preston I rang home, although it was two-thirty in the morning.

My brother-in-law answered, "How are you?" he said as if I'd been out for ten minutes. "Everyone's in bed apart from me, but I'll wake them."

"Yeah, I'm fine, but how did you know to wait up for me? I never rang, I couldn't find an empty phone booth that worked on Waterloo station."

"Oh a friend of yours rang his mum and she rang your dad."

"I suppose dad's in bed?"

"Oh yes, but he'll be up when you get back. I'll pick you up in about twenty minutes, okay?"

"Okay, I'll see you then."

My brother-in-law picked me up from the station and we drove out of town to the suburbs where I lived. "Glad to be back?" he asked, casually glancing across at me.

"You bet! You'll never know."

"Don't count on it," he answered "I've been in the Army."

I smiled, he knew the score, I could see that he knew how I felt, and it showed in his eyes. David was a quiet man at the best of times, we drove in silence and I was speechless for once.

It was with a strange feeling of relief that I looked at all the familiar sights as we passed them on the way home. I'd never thought of Preston as being anything but ugly, with its black dirty buildings pushed together, making it look gloomy and forbidding. We drove down the main street called Fishergate; I found myself looking at the shops that were most familiar, Lingards, the men's outfitters, where I'd bought all my clothes for school. I found my gaze lingering, almost lovingly, on the shop frontage, before experiencing some psychological insecurity as I realised what I was doing. Still, I liked its shape, the way the clothes were displayed, and even the way the letters were shaped that made up the sign.

I quickly came to the conclusion that I was just glad to be back and see the things that were part of my youth, but inwardly I knew that it was more than that. I thought about those we'd buried overseas, who'd never see anything again and shuddered. We passed Booth's, that unique grocer opposite the flag market, which purported to be the finest grocer in England, and I still wondered why I was pleased to see it? This was quickly followed by the arcade, which was built as a sign of grandeur and prosperity according to my father, who said it represented the prosperity of the people of Preston. I couldn't help but think that there were an awful lot of the population not represented in that sign, but I would never dare to say anything, I was simply too glad to be back.

"You really are glad to be back, aren't you?" David said with a smile. "Your mum's up, but I don't know about your dad. I woke him, but he didn't seem too pleased at the thought of getting up."

"That's about what I expected," I said with a grin, "he'll have had a bad night."

He laughed heartily before answering, "You wouldn't dare tell him that."

"That's quite correct. The sun's hot out east, but it's not that hot. My brain's still intact."

We both laughed. David stopped the car outside my father's butcher's shop. For some reason, I went across and looked into the window.

In the meantime David carried my baggage into the house, which was to the side of the shop. When he'd finished, he came and stood next to me.

"Funny isn't it, I've missed the old butcher's shop somehow. I think it's a part of me in a way."

He nodded indicating that he understood, but I doubt whether he really did. I ran my eyes over the shapes grooved out of the butcher's block through endless cleaning, and thought about how much sweat I'd lost on them. Strange as it may seem, even the colours were meaningful. I saw the cigarette burns on the ledge above them where my father placed his butt ends when customers appeared unexpectedly. I knew them all, and in some strange way, they were like monuments to my youth, for I'd grown up with them and they were a part of me. I recalled the times when I'd pinched his cigarettes without him knowing. I'd seen it all again and it was precious, so precious I couldn't share it with anybody. It was like stepping out of the mould for a moment, and seeing history as some part of eternity on the brink of time.

I went inside and into the hall, where my sister greeted me with a kiss and a hug before I went into the living room, where I greeted my mother with all the love I had. All this time my sister continued to chatter excitedly, asking endless questions without as much as a pause.

"Where's dad?" I asked.

My mother replied, "He's had a bad night Keith, nip into his bedroom and say hello."

I opened the door of his bedroom and switched the light on. "Hello dad, I'm glad to be back." I stopped, not really knowing what else to say.

Without sitting up, he opened one eye and squinted in the sudden light. "Nice to see you got back safely Keith; I'll see you in the morning, now turn the light off, I've had a bad night."

I went out feeling a little hurt and confused, before making my way back to the dining room where I joined the rest of my family who were drinking tea. "He hasn't changed much," I said with a laugh as I sat down, has he?"

"What do you mean?" asked my sister, before I hardly had time to finish the last syllable.

"Oh nothing, I've only been away for fourteen months, you'd think he'd get up at least."

My sister looked aghast, "What are you saying? You never did talk much sense, even before you went abroad."

I didn't answer her, thinking that whatever I said, it would change nothing.

Some days later, I tried to tell my father about what was going on in Malaya, but every time I tried he'd cut me short.

"Forget it. Malaya was nothing more than a skirmish compared to what I was in."

It wasn't just what he said, but the way the subject affected him. His whole demeanour would change. It was as if someone had pulled a switch. His eyes would cease to function normally; he would stare into space and speak as if to a stranger. But what was even more distressing, he would then enter into a deep depression that would last for days.

I mentioned this to my mother, she said that he was always like that whenever anyone mentioned war. All I wanted to tell him was that he wouldn't have liked the things going on out there, but I think he knew. I also wanted to tell him about the rumour I'd heard in the Regiment concerning Batang Kali.

One day I happened to hear some of the senior N.C.O's talking. Apparently some time before I got to Malaya, a detachment of Scottish Guardsmen, under the command of a Sergeant, had gone to a village because a nearby Police Station had been attacked the previous night. Some policemen had been killed, together with an eight year old boy. The guardsmen rounded up all the young men in the village, which numbered around twenty-eight. They took them behind one of the huts and told them to run. When they did, they shot all of them in the back. They killed all of them, even though some were still alive and pleading for mercy.

I listened, unable to take it in at first, knowing that the N.C.O's approved of their action, and were actually suggesting that this was the only real way that Malaya could get rid of Communists.

I also wanted to tell him that shortly before I got there, the British Army were in the habit of decapitating terrorists shot in the jungle, relieving them of the awkward job of carrying them out. In fact some of the Scots Guards had their photographs taken whilst holding up the heads of dead terrorists as trophies. I also heard about the killer squads, that operated under the Army's direction, to which they admitted to some time later. Apparently they went around the countryside killing without any real discrimination. I tried to tell people about these things but nobody seemed to want to listen.

The following Sunday, I went to church with the rest of my family. I remember sitting there listening to the vicar preaching about the symbol of light, and suddenly being engulfed in thoughts and memories that were far from the light, but which nobody wanted to know!